African Women Writing Resistance

WOMEN IN AFRICA AND
THE DIASPORA

Series Editors

STANLIE JAMES
AILI MARI TRIPP

African Women Writing Resistance

An Anthology of Contemporary Voices

Edited by

Jennifer Browdy de Hernandez
Pauline Dongala
Omotayo Jolaosho
Anne Serafin

The University of Wisconsin Press

The University of Wisconsin Press
1930 Monroe Street, 3rd Floor
Madison, Wisconsin 53711-2059
uwpress.wisc.edu

3 Henrietta Street
London WCE 8LU, England
www.eurospanbookstore.com

1   3   5   4   2

Printed in the United States of America

Library of Congress Cataloging-in-Publication Data
African women writing resistance : an anthology of contemporary voices /
edited by Jennifer Browdy de Hernandez, Pauline Dongala, Omotayo Jolaosho, [. . .] et al.
    p.   cm.—(Women in Africa and the diaspora)
Includes bibliographical references and index.
ISBN 978-0-299-23664-9 (pbk.: alk. paper)
ISBN 978-0-299-23663-2 (e-book)
1. African literature—Women authors—21st century.
2. Women authors, African.
3. Women—Africa—Social conditions—21st century—Sources.
I. Browdy de Hernandez, Jennifer.
II. Dongala, Pauline.
III. Jolaosho, Omotayo.
IV. Series: Women in Africa and the diaspora.
PL8011.A35   2010
809'.8896—dc22
2009046345

*To the generations of strong African women
whose lives and writings inspire and animate this book*

A woman writer must have an imagination that is plain stubborn, that can invent new gods and banish ineffectual ones.

Yvonne Vera,
from *Opening Spaces*
(1999)

Listening to the hopes and dreams of our people, I recall the words of a Mozambican poet who said, "Our dream has the size of freedom." My people, like your people, believe deeply in freedom—and, in their dreams, they reach for the heavens.

Ellen Johnson-Sirleaf, president of Liberia,
from an address to a joint session of Congress,
Washington, D.C.,
March 13, 2006

Contents

Contents

Part Four. Focusing on Survival: Women's Health Issues

Preface

Roots of the Collection

The four sister editors of this anthology came together in September 2005 with the goal of bringing the voices of emerging African women writers to a wider audience. With its specific focus on writing as a tool of resistance to the multiple challenges faced by African women today, *African Women Writing Resistance* is the product of the collective vision of the editors and the thirty-one women from thirteen countries and many linguistic backgrounds who contributed to this groundbreaking pan-African volume.

African Women Writing Resistance answers the clarion call of an earlier collection published by Jennifer Browdy de Hernandez, *Women Writing Resistance: Essays on Latin America and the Caribbean* (South End Press, 2004), which collected essays and poetry from that region's well-known and emerging women writers. Editing this first collection launched Jennifer on a global quest to follow the trail of women's resistance across cultural and geographic boundaries, always looking for clues as to how she, as a white American feminist teacher and activist, could become the most effective ally for women in very different circumstances from her own.

In 2005 Jennifer was thinking about putting together a class and an anthology on contemporary African women's writing. As events have a way of crystallizing when the time is right, she was also at this time getting to know Pauline Dongala, an exile from Congo-Brazzaville who became one of her students at Bard College at Simon's Rock; another Simon's Rock student, Nigerian Omotayo Jolaosho, who was then finishing her B.A.; and Anne Serafin, an African literature specialist whom she met at a Modern Language Association panel on female genital mutilation (FGM) in literature in 2004. Pauline, Omotayo, and Anne became enthusiastic partners in the *Women Writing Resistance in Africa* project, sharing with Jennifer a common vision of a book that would bring together many strong contemporary African women's voices, women writing about their lives, their challenges, their hopes, and their dreams.

The newly formed editorial group sent out a call for papers for the anthology in the fall of 2005, soliciting personal narratives, testimony, interviews, short stories, poetry, short plays, folktales, and lyrics by African women that concerned resistance to particular challenges or oppressions faced by women in Africa today. We suggested topics such as the effect on women of HIV/AIDS; female genital cutting; Sharia law; women's poverty and lack of access to education, health care, credit, and political power; armed conflict and rape as a weapon of war; displacement and exile; women's oppressions within heterosexual relationships; resistant sexualities; and intergenerational conflict and the tension between tradition and modernity. Submissions had to be written by women born in Africa, no matter their current location of residence.

Almost immediately a flood of writing began to arrive in our e-mail in-boxes, dealing with all the above-listed topics and more. It was obvious that the call for papers had tapped into a powerful, pent-up stream of African women writing resistance that was only waiting for the right channel to reach a world audience. With hundreds of pages worth of submissions in hand, the work of selection began, to which each of us brought her unique perspective. The book you hold in your hand is the collaborative result of many hands, hearts, and minds and of many hours of thought and labor. We send it out into the world in the hope that it will be the inspiration for ever-expanding rings of "women writing resistance" in Africa and worldwide.

Acknowledgments

Jennifer Browdy de Hernandez would like to thank all the women across the world, far too numerous to list individually, whose courageous and ongoing struggle for better lives for themselves and their families provides such an inspiring model of positive resistance. Closer to home, I would like to thank my parents, Joe and Sue Browdy, whose steady support and guidance continue to give me strength; my sons, Nico and Eric Hernandez, who have been patient with the hectic lifestyle of a mother who is also a professor and writer; and Sam Ruhmkorff, dean of academics, and my colleagues at Bard College at Simon's Rock, for their support of my ongoing work in comparative literature and gender studies. I would especially like to thank my friends and activist partners Vera Kalm, Judy Nardacci, Sharon Meyer, and Zoe Dalheim, in honor of our many hours of collaboration on nearly a decade of annual conferences celebrating International Women's Day; and my sister editors, who have made the demanding process of editing a big collection like this a joyful and stimulating labor of love.

Pauline Dongala would like to honor all the courageous women in the world who have experienced war, especially women who are still living in war zones. My work is dedicated to these strong women who have inexplicably lost their lives on the battlefield and to those who have lost their parents, children, husbands, brothers, and sisters. My thanks go to my mother, Elisabeth Bouanga-Milondo, who has always been my mentor, motivating me with her constant love. I am deeply appreciative of her for sharing her ideas in her contribution to this volume, which spans from colonial to postcolonial Africa. I would also like to thank Mr. Pierre Piya for interviewing Kaya a Mbaya in a remote forest village in the Congo. I know it was not an easy task. My thanks go to my sisters and brothers for our mutual support in times of despair and for sharing our joys. I am grateful to my deceased grandmother, Suzanne Nzobo, whose gifts of healing, prayers, and rituals brought great help to those around her. She still continues to positively affect the people she worked with and helps me to embrace life fully. My thanks go also to Emmanuel Dongala, my dear husband, who gives me strength and his loving support in many ways. I would also like to thank my friend Vera Kalm, who has helped to launch a sewing studio for single mothers and widows in Kinkala, Congo Republic, so that they can rebuild their lives. Thanks also to Sam Ruhmkorff and John McClaren for allowing me to pursue my bachelor's degree at Bard College at Simon's Rock and to Professor Jennifer Browdy de Hernandez, who has taken my hand to walk the path of my education and made me more aware of women's issues. Finally, I thank my coeditors for the joy of working together and bringing this project to fruition.

Omotayo Jolaosho would like to thank the generations of women whose lives engendered and continue to nurture mine: my mother, whose determination and perseverance constantly motivates me; my grandmother, Victoria Adebanke Bedu, who was the first to initiate me into an African childhood and womanhood and who remains my preeminent teacher; and my late great-grandmother, Marian Olapemo Odetola, whose spirit guides my path. The experiences of these elders and ancestors animate my life's work. Then there are those women who extend my family, my sister editors among them. I am especially grateful to Dorothy Hodgson, my graduate advisor at Rutgers University, who has been an invaluable resource in bringing forth this collection. Also at Rutgers University, Ousseina Alidou, Abena Busia, Fran Mascia-Lees, and Renee DeLancey provided a forum for us to discuss the collection in progress at the Center for African Studies. Finally, I would like to thank Ruth Hearns, Vernice Miller, Mary King Austin, James Sterling King, Okey Ndibe, Carlton Rounds, Suncadm Bey, and the many other individuals whose love, support, and commitment form the foundation upon which I stand as a scholar, artist, and human being.

Anne Serafin would like to thank everyone who has supported her study of African literatures. Several individuals and programs have been especially important. The National Endowment for the Humanities (NEH) provided the initial impetus for my interest with a Teacher-Scholar Award in 1991 to read and research African literatures in general during a sabbatical year. Then an NEH Summer Seminar in 1995 focused on African literature, politics, and film, guided by Leonard Markovitz of Queens College of the City University of New York. Barbara Brown invited me to lead and participate in numerous workshops as well as attend lectures and programs at Boston University's African Studies Center. Barbara and BU have been invaluable resources for my work in this field. In 1996 Beth Purcell of the Newton Free Library asked me to begin a monthly discussion group in African literatures. I am extremely grateful to Beth and to the ardent members of the group who have eagerly explored this topic with me for thirteen seasons. In the late 1990s, the Ghanaian writer Ama Ata Aidoo befriended me when I attended her class in African literature at Brandeis University. She served as a powerful inspiration as we sipped Zimbabwean tea in her little office, where I learned firsthand about some of the thoughts, emotions, and experiences that influence her writing. In 2006 Jennifer Browdy de Hernandez invited me to coedit, together with Pauline Dongala and Omotayo Joloasho, an anthology of African women writing resistance. This project allowed me the pleasure of reading the wealth of submissions following our call for papers and of working with Jenny, Pauline, and Tayo to shape our book. Lastly, I must thank James O'Hare for his unflagging interest, his astute observations, and his generous support and encouragement as each stage of our book has unfolded. Throughout our project, my esteem has continued to grow for the power, persistence, and talent that women around the world, particularly on the African continent and in its diaspora, possess.

Collectively, we extend our deep appreciation to Professor Abena P. A. Busia of Rutgers University for hosting the roundtable "African Women Envision the Future" at the Center for African Studies in April 2007 and for contributing in so many other ways to the strength of this collection. We would also like to thank the editors of the Women in Africa and the Diaspora series, professors Stanlie James and Aili Mari Tripp, as well as Gwen Walker, our editor at the University of Wisconsin Press, for their belief in and support of our project. We are particularly grateful to all of our contributors, whose hard work and clear-eyed vision this volume celebrates and honors.

Earlier versions of the following pieces have been previously published and are reprinted here with permission: Sybille Ngo Nyeck, "To Be or Not to Be a Lesbian: The Dilemma of Cameroon's Women Soccer Players," *Witness Magazine*, October 2003; Sefi Atta, "Hailstones on Zamfara," *News from Home* (Northampton, MA: Interlink Books, 2010), copyright 2010 by Sefi Atta; Nawal El Saadawi, "The Struggle to End the Practice of Female Genital Mutilation," www.nawalsaadawi.net; Juliana Makuchi Nfah-Abbenyi, "Slow Poison," *Your Madness, Not Mine: Stories of Cameroon* (Athens: Ohio University Press/Swallow Press, 1999); Khadija Marouazi, excerpt from *Biography of Ash* [Sirat al-ramad: riwaya] (Beirut and Casablanca: Afriqiyya al-sharq, 2000), copyright 2000 by Khadija Marouazi, translation copyright 2007 by Alexander Elison, published in *Words Without Borders* (www.wordswithoutborders.org), an online magazine for international literature hosted by Bard College and supported by the National Endowment for the Arts; Sokari Ekine, "Women's Responses to State Violence in the Niger Delta," *Feminist Africa* 10 (2008); China Keitetsi, excerpt from *Child Soldier: Fighting for My Life* [Mit liv som barnesoldat i Uganda] (Copenhagen: Ekstra Bladets Forlag, 2002), copyright 2002 by China Keitetsi and Ekstra Bladets Forlag, published by agreement with Leonhardt & Høier Literary Agency A/S, Copenhagen; Danielle Nierenberg and Mia MacDonald, "Don't Get Mad, Get Elected! A Conversation with Activist Wangari Maathai," *World Watch Magazine*, May/June 2004; Abena P. A. Busia, "Liberation," *Testimonies of Exile* (Trenton, NJ: Africa World Press, 1990).

Foreword

A Song in Seven Stanzas for Our Granddaughters

Abena P. A. Busia

1.

Tradition and the remembrance of things past,
Are a re-discovered country
Of things we struggle against;
Where as pygmy women we stand tall among the Bantu
And name ourselves Babongo.
We stand here, compassionate witnesses,
To witches who are just mothers, to mothers who are just loyal,
To those who wrestle snakes to feed their children,
And to grandmothers who keep faith enough with girls,
To make god change his mind.

2.

Young as we are, if we don't tell our stories who will speak out
    for us, when
We claim our bodies for ourselves and weep no more, when
We write to each other and teach ourselves, not
To trade our bodies for security, wealth, power,
Or whatever price they can bring, when
We call out and claim a love that knows no name and has no place, when
We learn "it is not rape if . . ."
We still love our daddy as his bewildering passion penetrates us
Shocking us to learn the forbidden pathways of ourselves,
And the things we struggle for.

3.

If we don't tell our stories, hailstones will continue to fall on our heads,
Thrown by fathers for the children to see—for we are not good women,
Thrown by Imams, by a judge's decree—for we are not good wives,
Thrown by other women in our husbands' lives
As they come in the morning cradling his children
Calling us witch, barren, bitch
And we find something to tie the chest with;
Challenging words to hurl back in battle,
And partners to hold us anyway,
Through the things we struggle against.

4.

If we don't tell our stories who will know we did not comply:
We did not wish our lives away, but stayed focused,
And staunched the cut of virginal blood,
To stop our daughters being slaves;
We learned to sing survival songs,
Through violence and rape and war;
We did not tell each other lies, or taste slow poison all alone;
And stitched for our dead not effigies, but new dolls
So our artistry shows only prayer heals despair,
Through the things we struggle for.

5.

When we share strategy through story
We empower ourselves to take a stand;
And bear witness through our words in blood and ink,
To wage peace as an act of faith,
To call out by name the things we fear.
Not just victims, or betrayed child soldiers —
liberated from the fires of oil, or greed, or power
We claim a collective love,
Plant trees or wage a campaign, sing songs or keep silence,
As agents of a just resistance now, and as in the past.

6.

Through bondage and through freedom we share our tactics,
And document. We write from every different place,
To reclaim our names, and inherited legacies we want to pass along.
We write to stay in places as we choose —
We who crossed the Atlantic all those yesterdays ago,
We who have come again today —
We who have stayed in place through generations,
We who will stay in place tomorrow —
Or move on: between generations, between cultures, between locations,
As we ourselves want, now, as in the future.

7.

We envision new futures for ourselves
As we weep with each other in silence or laugh:
We network behind shop counters, and on factory floors,
We engage across industrial landscapes, and in mining villages,
We reach out from fishing boats and commercial farms
We meet in schools, churches, parliaments and slums
And from dance floors to prison cells we are Ellen Johnson Sirleaf
    in the Liberian State House.
We are the tomorrow our grandmothers dreamed
We are grandmothers dreaming other tomorrows —
Our own compassionate witnesses: standing at the edge of time.

African Women Writing Resistance

African Women Writing Resistance

An Introduction

Jennifer Browdy de Hernandez
with **Pauline Dongala, Omotayo Jolaosho,** and
Anne Serafin

African Women
in the Twenty-first Century

African women are too often presented in scholarly and media accounts as passive, pathetic victims of harsh circumstances, rather than as autonomous creative agents making positive changes in their lives. Confronting entrenched social inequality and inadequate access to resources, women across the continent are working with grit, determination, and imagination to improve their own material conditions and to blaze a strong, clear path for their daughters and granddaughters. The contributors to *African Women Writing Resistance* are at the forward edge of the tide of women's empowerment that is moving across the African continent at the start of the twenty-first century. They look unblinkingly at the challenges they confront while also creating visions of a more positive future, using writing to bear witness to oppression, to document opposition struggles, and to share successful strategies of resistance. African women writers such as those included in this collection are moving beyond the linked dichotomies of victim/oppressor and victim/heroine to present their experiences in full complexity.

In many ways the twenty-first century is a good time to be a woman in Africa. African women, energized by the path-breaking 2005 victory of Liberian Ellen Johnson Sirleaf, the first woman president of any African nation, are educating themselves and entering politics and the professions in record numbers.[1] Another trailblazing African woman, Wangari Maathai of Kenya, won the Nobel Peace Prize in 2004 for her ambitious woman-based reforestation project, the Green Belt Movement.[2] *Gender mainstreaming* are the new watchwords at the United Nations and other international development agencies, which are finally beginning to give women their due as the pillars of any society, particularly in periods of crisis or rapid development.[3]

Though still trailing in numbers and recognition behind older, more established male counterparts,[4] African women writers have begun to appear on the world's bestseller lists, with debut novels by women writers such as Zimbabwean Tsitsi Dangarembga and Nigerian Chimamanda Ngozi Adichie building on the successes of previous generations of African woman writers,[5] including Buchi Emecheta (Nigeria), Ama Ata Aidoo (Ghana), and Mariama Bâ (Senegal).[6] Africana studies is growing as an interdisciplinary academic field spanning Africa and the African diaspora and is increasingly taking women's experiences and voices into account,[7] as evidenced by the recent publication of collections such as the multivolume Women Writing Africa series, produced by a collective of editors and writers at the Feminist Press; *African Gender Studies*, edited by Oyeronke Oyewumi; and *African Feminism: The Politics of Survival in Sub-Saharan Africa*, edited by Gwendolyn Mikell.

Still, there are many challenges for African women to confront. The scourge of HIV/AIDS has hit African women hard; their own rates of infection and death are high, and those who survive are left to care for the sick as well as for an ever-growing tide of orphaned children.[8] Other health-related burdens exist as well: maternal mortality remains high throughout much of Africa, due to a lack of access to modern health care facilities,[9] and other preventable diseases take their toll, including malaria, tuberculosis, and lesser-known but equally deadly and prevalent parasitical diseases, such as schistosomiasis, trachoma, river blindness, and elephantiasis.[10] Though some women are beginning to gain social recognition and political power, the vast majority of African women remain undereducated[11] and subject to patriarchal norms, both indigenous and imported, that keep them from reaching their full potential.[12] Domestic violence remains a significant problem, along with marital rape and child marriage—all issues explored by contributors to this volume.

Conflicts in African countries, such as Rwanda, Sudan, and the Democratic Republic of the Congo, have too often relied on brutal tactics of ethnic warfare, with the raping of girls and women of all ages commonplace and devastating.[13] Conflict has also led to the displacement of millions of African women, who languish in refugee camps all over the continent,[14] where they are often subject to sexual predation, in some cases by the very aid workers and peacekeepers who are supposedly there to help them.[15] Sex work and sex trafficking are also increasingly important issues for African women, as several alarming recent reports make clear by detailing the growing numbers of women and children lured into unsafe and exploitative sexual activity.[16] Luckier are those women refugees who have managed to flee to exile in the West, but this escape, too, brings its own forms of alienation and struggle. These are among the issues of concern to African women today that are thoughtfully explored by contributors to this volume.

Certain common themes of African women's resistance quickly emerge in the writings collected here. Early twenty-first-century African women from all over the continent write about their struggles to balance the demands of cultural traditions with the pull of modernity and their own desires for autonomy and independence. They write about their sexuality, which is often a fraught site of struggle and resistance for women of all ages, from young women exploring first sexual relationships, to women confronting societal intolerance as a result of their desires for and relationships with other women, to women entering into marriage for the first time. We also hear about mature women grappling with unhappy marriages, in some cases making the difficult decision to leave their spouses and children in search of their own happiness. We hear too about the inherent tensions of polygynous marriages and about the suffering of older women dealing with the cultural exploitation of widowhood.

Contributors to the anthology also focus on women's health concerns, such as the highly contested issue of female genital cutting; environmental degradation and lack of access to clean water; and the destructive impact of interethnic conflict and corrupt government. The writers included here aim to raise awareness about the issues rather than to promote any one answer or solution to the problems they describe. They are reaching out to join hands with a wider audience to prompt an open-ended discussion about conditions for women in different regions of Africa, in the hope that a gendered and localized analysis will lead to an appropriately focused response—or at least a broader, more inclusive conversation.

Many of the contributors to *African Women Writing Resistance* are relatively young and just emerging on the literary scene,[17] but we have also included a few of the activist "mothers" of the current generation of younger women, such as Nawal El Saadawi, Wangari Maathai, and Abena P. A. Busia, whose ongoing, path-breaking contributions to the empowerment of women in their home countries and on the broader world stage cannot be over-emphasized. In going through the many submissions we received for the anthology, we looked above all for women writing their resistance to contemporary social issues eloquently, forcefully, and with style. We made the choice to limit our pool to contemporary women writers who were born in Africa, in order to amplify the voices of African women who might not otherwise be heard in classrooms and other literary circles in the West. We did, however, include African-born women writers who are now living abroad, since so many African writers do leave their homelands in search of better educational or career opportunities or to escape political unrest or persecution.

We also looked for contemporary women writers who could represent a wide range of genres and cultural contexts. While not encyclopedic in approach, *African Women Writing Resistance* opens a series of windows into the lives of women from thirteen countries across the continent, from different cultural and linguistic backgrounds and many different walks of life, writing in genres ranging from poetry and fiction to memoir, essay, epistle, and interview. Most of the pieces included here were written specifically for this anthology, either in French or English; we also included a few excerpts from longer works published elsewhere that provide an important and unique contribution to our theme of women writing resistance.

Writing Resistance

How do these African women writers understand resistance? Generally speaking, resistance for these women is not a matter of armed political resistance movements, which are more often the province of men. For women across the African continent, resistance frequently takes more subtle forms. "To me, resistance means challenging beliefs, traditions, and values that place women below men in terms of being heard, making decisions and choices," says Zambian contributor Ellen Banda-Aaku.[18] Kenyan Ann Kithaka agrees, saying that "resistance means saying 'no' to the patriarchal system and values that continue to disempower, subjugate, and undermine my personal dignity. In all stages of my life, my thoughts and actions have been subject to societal dictates, where 'society' denotes the male figure—my father, my husband, my boss, my brothers, my pastor." Marame Gueye of Senegal defines resistance simply as "the political, moral, intellectual, and spiritual refusal to succumb to any form of violence or oppression."

Many contributors to this volume note that their personal struggles for dignity and empowerment benefit the larger society as well as themselves. Ellen Banda-Aaku works to enable women to "come out of the shadows and use their full potential to contribute to economic and social development and change in their communities, be it locally or internationally, formally or informally." Susan Akono of Cameroon highlights her resistance to the separation and segregation of human beings into arbitrary "races": "One is not always one. In my case, one is, at least, five. For while I am a pure black woman, I can silence neither the white part within me, nor the yellow, nor the brown, nor the red. In other words, I cannot silence my humanity."

For the contributors to this anthology, writing is essential to effective resistance. "Writing exposes the many challenges African women are resisting in the world today, and speaking out brings issues to the forefront so we are forced to question or address them," says Ellen Banda-Aaku. "By writing we become more aware of the values and beliefs holding us back, as well as those that can move us forward. Only by writing can we tell the story of the African woman. If we don't tell our story, who will?"

For poet Ann Kithaka, "Writing resistance is a process of discovery, emancipation, and reclaiming. It is about reclaiming my dignity, privacy, and freedom as an African woman and human being. It is about emancipating myself from historical, structural, and systematic abuse, oppression, and discrimination. And finally, it is about discovering my inner strength, my uniqueness, and my interdependence on other people." She continues, "Writing resistance is a reawakening of my consciousness through intercultural and intergenerational dialogue with other women writers around Africa and the diaspora, so that we can stoke the dying embers of feminism for the benefit of future generations." Resistance is not only a struggle *against* but also a struggle *for*, and many of the writers represented here present their positive visions for the future of African women—a future where resistance and struggle might give way to peaceful, productive, and equal coexistence with their men.

Writing provides opportunities for resistance that may be largely unavailable to women in their day-to-day lives. Thus writing can become a safe space for resistance—which does not make it any less powerful, as contributor Diana Adesola Mafe observes in the following anecdote:

> "Resistance" has generally meant "non-compliance" to me. In speaking about my resistance *as an African woman*, I know that my non-compliance is not always immediate, not always self-evident, and not always strong enough. Sometimes my non-compliance is all too introspective, all too silent. Audre Lorde warns us in *Sister Outsider* that, "Your silence will not protect you."
>
> I remember crossing the border from Canada into the United States by car a couple of years ago. Since I was not Canadian, I was required to go through passport control, fill out forms, and be fingerprinted and photographed as part of the US-VISIT security program. The officer who "processed" me, a white man, was patronizing and insulting. He spoke with exaggerated slowness, despite my Canadian accent, Western clothing, and obvious ability to speak English. When I filled out the two-sided green form, he inquired condescendingly about "how I had done that so fast," ostensibly marveling at my literacy.
>
> Inside, I was fuming—ready to whip out degrees and a résumé, thus proving my worth as an articulate, educated woman of color—ready to stoop to insults,

mock *his* accent and sneer at *his* levels of education and literacy. Instead, I remained silent and, yes, compliant, because I knew he had all the power in that situation—the power to turn me back, the power to detain me. Insulting him would have been juvenile and probably disastrous but if, as I believe, the purpose of resistance is to counter oppression, then I failed in that moment. I could at least have commented on his behavior and the fact that it was unnecessary. In doing so, I might have made things easier for the next woman of color he processed. Or worse.

Thankfully, that is where writing comes in. Writing *is* resistance, an opportunity to voice my non-compliance. Here I can make up for all those moments where I wish I *had* said something. Here I can anchor those past (and future) experiences, deconstruct them, learn from them, and perhaps most importantly, share them.

The Power of Collective Struggle

African Women Writing Resistance locates itself within the transnational, intergenerational, cross-cultural efforts of African women to voice their needs and desires, their sorrows and their joys, to each other and to the wider world. As education is a necessary precursor to writing, the call to African women to educate themselves and each other is frequently heard in this collection. Elisabeth Bouanga of Congo-Brazzaville, a grandmother in her seventies and the mother of anthology coeditor Pauline Dongala, recounts how, when she was young, "Women were not allowed to go to school; they were supposed to learn from their mothers how to work in the fields, how to cook and how to be good wives. It surely was a kind of education but it was too limited," she says. "Girls must go to school to be educated," Bouanga declares. "A woman, be she single, married, or widowed, must free herself and be capable to take on any profession."

This is a rallying cry heard all over Africa in these early years of the twenty-first century, as women organize themselves to join fully in the contemporary social, economic, and political life of their countries. Resistance is undoubtedly more powerful when it is collective, and women throughout Africa and the diaspora are joining together to improve the quality of lives for themselves and their sisters through many organizations, such as the African Women's Development Fund, Tostan, and FEMNET, to name just a few.[19]

What do the contributors to *African Women Writing* need and want from us, their readers? It is our belief that African women writers seek a broad-based audience with which to engage in the healing exchange of compassionate witnessing and empowering dialogue.[20] We present this anthology in the hope that the strong voices of African women represented in these pages will arouse the spirit of activist solidarity in women and men all over the world, encouraging us to work together to build a better future for us all.

Notes

1. A biography and set of speeches by President Johnson-Sirleaf can be found at the Liberian government site http://www.emansion.gov.lr/content.php?sub=President's%20Biography&related= The%20President.

2. For information on the current work of Wangari Maathai and the Green Belt Movement, see the Web site http://www.greenbeltmovement.org/.

3. For a good description of the theory and practice of gender mainstreaming, see the 2007 report by the United Nations Education, Scientific, and Cultural Organization (UNESCO), "UNESCO's Gender Mainstreaming Implementation Framework," available at http://unesdoc .unesco.org/images/0013/001318/131854e.pdf or the WomenWatch site, produced by the United Nations Inter-Agency Network on Women and Gender Equality, at http://www.un.org/womenwatch/.

4. A few of the male African writers who have achieved international fame and recognition are Ngugi wa Thiong'o (Kenya), Chinua Achebe (Nigeria), Nuruddin Farah (Somalia), and the winners of the Nobel Prize for Literature Wole Soyinka (Nigeria, 1986), Naguib Mahfouz (Egypt, 1988), and J. M. Coetzee (South Africa, 2003). The only African women writers to win the Nobel Prize for Literature thus far are Africans of European descent: Nadine Gordimer (South Africa, 1991) and Doris Lessing (2007), who was raised by British colonials in Southern Rhodesia, now Zimbabwe.

5. Tsitsi Dangarembga's first novel, *Nervous Conditions*, was published in 1988, won the African Commonwealth Writers' Prize in 1989, and is widely taught in colleges and high schools worldwide. Dangarembga has gone on to work in film as well, becoming the first black Zimbabwean woman to direct a feature film, *Everybody's Child*, about four African AIDS orphans in 1986. A second novel, *The Book of Not*, was published in 2006. Chimamanda Ngozi Adichie's first novel, *Purple Hibiscus*, a finalist for the Orange Prize for Fiction, was written while she was a student at Eastern Connecticut State University. A good survey of emerging African writers, both male and female, is available on the African Writing Online Web site, http://www.african-writing.com/aug/profiles2.htm.

6. Other groundbreaking African women writers include Bessie Head (Botswana, 1937–86), Flora Nwapa (Nigeria, 1931–93), Nawal El Saadawi (Egypt, 1931–), Zoe Wicomb (South Africa, 1948–), and Werewere Liking (Cameroon, 1950–). See the suggestions for further reading at the end of this volume for more specifics on these and other important African women writers.

7. The African Studies Association provides an excellent resource list of Web sites affiliated with Africana studies: http://www.africanstudies.org/?page=links_page.

8. Current information about African women and HIV/AIDS can be found, among many other sources, on the World Health Organization Web site, http://www.who.int/gender/hiv_aids/en/ index.html; the Global Coalition on Women and AIDS Web site, http://womenandaids.unaids.org/ default.html; and the IRIN news agency focus site on HIV/AIDS in Sub-Saharan Africa, http:// www.plusnews.org/.

9. See an excellent analysis of African maternal mortality and related issues in the article "Reproductive Health in the African Region: What Has Been Done to Improve the Situation?" by Tigrest Ketsela, a pediatrician with postgraduate training in public health and the director of the Division of Family and Reproductive Health in the WHO Regional Office for Africa (WHO/ AFRO), which is based in Brazzaville, Congo. The article is available at http://www.un.org/Pubs/ chronicle/2007/issue4/0407p71.html.

10. A good hub resource for information on African diseases of poverty is maintained by the

United Nations Special Programme for Research and Training in Tropical Diseases, at http://www.who.int/tdr/index.html.

11. See the UNESCO reports on progress toward achieving the Millennium Development Goals for educating girls, at http://portal.unesco.org/education/en/ev.php-URL_ID=34813&URL_DO= DO_TOPIC&URL_SECTION=201.html, as well as reports on the ways in which increased technological access can improve educational opportunities for African women and girls, available at http://www.elearning-africa.com/newsportal/english/news35.php.

12. Female genital cutting, a touchstone issue for many African women's rights activists, is an indigenous tradition in some African regions and is also practiced in tribes that have adopted Islam. Other patriarchal norms that continue to create conflict include the strict relegation of women to the private sphere (reinforced in earlier eras by the Victorian mores of the European colonizers) and the practice of polygamy. For information on female genital cutting, see the Tostan Web site, http://www.tostan.org/web/page/586/sectionid/547/pagelevel/3/interior.asp.

13. Rape was first acknowledged to be a war crime in the aftermath of the Bosnian conflict in the late 1990s, and UN Security Council Resolution 1325 was passed in 2000, officially recognizing the impact of armed conflict on women and calling on governments to include women in the peacemaking process and to provide the means for healing and reconciliation for sexually traumatized women. The full text of Resolution 1325, as well as analysis and useful links, can be found at the Women's International League for Peace and Freedom Web site, http://www.peacewomen.org/un/sc/1325.html. A series of articles, analyses, and multimedia resources on the use of rape as a weapon of war in Africa is available on the IRIN Web site, http://www.irinnews.org/InDepthMain.aspx?InDepthId=20&ReportId=62817. See also the useful 2006 report by Jeanne Ward and Mendy Marsh, "Sexual Violence against Women and Girls in War and Its Aftermath: Realities, Responses, and Required Resources," at http://www.unfpa.org/emergencies/symposium06/docs/finalbrusselsbriefingpaper.pdf, which gives a worldwide view of a problem acutely faced by African women. The Web site of Women for Women International, a nongovernmental organization (NGO) focused on improving the lives of women in postconflict regions, also provides much useful information on this topic: http://www.womenforwomen.org/programs.htm.

14. Excellent regional and country-by-country analysis of the situation of refugees or internally displaced persons (IDPs) is provided by the Internal Displacement Monitoring Centre at http://www.internal-displacement.org/8025708F004CE90B/(httpRegionPages)/BBA6119 B705C145802570A600546F85?OpenDocument. Additionally, a series of recommendations on improving conditions for women and children who have been internally displaced by conflict is available on the Brookings Institute Web site at http://www.brookings.edu/speeches/2004/~/media/Files/rc/speeches/2004/0526humanrights_mooney/20040526_mooney.pdf.

15. See the BBC Special Report "Peacekeepers Abusing Children" at http://news.bbc.co.uk/2/hi/in_depth/7420798.stm or the Human Rights Watch report at http://www.hrw.org/english/docs/2008/04/03/darfur18424.htm to get a sense of the scope of the problem.

16. See the UN High Commission for Refugees report "South Africa: How Heavy Is Human Trafficking," at http://www.unhcr.org/refworld/docid/48ced5e1e.html, for a window into this problem just in South Africa. Human trafficking is occurring all over the continent on an unprecedented scale, as is evident in the following 2003 expert testimony before the House International Relations Committee by a doctor representing Doctors Without Borders: http://physiciansforhuman rights.org/library/2003-06-25.html.

17. A number of online Web sites provide a great window into the leading edge of the African literary scene. See, for example, African Writing Online at http://african-writing.com/hol/profiles .htm; Words Without Borders at http://www.wordswithoutborders.org/?sec=Africa; African Writer at http://www.africanwriter.com/; *Farafina* magazine at http://farafinamagazine.com/fi4/index .php.

18. Contributor quotations in this section are from personal letters sent to the editors in response to a query, What does resistance mean to you?

19. Information about the African Women's Development Fund is available at http://awdf.org/ web/index.php/about-awdf. Information about Tostan is available at http://www.tostan.org/web/ page/556/sectionid/556/pagelevel/1/parentid/556/interior.asp. Information about FEMNET is available at http://www.femnet.or.ke/default.asp.

20. We borrow the term *compassionate witnessing* from Dr. Kaethe Weingarten of Harvard University, whose groundbreaking work on the value of a compassionate listener to heal post-traumatic stress is detailed in her book *Common Shock* (Penguin, 2003). A condensed version of her argument is available online at http://www.humiliationstudies.org/documents/WeingartenCompassionate Witnessing.pdf.

Part One

Engaging with Tradition

Many African women writers are engaged in an ongoing process of negotiating with the past in order to empower themselves in the present. While this is a theme that is sounded in several other sections in this anthology, part 1 brings together four pieces that focus directly on women's struggle to balance the often competing goals of honoring valuable traditional practices while rejecting those that keep them from prospering as individuals and as members of their social groups.

The first story in this section, "The Day When God Changed His Mind" by Eve Zvichanzi Nyemba of Zimbabwe, combines myth with politics in depicting the success of a young warrior woman in winning back her grandfather's kingdom, which he had lost through the treachery of an enemy. Set in a mythic time and place, the story celebrates a young woman who will not let anyone—not even her beloved grandmother—tell her that her place is in the kitchen cooking for her husband rather than in the field of battle on behalf of her people. Significantly, her initially recalcitrant, tradition-minded grandmother joins her in her struggle, and together with her husband, the son of the deposed king, the three warriors are successful, old and young working together to right an old wrong.

"The Old Woman," by J. Tsitsi Mutiti of Zimbabwe, is also set in an indeterminate time, but it seems closer to the present, and the issue at hand is the uneasy relation between the positive use of traditional medicine and the sometimes capricious use of superstition as a means of scapegoating innocent people. The unnamed old woman of the title is on her way to the city to bring a powerful amulet to her son, a politician who has been jailed for corruption. Along the way, she herself is made the target of someone else's superstition, when a medicine man accuses her of bewitching some crying babies on the bus. She manages to evade the charge, but the story leaves us with lingering questions about ongoing negotiations of the past in contemporary African society.

The third piece in this section moves away from fiction, providing a space for a voice rarely heard in the annals of African women's literature: that of a Babongo woman, from the Congolese ethnic group formerly known as Pygmies. Kaya a Mbaya tells the story of how traditionally the Babongo people have been mistreated and practically enslaved by the Bantus, the larger and more powerful ethnic group in the region. Babongo women have worked hard to raise their families in dignity, despite the handicaps of discrimination and lack of access to education and health care. Her story shows how hard it can be to maintain positive cultural practices in the face of oppression and desperate poverty.

In the final piece in this section, Elisabeth Bouanga, a Bantu woman from the same region of the Congo as Kaya a Mbaya, tells her story in an interview with her daughter, Pauline Dongala, a coeditor of and contributor to this anthology. Though the Bantus may be privileged in relation to the Babongos, Elisabeth Bouanga's story shows that even women from privileged backgrounds struggle with cultural practices designed to keep them disempowered. When her husband died, Bouanga was left a widow with a co-wife and fourteen children to support between them. Following tradition, her husband's family wanted to marry the two women off within the family or force them to pay back their dowries. Bouanga resisted and sought the protection of the police, who interceded in her favor, allowing her to keep her house and her widowhood. After her co-wife remarried, Bouanga kept all fourteen children and successfully raised them on her own, focusing all her efforts on securing for them the formal education that she herself had been denied.

Taken as a group, the stories in this section illustrate the power of women not only to resist harmful traditions but also to begin to create new cultural practices that will better serve themselves and their daughters in the future.

The Day When God Changed His Mind

Eve Zvichanzi Nyemba

She stood tall and mighty, high and proud. The clouds had gathered and a cool refreshing wind washed over her. She shivered slightly but did not change her position. She was standing on one of the majestic Nyanga mountains. She looked down from the mountain top. The distance was enough to make anyone shiver, but Tamara was a warrior and this was her kingdom!

Tamara wore the traditional garb well known to the Ndau sect. Her hair was long and plaited. Her skirt was of leopard skin, rough and oily as it rubbed against her long, slender legs. Her chest was covered by finely strung cattle hide, and she had bangles on her right arm. On her back, Tamara carried a small sack, where she put her bows and arrows. She was a true warrior, but a warrior without recognition, a leader without followers. Yes, she was alone in her quest to claim back what was rightfully hers, to take what had been stolen away from her—the throne. It belonged to the Chideya family. She might be a mere woman in the eyes of all who saw her, but she was more than what people saw.

Since time immemorial, a man had always ruled over the Ndau kingdom. A woman's place was at the cooking fire, Tamara had heard her grandmother say so many times.

"Not me," she had said, shaking her head violently. "My place is on the throne. I'm a princess. A leader of the Ndau people." She hissed softly and the dog that lay beside her suddenly stood as if agreeing with her. She patted it slightly and then, as the clouds continued to gather, she said, "Shumba, let's go," and she ran all the way to her hut, the dog on her trail.

Mbuya Chideya raised the calabash to her lips and drank the luscious liquid. She handed the calabash to her husband who took his fill of the porridge-like maheu drink. As she wiped her mouth, she murmured, "I don't understand our Tamara girl at all. She does not behave like any normal girl would. She spends hours and hours in the forest hunting. Her place is here with me at the cooking place preparing a fine meal, not chasing after a man's job."

Sekuru Chideya raised the calabash from his mouth, cleared his throat, and gingerly said, "Let her be. Her heart lies elsewhere. Don't you see that she was sent from the heavens above? Does any boy her age match her? Do you think it's normal? We should thank God for her."

"I am beginning to see that you are losing your mind," Mbuya Chideya said as she added logs to the burning fire. "Tamara is a very beautiful girl. No man looks at her once and forgets her. There have been many suitors seeking her hand in marriage but lo, she spends the day doing a man's job! Soon no one will come after her. She is a disgrace to this family! How can you say she is a gift from God?"

Sekuru raised the calabash to his lips again and took in the rich liquid. He shook his head in protest at Mbuya's argument. Finally he bellowed, "Do not forget that the throne rightfully belongs to this family. Remember how the throne was stolen from us!" He suddenly looked much older than his age, but his voice was firm.

"My father was king of this territory," he said more calmly.

"Who doesn't know that?" Mbuya interrupted him.

He raised his hand to still her voice and then continued, "He was a brave warrior—" Just as he was saying this, Tamara entered the hut, gasping for breath. She knelt and said, while clapping her hands, "Good evening, Mbuya and Sekuru."

"Ah! Here comes my favorite granddaughter. Come and sit beside me," Sekuru Chideya cried.

"Good evening Tamara," Mbuya said. Her voice hardened. "This behavior of yours must stop," she added sternly. "You are now a grown woman, ripe for marriage. Forget about playing tomboy for a change. Chandinakira came to see you. He said he will come back tomorrow."

"I don't want to see him!" Tamara cried.

"You will do as I say," her grandmother ground out between gritted teeth.

"But Mbuya, I don't want to become his fifth wife!" Tamara said vehemently.

"What do you want to become? The laughing stock of this compound?" her grandmother retorted.

"No, Mbuya! You have always known where my heart lies—"

Mbuya did not let her finish. "Which heart? The talk about war and king-doms is for men. No man will ever allow a woman to rule over them. Wake up, Tamara! Tomorrow you will see Chandinakira and that is final."

"No!" Tamara wailed.

"I will not have you disobey me!" said Mbuya, now visibly angry.

"Let her be," said Sekuru again, coming to Tamara's rescue. Mbuya rose angrily. "You tell me 'let her be,' are you going to marry her yourself?"

"It is right for her to seek what she desires. Let her fulfill what God sent her to do."

"To hell with God!" Mbuya swore violently.

"You see, my father, he was a brave warrior—" Sekuru continued, ignoring Mbuya.

"I don't have to listen to this!" she said as she headed for the door. She stopped, turned, and then said, "I wash my hands of Tamara. You do what you want with her, since you feed her with this rubbish that one day she will rule over the Ndau people. Will teaching her about the methods of warfare earn her a husband? Why are you encouraging her? I am sure your father is turning in his grave!" She stormed out of the hut.

"My father drove away the Samanyika," Sekuru continued, as if nothing had happened. Tamara crept closer to the fire, reveling in the story she had heard so many times.

"He brought peace and liberty to the Ndau kingdom. He conquered the Zezurus, the Vakorekores, and even the Nyanjas. All these fine-looking beasts the king now owns were won by my father in great battle. Up to this day, the Ndau are feared because of him.

"No one in this kingdom could throw an arrow like my father. He never missed. No one could run like a cheetah but Chideya himself. No could fight like a mighty lion and conquer thousands like him."

Sekuru was silent before he continued, "Chideya had ruled for just two years when his own *jinda* [general] became jealous. What a coward Rushowe was! He waited for Chideya's weakest moment. He had just won the war against the Zezurus, but he had been stabbed savagely. Rushowe went to my father's hut in the night where he was recuperating. He did not see me behind him. He took some fire and lit the roof of my father's hut as I looked on helplessly. I hid myself in the bushes nearby. After some time, Rushowe wailed bitterly, "Fire! Fire! Please bring water! Water!"

Tears suddenly filled Sekuru's eyes, "No one could save him. I tried to tell everyone what had happened but no one believed me. They said I was just a child who didn't know what to say. When I grew up, I tried to fight Rushowe, but he was too strong for me." He pointed to the huge, fearsome scar on his chest. "He drove me out of the king's kraal and threw me in this wretched compound. That is when your grandmother gave birth to your father. When he grew up, Rushowe's son became jealous of your father and slaughtered him. He made it appear as if he had been wounded in battle. Your mother committed suicide when you were an infant suckling from her breasts. She was heartbroken. Who could blame her?"

A thick, oppressive silence fell, a silence you could hear. After a few painful moments, Tamara picked up the story. "And now Rushowe treats us like trash. There has been no rain for the past three years, but he demands that we give him two-thirds of our meager produce. The people are dying from hunger and disease and does he care?" She stood up and paced the hut restlessly.

Finally she proceeded. "Tonight is the night of victory. Tonight the Ndau people will know no hunger. Tonight is the night of redemption." Together with her grandfather, she chanted:

> Chideya! Chideya!
> The name that thunders.
> The ones who bellows.
> Kingship belongs to you!

The two danced as the flames leaped into the air, covering their bodies in sweat. Mbuya reappeared at the entrance, her eyes fixed on the two in awe. Soon she could not contain herself; she joined in their dancing and merriment.

After the dance was over Tamara announced, "I'm ready, grandfather. Give me your blessing. Tonight is the night of restoration!" She went and knelt before him.

"Go with all my blessings, granddaughter," Sekuru said.

Tamara stood and went to hug her grandmother. "I know you say that a woman's place is at the fireplace, cooking for her husband and children. It's not that I do not desire that, but first things first. I will not rest till the throne is in my hands, where it belongs."

"Go with God," Mbuya Chideya said, tears welling in her eyes. Somehow the magic of the moment had made her realize that nothing she could do would ever stop Tamara from pursuing her dream.

As Tamara went out, her grandfather's voice stopped her. "Wait! I am coming with you," he said as he took up his spear and shield. He threw a sack full of arrows over his shoulder.

"I'm coming too," Mbuya said suddenly, and picked up her axe. Both Tamara and Sekuru stared at her in surprise but neither said a word.

The king's court was quiet as midnight approached. Everyone was asleep, save for the guards who roamed about the palace. Tamara was lying flat on her stomach on top of a small hill as she watched the guards. She had counted them all. There were twenty.

"Let's go," she whispered to her grandparents.

The guards at the first entrance saw a movement in the undergrowth and wondered what it was. One decided to go and check. He scanned the bushes but he saw nothing, changed his mind, and was about to walk away when he heard a weak wail. He looked again, his pulse quickening annoyingly. That is when he saw the old lady. She was holding her stomach with her left hand as she limped pitifully. He put down his spear as he went to help the poor soul, but before he had reached her, an arrow had found its way through his heart and he fell with a thud.

A second guard emerged, but before he could go far, an arrow went right through his throat, rendering him cold and lifeless. The silence of the night was quickly restored as if nothing had happened. At the second entrance, Tamara limped as she approached the line of six guards.

"What does this girl want?" one guard growled.

"She seems hurt," another answered.

"She looks like that infamous Chideya girl. I wonder if she has come to take the throne?" The guards roared in laughter. Before their laughter had died down, an arrow had plunged itself into the throat of the guard who had last spoken. His smile froze and his eyes became still as he fell, blood gushing from his mouth. While the guards were distracted, Tamara hid herself in a nearby shrub. Well hidden by leaves, she aimed her arrow at the next guard and continued to fire until the last guard fell.

The main entrance was the most difficult one: there would be twelve guards. Mbuya ran toward the guards, her hands on her head as she wailed uncontrollably. She fell down in front of one of the four guards lounging outside.

"What is your problem, woman?" the guard growled. While the attention of the guards was focused on the howling woman, they did not see an old man and a young girl run stealthily up to them. When the first guard looked about, it was too late—a spear was shoved into his body.

Tamara swiftly axed the remaining guards. A fifth guard saw this from afar and shouted from the top of his voice, "Invaders! Invaders!" Tamara released an arrow, swearing violently. It went right through the guard's stomach, but he had raised the alarm and the remaining guards ran toward them from all directions. Sekuru raised his bow and arrow and aimed. Tamara did the same. After they had killed five more guards, the silence of the night was restored.

Where were the other two?

As they entered the gates of the palace compound, a foreboding silence greeted them. They went straight to the king's huts. Women and children were beginning to come out of their huts as if they were welcoming the new intruders. Tamara bravely led her grandmother as they went to the king's huts. Suddenly, Tamara and Mbuya were pushed violently to the ground from behind. An arrow passed above Tamara's head and when she got up, she saw a man fall with an arrow in his back. The nineteenth guard.

Tamara silently thanked her grandfather, and they continued on.

The king's hut was strangely unguarded. Tamara knocked sharply on the door. There was no answer. She took a few steps back and, using her right foot, hit the door with all her might. The door flew open. The king lay sprawled on the floor with his eyes wide open staring at the roof. Without warning, an earth-shattering sound broke out as a huge calabash fell and broke, exposing the queen and the twentieth guard who had been hiding behind it. They looked frightened.

Tamara growled, "Get to your feet."

Sekuru grabbed the guard and pointed his spear at his abdomen while Mbuya held her ax by the queen's throat.

"Now," Tamara said decisively, "which of you two killed the king, and why?"

"It was me," the guard said.

"No it was me!" the queen shouted.

"Don't waste my time or I will have both of you hanged," Tamara said severely.

"I killed him," the queen said. "I plunged a knife into his heart. He was going to marry another woman and bring shame to my family by sending me back, since I could not bear any children."

"And you," Tamara shouted at the guard, "what was your involvement in this?"

"I love her! She wouldn't listen to me when I told her not to kill the king," he answered, his face ashy with fright.

"Both of you get out, before I change my mind and decide to hang you," Tamara said.

Sekuru, Mbuya, and Tamara followed them outside, where a huge crowd of people had gathered.

"Today, I have taken over my father's kingdom," Tamara said, addressing the crowd. "This kingdom was stolen from my family a long time ago." She went on to repeat the famous story of Chideya. When she was through, her voice was hoarse as she shouted, "Who is with me?"

"Long live Tamara! Long live the princess!" the people chanted. They were happy that the brutal king had been overthrown. They had longed for this moment for a long time, and it did not bother them that it was a woman who had defeated Rushowe. They were confident that Tamara would follow in her father's footsteps and be a just ruler.

As they continued to chant and sing their praises to her, ten powerful men emerged from the crowd and stood by Tamara's side. "We are at your disposal, your majesty," said one loudly. "We will become your guards."

There was shouting and ululating as more men arrived and joined the queen's guards. Mbuya Chideya smiled joyfully as she hugged Tamara and said weakly, "Today is the day when God has changed his mind, for look now! A woman rules."

Glossary

maheu	a porridge-like drink common in Zimbabwe, made out of mealie meal
sekuru	grandfather
mbuya	grandmother
jinda	a Shona general
Ndau	a Shona tribe found in Zimbabwe, prominently in Chipinge, Chimanimani, and Mutare
Zezuru	a Shona tribe found in Zimbabwe, particularly in Murewa, Buhera, Zvimba, Wedza, and Guruve
Korekore	a Shona tribe found in Zimbabwe, particularly in Hurungwe, Chinhoyi, and the Mashonaland West Region
Ndebele	a tribe that speaks a dialect close to the Zulu language; although they are found in most parts of Zimbabwe because of migration, they are usually found in Bulawayo

The Old Woman

J. Tsitsi Mutiti

Give me hope that
Help is coming
When I need it most . . .
Tracy Chapman,
"Let It Rain"

Since this morning when she woke up, something has been weighing heavily on her, a premonition. Of course, you might think to yourself, anybody in your circumstances would feel things weighing them down. But really it is not that. It is true her son and his situation have been weighing heavily on her mind. It has not been easy to raise three children singlehandedly. Beyond that, she can see history repeating itself. The same politics that made her first a grass widow, then a real one, look set to leave her bereft of a son now. She has been to see him several times in prison and things are not going well for him. He has even been denied bail. Considering what a star he had been in the party previously and how he had been rising, things are not at all well.

Her consultations with Sekuru show that this is going to be an arduous battle even though he has promised that they will win in the end. When she looks at the charm, it does not look so impressive considering that it cost her a whole cow; she just hopes it works. It had better work after the big risk she ran in going to see a *n'anga*; she, the leader of the Sacred Heart Society at church!

22

She carefully wraps the ointment in her old petticoat and packs it in the bottom of the bag. The amulets she wraps in her *doek* and puts in the side pocket. She decides to go to Harare on Monday, since Ticha's court day is Tuesday, so that she will only have to stay a day with that wife of his.

At the bus stop she and her baggage make a sad little island; the wide berth every young person gives the old and unattractive is always so obvious. Pity for them they can't maintain it in the bus where they have to sit squashed up three to a seat. When the bus finally arrives, she manages to get in first and comfortably, since nobody wants to be pushing and shoving against her old body. In the bus she eventually settles in the far corner after squeezing past a surly young woman dressed in bright, new-looking clothes. Lost in thought, she no longer sees the dusty scenery flashing by. Her son, languishing in jail for the past several months, denied even bail, weighs heavily on her mind.

I was never very happy with the way he shot so quickly to prominence. It was frightening to see the way he, who had struggled so beforehand, was suddenly able to build a beautiful, expensive house and buy two shiny new cars in such a short time. To my questions he answered, "Amai, is this not what you sent me to school for? I am educated after all and with all my degrees I should make money! Ko, do you think my ancestors are sleeping? What, aren't I a dutiful son? Don't I remember to honor my ancestors?" Ah, so it was your degrees, was it, mwanangu? What are you doing now in jail?

She sighs and gradually becomes aware of a commotion near where she is sitting. Loud wailing is coming from somewhere behind her and she glances back to see. A young woman on the seat behind her is rocking a howling baby in her arms and humming to quiet it. The baby continues to wail furiously at the top of its lungs.

"Why don't you feed him?" a male voice near her suggests. It rather amuses her how that seems to be the height of male knowledge of baby care. Is the baby crying? Why don't you feed it?

"Yes, feed him. You young mothers abuse your babies letting them cry like that! He must be hungry. Go on, then, feed him!" another impatient male voice joins the chorus. That is their best advice, it is.

Shyly, the young woman withdraws a plump breast from her blouse and puts the nipple in the baby's mouth. She covers the baby with a corner of its shawl, while it suckles to the accompaniment of "I told you so's." The respite is brief, however, as the infant soon spits out the nipple and lets out a wail loud enough to wake the dead. Another baby nearby immediately joins in, and the two begin to bawl in unison. It really is nerve-wracking the way they are crying, with the mothers frantically trying to hush them.

Soon there is an uneasy buzz in the bus, together with furtive glances thrown in her direction. Gradually the stares become openly accusing. Worried, she ponders.

At my age it is easy for people to believe that you are capable of any sort of evil-doing. How else have you managed to outlive all your age mates and so many of your juniors? Truly, living long is not always the blessing it is made out to be. How much easier it is for strangers to accuse one when even one's own nearest and dearest cast the same condemning looks. Even my daughter-in-law: first it was my fault her husband did not succeed in life. Now that his dizzy flight to success has ended in such an ignominious fall, it is my resentment that has done that too. Of course I never wanted his success, for what mother wants another woman to enjoy her son's money? That is what they believe, all these young women. To hear her, you would think that she never wanted to be my son's wife! Doesn't she realize that she will grow to be a mother-in-law in her own turn? Once people are convinced of your evilness nothing will ever change their minds.

The bus stops suddenly and she wonders why they are stopping, as they are in the middle of nowhere and there is not a commuter in sight. The next moment, the conductor's announcement throws her into consternation.

"Everybody get down with your bags and stand next to them. We have *Tsikamutanda** in here with us and he says that he has smelled something evil on this bus. If we do not follow his advice we will not get where we are going."

Tsikamutanda! The scourge of all witches and sorcerers and their ilk throughout the country! She had never seen one before but she had heard enough about them to make her uncomfortable with what she is carrying, and

---

*Tsikamutanda was the name of a highly acclaimed traditional healer in the Mashonaland region of Zimbabwe during the 1980s (the first decade of Independence). The name was derived from his method of sniffing out witches and other evil doers: it was a sort of trial by ordeal where he would make people step over a stick (*kutsika mutanda*) and those guilty would fall. He would then discover that they were carrying all sorts of sorcery charms or fetishes. The Tsikamutanda phenomenon captured the popular imagination and spawned many copycat operators throughout the country. Now it is a virtual institution and the term is a professional name adopted by those engaging in witch hunts, as well as a generic term to refer to those who practice witch hunting even if they do not specifically employ the name.

what she sees of this one is hardly reassuring. It is not evil or witchery that she carries, but one can never be too sure. Besides, a man that young, hardly more than a boy really, can only be thought a great seer in today's world. The youth are taking hold of everything. She slowly hobbles down the steps with her bag and joins the queue, with the babies' howling in her ears. While they are in the queue, the conductor is busy shouting, "All you people come on, hurry up! Everyone next to his bag! Now whose bag is this? Whose bag is this? WHOSE BAG IS THIS?" It looks as if that particular bag had been abandoned by its owner. Everyone wonders what it contains.

"Whoever owns this bag, come forward before you are exposed. Face up to your things and come and claim your bag." No one steps forward. Would you?

"We will start with this bag then. Those of the night do not like their things exposed to the light. Do not look unless you know yourself strong." Tsikamutanda kneels down and opens the bag gingerly, feeling inside it as he mutters to himself in a strange language. The old woman is not sure whether it is the strange object covered in black and red beads or the dramatic manner in which he whips it out of the bag that causes the sensation in the crowd. Some women scream and run away, disrupting the queue.

"Now you ladies! Why do you want to see things for which you have no heart? Your chests are too weak for some sights. I told you not to look if you can't stand it." But even if they cannot stand the sight, who would want to miss out on the exciting rare sight of *tokoloshis*, those fabled goblins of the other realm?

Oh, why today of all days does this have to happen? You, my husband, who have gone ahead, do not let me or your child down. Tembo, is this why you left me to bring up this child alone? What am I to do if he is jailed? Can I possibly look after that wife of his and his small children? Tembo, you know how she wants all these expensive things and she has nothing. What sort of father are you? You left me to raise them alone, and now you can't even cast your protective shadow over your child? Holy Mary Mother of God, who promises to intercede on behalf of us sinners, make my son's things safe. Maybe if Tembo was unwilling or unable to help, then at least Mother Mary would.

She watches Tsikamutanda closely as he moves closer and closer to her and holds her breath. From the way he smelt out those first objects in the unclaimed bag it appears he genuinely can smell out bad *muti*, or juju, as the young ones now call it. About three people before her, he lets out an appalling hiss and grabs at the woman before him. His hand shaking, he withdraws a shriveled piece of dried skin.

"The spirit of your grandson whom you ate cried out to expose you. Have you no shame eating your own? What sort of hen are you, feeding on your own eggs?"

Suddenly there is a huge space between this woman and the others who had been standing next to her. The young woman with the crying baby looks at her as if she were a maggot and spits.

All too suddenly, Tsikamutanda is upon the old woman. He grabs her bag, opens it, and his unerring hand finds something and pulls it out. It turns out to be a piece of roast chicken wrapped in newspaper.

"You, Ambuya, are a clever one. This time you have defeated me; turning your evil muti into harmless-looking meat. If this is really meat, eat it now before these people and prove your innocence."

Gladly did she eat that piece of chicken! Soon afterward everyone was back on the bus and on their way. The other passengers feel badly about Tsikamutanda's accusation, but she keeps her peace, focusing again on her mission.

A day later, her son is out of jail. They finally allowed him bail. Whether it is thanks to the n'anga's muti or the spirits of his father and those gone before or to Tsikamutanda or to Mother Mary, she will never know. What she knows is that when the time comes for his trial she shall be making the journey to Harare again.

Interview with
Kaya a Mbaya,
a Babongo Woman

Pierre Piya-Bouanga

Kaya a Mbaya, a Babongo woman of approximately forty years of age, was born in the forest of Tele in the district of Sibiti. She now lives in the forests around the village of Missama, also in the district of Sibiti, in the Republic of the Congo. Kaya a Mbaya is married and mother of several children and grandchildren.

The minority people called Pygmies by the colonizers are called Babongo in the local language (singular: Mubongo). Physically, they do not correspond anymore to the portrait of them painted by the early European explorers: today the Babongo people are taller than they used to be (1.2 to 1.5 m) because their morphology has changed through sexual contact with larger people. Most Babongo people live in or near the forests, where they carry on their traditional activities of hunting and gathering. They reside in more or less sedentary villages, together with the other major ethnic group in the Congo, the Bantus.

This interview took place in January 2006.* Because of the widespread suspicion between the Pygmies and the Bantu communities, it was difficult to gain the trust of Madame Kaya a Mbaya. My mother first approached the Pygmy community with some gifts that I sent, and after visiting the village two or three times, she was able to begin to forge some lines of communication, if not of actual friendship, with Kaya a Mbaya. The path thus smoothed for me, I approached the village myself to conduct the interview, leaving my motorcycle at the edge of the forest and walking half an hour further into the forest to arrive at my destination. The interview was rather long, between eight and fourteen hours, including the time that was needed to overcome her distrust, as well as the time it took me to write down her responses, since I did not have a tape recorder. I spoke in Kiyaka, a language that the Pygmies in this area understand quite well, and she responded in the Pygmy language, which my mother and I understand fairly well.

What are your current relations with Bantus?

Bantus consider the Babongo as subhuman, second-class people. Very rare are those among them who consider us as human beings. Take, for example, the case of marriages between Bantus and Pygmies: they are almost nonexistent. You can count them on the fingers of one hand. In those marriages, it is the Bantu man who marries the Pygmy woman, whereas no Pygmy man is allowed to marry a Bantu woman. Bantus say that we are swine, that we smell bad, that our woman emit bad odors, that we do not wash ourselves. Moreover, they accuse us of being lazy, liars; in short, good-for-nothings.

In fact, the laziness they attribute to us is due to the fact that we easily find our livelihood in the forest that is our home. In the forest, a Mubongo finds all that is necessary: honey, mushrooms, game, fruits, fish, wild vegetables, and even medicine. But now, you see, our forest is being destroyed. Where will we live? Where will we go to find our food? Even the animals, to whom we were very close, are running away from us and becoming very rare.

But let me go back to my subject: a Bantu man is ashamed to show publicly that he carries on an intimate relationship with a Pygmy woman, and yet they are secretly crazy about us—especially at the time of our dances, when they come to admire us.

A Mubongo does not have the right to look a Bantu straight in the eyes. When a Bantu and a Mubongo meet on a road, the Mubongo must give way

---

*This interview was commissioned by Pauline Dongala. It was translated into French by Pierre Piya-Bouanga, then into English by Jennifer Browdy de Hernandez.

and let his "Master" Bantu pass. They do not eat the food prepared by us; they say we do not know how to cook.

Are there cases of rape in your society?

The women of my generation and certainly our ancestors did not know this phenomenon. But today, the young Bantu people, because of the loosening of moral standards, will wait for our girls when they go to the river or the fields and make advances to them. When the girls refuse this kind of relations, the Bantus beat them. A raped or beaten girl, when she returns to the village, prefers to keep silence; she does not speak to her parents about it for fear of reprisals. It is especially the young Bantu who are addicted to drugs who do this kind of thing. Nonetheless, it is still fairly rare. When Bantus go with our wives, they bring along their diseases. We heard about this new disease which kills . . . AIDS. We have even written songs about it to warn our young people against it. In these songs we tell our daughters to avoid any sexual contact with the young Bantus.

Do you use condoms? [The interviewer shows her one and shows how it is used.]

No, it is unknown to us. Our men say that they do not need this thing to cover their male body. . . . [*She shows some discomfort at talking about this even though there seems to be a malicious glint in her eyes.*] When a Bantu gives the disease to one of our women, he flees the village. It is a shame. The sick woman is abandoned to her sad fate. We do not go to the hospital because we do not have money to pay for the drugs; we treat ourselves with the plants, wood, and certain animal parts. Moreover, during the civil war, even the Bantus came here to ask us to cure them with our plants and medicine. They abandoned their villages to live in the forest because of the war.

Do you often have cases of adultery with Bantus?

When a Bantu is caught in a case of adultery with a Pygmy woman, he is brought to the village chief. He is judged and must pay a fine. Some of them, because of shame, prefer to make an amicable settlement by secretly paying the offending Pygmy husband, instead of standing judgment in front of the whole village; they do not want the story to be spread.

What type of relation exists between a Mubongo woman and her husband?

The Mubongo woman is proud of her tradition, because our tradition has always respected the position of the woman in a marriage. In our tradition, it is the man who leaves his parents to join the family of the woman he marries. It is not like you Bantus, where the woman will join her husband. Divorce is rare, just as a man leaving his wife is rare. A Mubongo loves his wife and his children. In our society, there are no sterile men or women. We also have our children very early.

Do sexual mutilations exist in your society?

[*Astonished*] This practice is unknown in our society. If that existed, no Mubongo woman would accept it! How is that done?

What relation exists between a Pygmy woman and a Bantu woman?

They are sustained relations. A Bantu woman who recruits us to work in her field makes us work from morning to evening for 500 F CFA [Franc de la Communauté Financière d'Afrique]. The woman also gives us sufficient food in addition to the money. In times past, for working a peanut field she would give us a *pagne* [traditional dress]. But now things have changed because of the market in Sibiti. In this market, we easily find secondhand clothes which enable us to dress ourselves and our children. You see, all my children are clothed. Before there was this market they were completely or half naked. Things have changed!

There is something that I have to say: while Bantus use us on their plantations, we forsake our own fields. In the end, we find ourselves without food and we are forced to go buy manioc from the Bantus! One of us, Ngounimba, a Mubongo, a Pygmy and proud to be one, came here to encourage us to work our own fields and to cease depending on Bantus. Unfortunately, they did not leave us the necessary tools. We need machetes, axes, shovels. Please go and tell those who sent you that even the food they send us as aid, like rice and beans, is hijacked by the Bantu. And yet these were intended for us! [*She says these last words with force.*]

Do your children go to school with the Bantu children?

Yes, but they do not spend much time there because they cannot buy the books. We cannot thus ensure the schooling of our children. We have to pay the young teachers and for the other school material. That costs a lot. We do not have money. Don't they know our difficult living conditions?

Are your children bullied or harassed by the Bantu children?

Yes, [they were] at the beginning. But things have changed. Our children used to sit on the last benches because the Bantu children refused to sit down beside them. But today, they live together at the village, out of the forest. They play ball together. You know, our children can run, and they score more goals than Bantu children! [*She leans over and points to a board on a wall in the village.*] You see over there? These letters on the boards of our walls are written by our children! [*She says this with unmitigated pride.*]

Do the Babongo children take drugs?

Oh yes, increasingly so! The contact with Bantus and modernity has brought along these new practices. You know, we are people of the dance, we are dancers. Our children do not dance our traditional music any more. They go to Sibiti during the festivals, to dance the modern dances with Bantus. They spend the night there and drink Kelé-welé and Koroto [local wines drawn from palm trees]. Then they all become wild! They become insane! And then they take all kinds of grass and even *diamba* [Indian hemp]. In Télé a young Mubongo became crazy because of this grass. You know, we do not know moderation in our society. We do everything with exaggeration. When we dance, it is all night. When we drink, even the women get themselves drunk! However, it is rare to meet a Bantu woman drunk in the village.

What do the parents do to educate their children and to put an end to this state of affairs?

Can you educate a child who is addicted? For us it is a lost child, a child who has become useless for the family. Even Moukila, the village healer, cannot do anything. Really, our young people are bewitched by the bad spirits.

Where do the Babongo women deliver their babies?

Our wives deliver their babies in the forest or in the village. Seldom at the hospital. Babongo are very poor. At the hospital in Sibiti, you have to pay for many things. All of my children were born here at the village with the assistance of our own midwives. We do not know the maternity hospital. There they ask us for many documents we don't have, such as identity papers. My husband and I do not have any.

There is however something that I have to say: once in a while a Mubongo woman will have difficulty delivering her child. There are some goodwill Bantus who will help her go to the hospital to be operated upon. Thus, the mother and the child will be saved.

A final word?

[*She concentrates and gives up her merry and relaxed attitude.*] Yes, I will say that Bantus must respect us more; they should give us the same consideration they give to their wives. Times change, we want to be treated as equals. We want to be human beings, like them. We want to walk together with them toward the future because both of us have no choice but to cohabit, to attend the same places of prayer, the same schools, the same playgrounds. You see, even our women do not go fishing anymore, they prefer eating commercial fish. We Babongo want to safeguard our culture, our natural environment, and our practices, while adapting to modern times. Can you believe that for a debt of 100 F CFA a Bantu can come to a Pygmy village and seize five or six hens? This is unjust. We want to live quietly, on good terms with all.

One last question: Do you have associations to defend your rights?

[*Smiling.*] We are dispersed. We find ourselves together only at the time of the great festivals. We live in dispersed communities, so how can we come together as an organized group to deal with our problems?

Interview with
Elisabeth Bouanga

Remembrance of Things Past

Pauline Dongala

Can you tell us who you are?*

I am Elisabeth Bouanga Milondo. My parents gave me the name of Elisabeth Boulah Mpoumou when I was born. After I was married, my husband decided to give me the name of Bouanga Milondo as a testimony of our love. Later my grandsons and their friends nicknamed me Betoula. I was born in 1931 in the village of Bikie, which lies in the district of Sibiti, located in a district of the Republic of the Congo called Lekoumou.

---

*The interview was conducted in French during a visit Mrs. Bouanga made to her daughter Pauline's home in Massachusetts in 2006. English translation by Jennifer Browdy de Hernandez.

Tell us about your birth.

I was born under a banana tree; my umbilical cord was cut immediately with the leaf of a plant called *kenguere*, which has razor sharp edges, and then buried. This is what my parents Suzanne Nzobo and Missimi Noah told me. They also said that they planted a banana tree at the place where the umbilical cord had been buried. A child born healthy, without any physical impairment, has to go through certain rituals and prayers in order to be protected by nature, by plants and leaves, so that no malevolent act can hurt her.

Now tell us about your childhood.

I come from the Mbingui clan, a very powerful clan of *mfumu* [chiefs]; because of that I am myself a chief also, according to tradition, and so are my children and their descendants. My parents were important traditional healers. People from faraway villages came to their place to be cured. My father was also known as a great hunter. When I was about six years old, my mother pressured my father to send me to primary school. I was a very good pupil; I knew the French alphabet well. I could recite very well the French recitations that they asked us to memorize. One well-known one is "Ma main" [My Hand]: "Ma main, voici ma main, / elle a dix doigts, en voici deux, etc." [My hand, here is my hand, / It has five fingers here are two, etc.]

How long did you go to school?

I did not go to school for long. One day the master struck me so badly with a whip that I was injured. That evening, my father decided to withdraw me from the school. It should be said that in that time, and even later, women were supposed to remain at home to do domestic work and work in the field. School was reserved for men. I always obeyed what my father said, so I stopped going to school without further thinking.

What did you do, how was your life after you left the school?

I stayed with my parents. I learned how to cure people with traditional plants, how to cook and to work in the fields. My parents loved each other very much, and there was love in my family. The respect and the love of your fellow man was the rule in our house. I had a very good childhood. Prayer was also very important for us.

Speaking about prayer, in which religion were you raised?

When I was growing up, I remember vividly that we prayed in our house and my parents called upon the ancestors every time, and we also prayed to Nzambi ya Mpungu. When there was a problem that required a spiritual intervention, my parents invoked the names of ancestors we called *outa mou kouh*. Marriages had their rites as well, such as "getting a baby out." Three months after the birth of a baby, a mother can take the child out of the house and take him along with her everywhere she wants to. There were rules for everything, for example, not to sweep the house after nightfall and not to call aloud or shout the name of a person after a certain time in the evening. The ceremonies performed during weddings were important because they brought together the two families as well as their ancestors, who then became common to both families. There was also the dowry given by the man's family, as well as the wine drunk and poured in a corner of the house to pay homage to the ancestors—all these were part of important rituals.

But I see that now you are a Christian, how did that happen?

Well, one day, I remember clearly, there was an eruption of white people in our village. They went from house to house, accompanied by soldiers. They collected the baskets, the dried plants that we use to cure people with, the animal claws and skin—all of the things we used for our worship and our traditional medicine. The interpreter who accompanied them said in our local language that all that we had in our houses was not good in the eyes of God. Whole villages were thus "cleansed."

They then built a small shed and told us it was now the place where we would have to gather and pray every Sunday. They taught us new songs. The following months, other whites came to speak about God on behalf of their denominations. My family and I found ourselves in the Evangelical Church of the Congo. My uncles Nzoulou-Mouko and Moungalla Itourou went to the Salvation Army instead. Certain people who were attracted by other denominations left their first affiliation to join those of their friends or parents. I was baptized and later I was in charge of many duties in the Evangelical Church of the Congo in Dolisie, and still today in Bordeaux, France, where I now live.

You spoke about traditional religion and the conversion to Protestantism imposed on you by the white man. Can you tell me what is bad and what is good in each form of worship?

I will answer this question briefly because it can be the object of a long debate. I would say that regarding spirituality, traditional religion is not all negative. Today I am a convert; I have accepted the way of the Evangelical Church of the Congo. I chose the Protestant faith and its precepts, and I accept Jesus Christ as the Savior.

Can you tell us of your struggle as a woman?

At age fourteen or fifteen, my parents married me to Daniel Milondo. It was a marriage arranged by my parents, as was the practice of those times. My husband then decided to leave the village with me to go settle in Gabon, a neighboring country. In those times, transportation was not well developed. To go to Mayumba, we had to travel long distances by foot, then in a truck, then in a dugout canoe. It took days and nights for us to reach our destination. My husband paddled, and we stopped during the night to rest on small islands and then continue the next day at dawn. One day on our way a hippopotamus attacked us, but we got out of that safely thanks to the intelligence of my husband, who managed to change the course of the animal. Once I arrived in Gabon, I gave birth to my first daughter. We had nine children in all.

And what did you do after you left Gabon?

After our return to our native land, my husband joined the police force; he then married a second woman with whom he had five children. When he died, he left us with fourteen children.

How was your life after the death of your husband?

The real struggle started at that point in time. With my husband alive, we had all that was necessary to live a normal material life. In Africa, especially in my part of Africa, the rights of widows are never respected. With his death, my family-in-law stripped us of everything, including money, and told us to leave the house. Their goal was to strip us completely because our children were not theirs; traditionally the children belong to the family of the mother. They proposed new husbands to us from the family of our late husband. To the second wife, they proposed two nephews; to me, a cousin of his. If we did not marry the husbands they chose for us, the alternative was to pay the dowry back or go back to the village with the fourteen children.

As I did not want anything to do with their plan, I went to the police to ask for help and thwart their projects. The police intervened in our favor and restored our rights. I therefore kept the house, but a house empty of everything because all our possessions had been taken away by my in-laws. Two years later, the second wife, who was much younger than I, decided to remarry. She went away and left me all her children. I took care of the fourteen children and, later, the grandchildren.

How did you manage to feed and raise fourteen children?

My daily struggle was how to manage the survival of a large family of more than fourteen members without financial security in a country where government institutions did not provide much support for single mothers. The small pension of approximately 7,500 F CFA [15 U.S. dollars] that came from my husband, and which I was supposed to receive once every three months, was seldom paid. But there was also joy in my family, and all my offspring were happy. The acceptance of the fact that I did not have anybody to count on made me focus on my principal goal: to see my children succeed in their studies. This gave me strength. I invested myself totally in their education. To achieve this, I worked in the fields, I sold fruits and vegetables from my fields, and I bought produce from the countryside and resold it in the big cities.

One anecdote. One day in the forests of Passi-Passi in the Niari region, after a good harvest, I had twenty-five bags of groundnuts that I had to take out of the forest where my fields were and bring to the main road where I could find a vehicle to carry them to the large city. As I was walking on a wet path of the equatorial forest, where the trees formed a roof that does not let you see the sky, I was walking with my head bent under the groundnut bag. Suddenly I heard a heavy noise behind me. A boa had prepared a trap and was waiting for its prey. Fortunately for me this day, I did not fall into its trap; the giant snake had aimed badly at me.

Another anecdote. In a fishing party at Mafoubou, a forest zone around the city of Dolisie, we built a dam to divide the water into two ponds. After having emptied the first pond and caught all the fish, we had to dig holes to catch the crabs and catfish that were hiding. I put my hand into one of the holes, and instead of bringing out a crab or a fish, I brought out a snake!

You are really a courageous woman to have been able to cope so well.

I had faith in God in everything I did. I prayed a lot and I put my children under His protection. I had always had a positive attitude toward what I did. Today, I can say that my efforts have paid off. My children are all grown up now; I am happy with the work I have done.

Have you experienced any disappointment in your life? If so, how did you manage to cope?

Of course I have: the loss of my husband and the successive civil wars we had in my country, which have brought many deaths in my extended family. I had two children killed, as civilians; I had my house looted and burned down. Those are terrible things to live through, especially for all those women who have lost husbands and sons. These ordeals are harder for women because they are always the ones who suffer more during wars.

As I said at the beginning of this talk, I pray a lot, and prayers have helped me through all these hardships.

What piece of advice can you give to today's women?

I would tell them that times have changed and that they have to adapt. In the past, women were passive and did not know their rights. Today's women must know their rights! In my time, women were not allowed to go to school; they were supposed to learn from their mothers how to work in the fields, how to cook, and how to be good wives. It surely was a kind of education but it was too limited. Girls must go to school to be educated. A woman, be she single, married, or widowed, must free herself and be capable to take on any profession. I would also add that the rights of widows must be recognized in Africa, especially in my country.

Part Two

Speaking Out
Young Women on Sexuality

In this section, the complicated terrain of sexuality is mapped by women from a range of African countries. The common denominator among these stories is the struggle of women to define for themselves the terms under which their sexuality enters into play in the realm of social relations. These women writers bear witness to the many challenges African women face today regarding their sexuality.

In "Woman Weep No More," Sibongile Mtungwa describes her coming of age in a small village in South Africa, where girls were taunted by their age-mates if they did not follow the custom of engaging in thigh sex, or sex without

intercourse, before marriage. Young men may have many such premarital partners; young women are expected to limit themselves to just one man, to whom
they may eventually be wed. In young Sibongile's case, she stays with her first
boyfriend for many years but ultimately decides not to marry him, a decision
that brings the reproaches of her family and the fury of her boyfriend, who attempts to kidnap her and force her into marriage. She saves herself by going to
the civil magistrate for a restraining order but remains bitter over the system
that sought to entrap her from the moment she was considered old enough to
engage in sexual practices.

"Letters to My Cousin" is presented as a series of letters from an older
woman to her younger relative, warning her of the dangers of getting involved
with an older man who may or may not be married and may or may not be
carrying the HIV/AIDS virus. The author, Catherine Makoni of Zimbabwe,
seeks to provide the guidance that can be sorely lacking for young girls in many
contemporary African contexts, as they seek to move away from the traditions
of their parents into the uncertain waters of urban African society. In "Story of
Faith," Mamle Kabu of Ghana presents a kind of modern-day fable of the difficult decisions faced by even those privileged African women who are able to go
to university. The protagonist, initially a modest, studious young woman,
learns from the example of her roommate and other students that the way to
get ahead in her society has more to do with using her body than her mind—
with, in this case, disastrous consequences.

Two pieces in this section give voice to a segment of African society that is
still rarely heard from: lesbian women. In "To Be or Not to Be a Lesbian: The
Dilemma of Cameroon's Women Soccer Players" by Cameroonian writer and
activist Sybille Ngo Nyeck and "My Name Is Kasha" by Ugandan gay-rights
activist Kasha N. Jacqueline, two young women describe the challenges they
and their sister lesbians face in acting on their sexual desire for other women in
societies that remain resolutely hostile to any departure from heterosexuality.

In "Lovesung for a Father," Nigerian writer Zindzi Bedu relates the disturbing story of a young girl's awakening to sexuality at the hands of her own
father, otherwise seen as a paragon of immigrant African society in the United
States. Her mother and grandmother in Nigeria, who send her to the United
States to seek education and opportunity with her father, know nothing of the
repeated rapes and beatings she suffers with him and are powerless to protect
her. A similar story of powerlessness is told in the poem "It's Not Rape If . . ." by
Kenyan Ann Kithaka, a somewhat tongue-in-cheek description of the blurry
boundary between sexual harassment and rape, for female employees as for
wives. Yet in the act of writing about these situations of apparent powerlessness, the authors enact resistance to the oppressions they describe and give
themselves and their readers the courage to fight back.

Closing this section is a series of four poems by Cheshe Dow of Botswana that sound a slightly more positive note, as the narrator reflects on her relationship with her own body and her ongoing struggles to find a man who will love her for her intellect and emotions as well as for her physical beauty. This seems to be a call repeated by many African women today as they work to level the playing field in their relationships with men, seeking love and commitment without compromising their own self-respect and dignity.

Woman Weep No More

Sibongile Mtungwa

My roots lie in the village of Sibizane, three hours drive from Durban, South Africa. My grandmother and my mother struggled to raise us with the ability to face a world that they knew was tough. For them, life was to get married if you were a young woman, and to work in the mines or cities or stay home and look after a healthy herd of cattle if you were a young man. Work, livestock, and marriage were the sources of pride or failure among the residents of Sibizane. This was the society I stepped into in my teenage years.

One afternoon when I was sixteen, I went to the Umzimkhulu River to fetch water as usual. I met two young women of my age group. Zenzile asked me, "Sibongile, who is your boyfriend?"

"I don't have one," I answered.

They both shouted at me "You are lying!"

"It's true!" I protested.

Khethiwe then accused me, "I suspect when my boyfriend comes to you asking you to call me for him, you first give him a bite [have thigh sex with him]. If you don't stop this habit of yours, we will fight you."

I was shocked. I did not want a boyfriend because I knew my uncle would beat me to death. Also, I wanted to be a nun.

When we were collecting firewood and the weather was hot, we normally walked bare-breasted. On one of these days, two young women, Ntombi and Nomusa, confronted me.

"Why are your breasts so straight?" Nomusa asked.

"That is just the way they are," I answered.

"You mean to tell us that you have not slept with a man since your first period?" Ntombi asked. (Sleeping with a man meant thigh sex. Sexual intercourse is not sanctioned for young women before marriage.)

"Of course I have not slept with a man," I answered. I did not know what the breasts had to do with sleeping with a man. They squeezed my breasts and both confirmed that they were hard, so it meant no man had slept on them. They looked at me with eyes of disapproval.

That painful experience left me feeling confused and ashamed of myself. It taught me that to be a woman of my age and accepted in my community, I needed to have a boyfriend; otherwise I was in trouble with my peers, and perhaps with my parents too.

I was afraid of being rejected. So I started to think whom I would choose of all the young men who were proposing love to me. I was afraid of any young man who was much bigger than me in case I would not be able to defend myself if he wanted to have sex with me. I decided to get involved with Vusi, who was five years older than me. Now was the time to practice all the things the *iqhikiza* (the older girl who is the advisor to girls in the village) had taught me about relationships. It was the time to learn to love and why to love.

Control was awakened in me at this stage. The iqhikiza had taught me the rules of being with a man. "When you sleep with him, you always sleep on your left arm. That is to make sure that you will be able to defend yourself easily if necessary, using your right arm, which is powerful. Put his penis between your knees and the middle part of your thighs, not more than that because you can get pregnant. Wipe yourself downwards to avoid pregnancy."

The first day I had thigh sex with him, I forgot all those rules. I slept on the wrong side. That was bad because he could have interpreted that as a sign that I had previously had intercourse and it was difficult to change the habit. But luckily Vusi told me I was on the wrong side. I felt very embarrassed. But there were many other things about boy-girl relationships that I learned from him. I was eighteen years old. The nine years I spent in that relationship were full of moments of learning, awakening, questioning, and action. The learning stage was when I learned to deal with peer pressure and community expectations. At that time I did what my community expected me to do.

Vusi had other girlfriends. That was allowed in the community. It was acceptable for the girls who were sharing the same man to be friends since it minimized conflicts. It was the man's pride to have many girls and maintain them as virgins. But for a woman to be found with more than one boyfriend was taboo. She was insulted and called *isifebe* (loose woman). If the two young men discovered that they were sharing the same girl, they would take her to the Umzimkhulu River in the middle of the night to wash her private parts as a way of removing *ubufebe* (promiscuity). They would insult her for hours while she was washing, saying, "Tonight you are going to take your ubufebe out. You are a dog. You are a pig and a bitch. Your vagina is insatiable." If the girl could not use up the bar of soap in the freezing water (it was sometimes minus four or five degrees Celsius), they would beat her.

I learned to like some of Vusi's other girlfriends because they were good, but I hated others because their values did not match mine. I accepted the other girlfriends for some time. but then began to question why I was tolerating the situation. It was 1996 and I had started to work for the Women's Leadership and Training Programme as a center worker in Centocow. I was beginning to realize that there was more to my life than being a housewife whose purpose was to serve her in-laws. Those were significant times, when I followed my feelings and wisdom. I realized that I had been pleasing my boyfriend so that he could have a high status in the community.

In 1997 I ended the relationship. I told my grandmother and my brothers and sisters. It was a great moment to be on my own. I was free from pleasing him or from having to live up to the expectations of other people and my peers. My eyes had been opened to other possibilities and new ways of enjoying myself.

Unfortunately that freedom did not last even a month. One afternoon we were on our way back home from a traditional ceremony. I met a young woman friend who asked to accompany me on my way home. My home is next to many *dongas* (dry gulleys) and I was using a path to avoid meeting Vusi. Suddenly Vusi appeared between two dongas with a friend. They told me that one of my friends had told them that I was accusing them of a number of things. I was very angry. They told me to go with them back to the road so that we could meet the friend and solve the problem. I agreed, but when I asked where he was, a car drove up and they forced me into the car. I cried a lot. I cried about many things—the people I was going to meet that evening and my feeling of power-lessness. I did not want to leave my home. I cried because I was going to miss my freedom and space. I thought it was the end.

I arrived at his home and some herbs were put onto hot coals, and I was forced to inhale the smoke. Vusi told me he was not going to make me lose my virginity because he had abducted me to pay *lobola* (dowry) to my family. And I should stop thinking that I was free to get involved with other young men. The following day I was told to write the letter that the negotiators were going to take to my home.

My first letter was written like this: "My grandmother and uncle, I am here at Vusi's home and I want to come back home. It was not my will to be here. Your daughter, Sibongile."

They told me that they could not take that letter home because they were going to be beaten up. They tore up that letter. I was confused about what to write next, but the second letter was written like this: "My grandmother and my uncle, I am here at Vusi's home and I want these people to come and negotiate lobola with you."

That was not true in some ways, but when I talked to Vusi, he told me that he was willing to stop being involved with other girls. He promised to be faithful and to respect me, and I thought that he was serious. They went to my grandmother and uncle and returned with the news that they had been accepted at home. I was very sad to hear that. I had hoped my relatives would request that I come back and tell them in front of the negotiators if it was really my will to get married to Vusi. They knew that young women were often forced to write those letters. I felt very powerless. I was left with no option but to accept Vusi's apologies and my parents' decision to accept the money from the negotiators.

On my second day in Vusi's home, my grandmother came. I heard her talking outside. "Where is Sibongile? I want my child. Even if you are paying lobola, I want her home today." She kicked open the door where I was and said, "Sibongile, stand up. Let's go home."

I was very happy. My power came flowing back and I stood up and followed her. Other women from Vusi's family told her that they were going to accompany me home. That evening I slept at home. It was a relief. At least I was still going to attend workshops and continue with my work, and I was hoping to learn to love Vusi again. I had the space to think and adjust.

But Vusi did not keep his promises. Things went from bad to worse. He continued to have girlfriends all over, including some of the group members I was working with. I felt that he was not respecting me. By the end of 1998 I knew that I was not going to stay with him. But I was afraid of what people were going to say if I broke off the relationship. I tried to talk to my mother about it.

"Ma, what will happen say if I decide not to marry Vusi?"

"That will be very bad. People will think you are crazy. After all who is going to pay back the lobola?"

One of my relatives told me, "To get married is a sign of good luck these days. People will think you are mad if you do not get married."

I knew that I was on my own and that my family could not understand my feelings of dislike for Vusi. In October 1999 I attended a Grail formation workshop where I realized that I had to face up to the situation and act. (The Grail is an international women's organization founded in 1921 that I still belong to today).

In December I went to a week-long training class of health workers in Pietermaritzburg. When it was time to go home, I told my colleagues that I was going to visit some people and was not going back home with them. I went to stay with a friend in Durban, and then in January 2000 I went to Kleinmond, where I lived with a Grail member for six months.

That was a very difficult time for my grandmother, my mother, my brothers and sisters, and some friends. Vusi harassed them so they would tell him where I was. Of course it was fortunate that they all had no idea where I was. I did not tell anyone. I was on my own in that decision and I could not trust any person in Sibizane. My grandmother got very sick for the first time, and I was worried that she was going to die. A close friend, Gugu, was insulted and accused of knowing where I was.

Later that year, in September 2000, I decided to come back to my home district. I began working for the Women's Leadership and Training Programme at Reichenau. I was not able to visit my home because I was scared of being abducted again. In July 2001 my uncle, Vusi, and two of his cousins came to my work place to take me home. I agreed to meet them with Sister Virginia Didi, Marilyn Aitken, and Mbali Khathi protecting me.

Vusi and his two cousins said, "Sister-in-law, we are here to take you home. Whatever the problem is, it needs to be resolved."

I replied, "I am sorry, but I am not going home with you. I am at work and I have already told Vusi that I am no longer interested in him and will not marry him. I am sorry that he has brought you here. He knows that I do not love him anymore. I am telling you the truth even if he has not told you."

I told them I was not Vusi's wife or girlfriend and that they should go to my home and fetch the gifts and cash they had given my family during the lobola negotiations. My grandmother had given me the strength to be very firm when she told me, "There is no way we can force you to marry him if you don't like him anymore." She was with my elder sister and my mother when she told me this. She was very brave to advise against the cultural norm by setting me free from the bondage of marriages that are the result of abduction and unfair cultural practices.

In August 2001 I went to a story-telling event at Centocow with other people from Reichenau. I saw Vusi and he asked me to talk to him about how they were going to get their lobola back. I saw a car parked next to the office where we were and two men walking toward us. I realized that they were going to try to abduct me again and I tried to run away. But they caught me and forced me into the car. I cried and fought off the three men. When some people tried to intervene, Vusi shouted, "I am going to stab anyone who tries to help her."

Forty women of all ages stopped and watched the "show." I bit Vusi's hand until he let me go. One of the men said "Let's leave her, before they call the police." They were indecisive, and I managed to escape.

I was so angry that I tore my clothes while I continued to scream hysterically. When I reached the office nearby, I fell down and cried so loudly that I could not hear anything. The police came and told me there was no case because he had not hurt me. I felt powerless again. What kind of system is this that does not protect women? What kind of system is this that waits until women are hurt before taking action? Soon after that, I sought a protection order against Vusi to enable me to visit my home. A woman official of the Women and Child Protection Unit in the Pietermaritzburg magistrate's court told me "There is nothing we can do because he has paid lobola. He is looking for his wife. You just need to hide from him or go to the tribal authority." I was shocked to hear her say that because South Africa has very good laws to protect women and children.

I was very angry and pursued the matter in other ways. I went to the Himeville magistrate, who listened to me and believed me. He called Vusi and told him that if he touched me, or people close to me, he would be immediately arrested. He made him sign all the papers. That was the end of the saga in one way. At least I knew someone was listening to me and that justice had been done. It was sad that we were not able to talk and resolve our conflict without including the magistrate, a foreign system for both of us. There could have been other ways to resolve the conflict, but Vusi had been unwilling to admit that he was wrong.

Some members of his family accused me of being a rude, cruel woman. They stopped talking to me and spread many stories about me in the community. Other people blamed the workshops I was attending for making me "uncontrollable."

I became a free woman again. I learned to live like a normal human being, not having to hide and run constantly. I continued with my work on gender, environment, and leadership training. I travelled to countries in Africa and Europe, as well as to the United States. In the meeting I attended at Rutgers University in 2002, I learned that women from Pakistan, India, Costa, Rica, Brazil, Nicaragua, and the United States were all encountering problems of male domination, as well as cultural or religious oppression. I knew I was not on my own. I was in the midst of women fighting for their human rights and their dignity as citizens. I have learned a lot from these experiences, and I am now able to share the light with other women who are searching for their own ways in different cultures and circles.

Letters to My Cousin

Catherine Makoni

Brief Biography

My name is Catherine Makoni. I am a thirty-two-year-old woman living in Zimbabwe at a difficult time in my country's history. I am a lawyer by profession and in addition to my law degree, I also hold a master's in women's law from the Southern and East African Centre for Women's Law, at the University of Zimbabwe. I am at present working with the Catholic Agency for Overseas Development (Southern Africa office) as a regional program officer for justice and peace. I have worked in the women's rights movement in Zimbabwe for a number of years and in this capacity have worked with women in difficult circumstances—women who have been subjected to violence and deprivation by their intimate partners. But I have also been there to witness their triumph over adversity.

Brief Background and Synopsis

In working with women of different ages, I have been particularly struck by the disconnect between older and younger women and between survivors of violence and women who were still grappling with violence in their lives. I was also particularly struck by the fact that in a country with an HIV prevalence rate of 20 percent, where parents are dying and leaving their orphaned children, we continue to see girls making the same mistakes that their mothers made, falling into the same patterns of conduct so that their lives play out in the same vicious cycle. This is what inspired the piece that follows, which is partly biographical and partly a fictionalized account. It started off as a discussion with my young cousin through e-mail, and then it grew a life of its own when I decided to tackle some of the challenges facing young women today. Because of the disconnect between the generations, they feel like the problems they are facing are unique, when in fact, we older women have also been through them.

It was interesting that while I could speak freely, my cousin was not able to open up to me until I started using e-mail. I would ask her about the "sensitive" issues, like whether or not she was sexually active and whether she and her sexual partner had gone for HIV tests, and generally she found it easier to talk about these issues via e-mail (I have found it an interesting use of technology!).

This piece is therefore in part an account of our conversation, but beyond that, it deals with some of the challenges young women face getting into relationships today—challenges like relationships with older men, negotiating safe sex, talking about HIV testing, violence, and poverty, as well as the political and economic difficulties in Zimbabwe and their impact at a very personal level on the decisions young women make.

Letters to My Cousin

Dear Jane,

I was shocked the other day when you told me about your boyfriend. But first let me clarify one point. I was happy you felt you could confide in me—I would like to think you will always feel free to come to me when you need someone to talk to. That is what sisters are for. But after you hear what I have to say, I fear you will not want to.

But back to why I was shocked. Perhaps shocked is the wrong word. I was sad. I still am sad. You are twenty-one years old, Jane. You told me your boyfriend is thirty-one years old. In fact he turns thirty-two in two months.

That is an eleven-year age difference. He is working; you are a student. That eleven-year gap has all sorts of implications, Jane. Your relationship will always be unequal. He has done a lot of things that you have not and experienced a lot of things that you have yet to experience. He probably has more money than you. Is that why you are having a relationship with him, Jane? I know the life of a university student is tough. I know that since the government privatized accommodation and canteen services, you have had to buy all your meals, but I thought that as your sisters, we always try to help you out. Have we let you down then? Is our assistance not enough to meet your needs? If that is the case, you could have come to us, Jane. We could have discussed this like family. I know I don't have a lot of extra money, things being what they are with our economy, but surely we can try? You are not a burden, Jane. You are family. We all help each other when we can.

When I asked you if he was married, you said you did not know. You didn't think to ask because you assumed he wasn't, otherwise he would not be asking you out. Sometimes I forget your naiveté and the sheltered upbringing that you have had. But moments like these bring it back. This is Zimbabwe, Jane. Men marry young in our country. Trust me, I know! Not everyone is nice and honest. There are men who will prey on innocent young girls. Please ask him whether or not he is married. It's the least you can do for yourself. I'm guessing he is going to say that he was married but is either separating from his wife or he is divorced. But let's find out first, shall we?

Your loving cousin,
Patience

Dear Jane,

So, you asked him if he was married like I requested? No? It has been three weeks since I raised this, Jane. Are you afraid to raise it? He is your boyfriend. You are supposed to have an open and equal relationship. Please, please ask him. I have been there, Jane, I know it is difficult. We are supposed to be equal, but we are not. I am not trying to make you do the impossible; I'm just asking you to be brave and to ask him. If it were not so important, I would not be telling you to do this.

Your loving cousin,
Patience

Dear Jane,

So you finally asked him? I'm glad. I know it could not have been easy for you. So what did he say? That he used to be married but is divorced? Really? And he has a three-year-old daughter with whom he lives? And who looks after this three-year-old? He does? Is this a Zimbabwean man, Jane, or does he come from Norway? A thirty-two-year-old, black Zimbabwean man looking after a three-year-old daughter? This is certainly a first! I'm not sure whether to laugh or cry. Did I not tell you so? This is such an old story, honey. Believe it or not, I have heard it before. A lot of men have tried that spin not only with me but also with a lot of other women.

You know my friend Barbara, the doctor? Her last boyfriend told her that story. She went out with him for three months before she discovered that he was lying. Like your boyfriend, Barbara's boyfriend would not take her home. And like your boyfriend, "he did not want his children meeting his girlfriends until he was sure that the relationship was 'going somewhere.'" In case you don't get the meaning here, let me be blunt. The only place that man wanted the relationship to go was to Barbara's flat and specifically to Barbara's bed! He did not care about her. He most certainly did not care about developing any deep and meaningful relationship with her.

It's a classic lie that some men in this country are so fond of. And there is no such thing as a "divorce certificate"! You only get a marriage certificate, and when you divorce you get a divorce order. But for interest's sake, why don't you bring it and I will get my lawyer friend to look at it; we can always tell if it is genuine or not. He is lying, Jane. It's as plain as the nose on your face, and you would see it too if you were not so infatuated.

But all these things do not worry me, Jane. I know hundreds of women have gone through life as second or third wives. It happens. I most certainly don't want that to be your fate, but if it is the path you have chosen for yourself, I would just have to learn to accept it, wouldn't I? An important part of growing up is making your own decisions. Even if a couple of years down the line, you were to discover that you made a mistake and you wanted out of that relationship, I would help you. It would be reversible.

What I am afraid of, Jane, is AIDS. Do you know the statistics for HIV infection for girls in your age group? Girls from fifteen to twenty-four years are three to four times more vulnerable to infection than boys in the same age group, and do you know one of the reasons why they are so vulnerable? It is because they have sexual relationships with older men. Men who have been around the block and who might already be infected with the virus. Men on whom they might be dependent for monetary support. Men with whom they will find it difficult to negotiate for safer sex. Just think about it, Jane. If you found it so difficult to ask him whether he was married, what makes you think you will find it easy to resist him when he demands sex? Do you honestly think you will be able to demand that he uses condoms when you do have sex? I doubt it.

I am happy that you went for an HIV test yourself. But it is useless to go by yourself, Jane. You do not have sex with yourself. Both of you have to go for

HIV tests. But do you see what I'm talking about here? What kind of relationship do you have if you are afraid to ask him to go for an HIV test with you? We are talking life and death here.

It would be a tragedy if you were to contract the HIV virus at the age of twenty-one. But do you know what the greater tragedy would be? It would be not learning anything from the lives of our mothers. Your mother was the nicest person I have ever met. Do you remember the testimonies during her funeral? That she was humble, gentle, kind, and meek. Do you remember people saying what a good and faithful wife she was? How even when she was in pain she would struggle to her knees to pray? She died, Jane. She followed her husband, your father, to his grave. And that could easily be your fate too if you do not learn from her life, from the lives of all our mothers. Perhaps they did not know better, but we certainly do. Perhaps she didn't have a choice, but you do. I know you carry an intelligent head on those shoulders. Use it!

Your loving cousin,
Patience

P.S. Before you protest, let me anticipate and preempt your protests. No, I am not your mother, but our mothers are gone, and in their absence what's to be done? All of us have to step in and advise you the best we can. And it is just that, Jane, advice. No, I'm not perfect; I have made a lot of mistakes in my life. But you do not have to make the same mistakes. That would be stupid and I know you are not stupid. No, I am not married. But you know what? I would rather remain single than be in a relationship that disempowers me.

Your loving cousin,
Patience

Dear Jane,

I spoke to your friend Karen the other day. She came by the flat looking for you, but you had gone into town. I took the opportunity to talk to her about life in general. I'm trying to understand you better. I know that we are not that different in age, but I feel that maybe the environment that you are now growing up in has changed from when I was your age. My conversation with Karen was an eye-opener. One important lesson I learned is that the more some things change, the more others remain the same. It was interesting to learn that there is still so much pressure on young girls to get married. She told me about one of your friends, who had been in an abusive relationship for the past three years, ever since she was seventeen. She went ahead and married that man! Did I ever tell you about my friend Khanyi? She also married an abusive man, back when we were at varsity. She divorced last year. Two children and ten unhappy years down the line. Like I said, the more things change, the more they remain the same.

I asked Karen whether female law students like her would be interested in participating in the activities of the Zimbabwe Women Lawyers Association, for example, working on the Domestic Violence Bill. Do you know what she said? She said they might be willing, but only if they considered it "fashionable." Really? And this from a person whose friend is in an abusive relationship? Karen is a law student. She is obviously very intelligent. But I really wonder if she has any life skills? I must admit that I am struggling to reconcile her obvious academic intelligence and her obvious social immaturity. For instance, she feels being liked is more important than celebrating her achievements. Is it true that students will laugh at you if they regard you as being "too serious" about your studies? Is this true of all of you? Is it true that boys at varsity are always saying that female students should secure a man before they leave college, because no one "out there" wants a woman who is "too educated"? Is this what they say? Is this why you feel you have to have this relationship of yours? So you can have someone to marry you when you leave university? Isn't that a strange reason to be in a relationship?

Remember what you told me when I asked whether your relationship with this man was serious? You said that it was and that he had indicated that he wanted to marry you. It scares me, Jane. You are twenty-one years old. You are still at school. You do not have a cent to your name. Should you even be thinking about marriage? Shouldn't you rather be worrying about getting a job once you graduate? Do you realize that estimates are putting the unemployment rate in our country at over 80 percent? Do you realize what the implications of this are? Do you ever discuss this with your friends? Have you ever noticed the crowds of people who pour out onto the streets every evening around 7:30–8 p.m.? Have you ever thought to ask why it is that so many people throng private colleges every evening? Did you ever think that a lot of them would kill for the opportunity that you have, to go to school and only worry about school, without also worrying about the work that you left unfinished on the desk and the family whose needs you cannot meet? Did you ever wonder why a lot of them feel that they have to keep learning and improving on their qualifications? Shouldn't you and your friends be concentrating on this? Forgive me if I'm preaching, but I just get exasperated sometimes.

In case you feel I violated your privacy, let me assure you that I did not discuss you with your friend. We just had a general discussion about life. Like I said, it was just me trying to understand you, your world, and the choices you are making in your life. I'm not sure I am any nearer that goal, but some things certainly are clearer.

Your loving cousin,
Patience

Dear Jane,

I have noticed that you have been subdued ever since we started discussing this issue. I hope you are not angry with me. I know I tend to express my views rather strongly but I mean you no harm. It's your best interests that I have at heart. My personal ethos is that there are some truths that people need to be told. I would not be a good friend or sister if I did not tell it to you straight. I do not believe in sugarcoating issues. I guess if I were in the West, I would be a proponent of tough love. Unlike some of your "friends," our relationship is not a popularity contest. I will not tell you what you want to hear just to score points. I know you have given me a not-so-flattering nickname, Dr. Killjoy (did you honestly think I wouldn't find out?). It is OK. I know one day you will thank me for this.

Anyway, my very last words on this issue (at least for now!) are these: I don't doubt that that man is lying to you. I never did see the "divorce certificate" that you promised to get from him. You didn't show it to me, because he never gave it to you, did he? And my guess is you still don't know where he lives, do you? I guess you still see each other in back of darkened movie theatres and at seedy lodges around town, where he is unlikely to run into run into anyone who knows him and where you will never meet his wife, the mother of his three-year-old daughter.

If I had my way, I would advise you to leave this man. This is a toxic relationship. My old university professor always used to say, "A relationship should enhance your life; if it doesn't, then it's bringing you down and you should terminate it." I agree. I know a lot of people will say that I should not get involved to this degree, that I should not tell you what to do, but let you decide. This is the reasoning used by mothers in our society, when their daughters tell them that they are being abused by their husbands. Our people believe that a mother should never tell her daughter to leave an abusive husband. That is tantamount to breaking up her daughter's marriage. An unforgivable sin.

But how many mothers, after their daughters have died at the hands of their abusive husbands, have wished that they had whisked their daughters to safety, and society be damned? How many mothers have stood over the graves of their daughters, mourning the premature death of a daughter who took her own life because living with an abusive spouse was just too painful to face, and wished they had grabbed their daughter by the hand and run for dear life?

I am inclined to put my head on the block and tell you upfront what I think you should do. You know I have always gone against the grain (I guess that is why I am thirty-two and still unmarried). Of course I cannot call this man and give him a piece of my mind, but I will tell you what I think. To make it easier for you to digest, I will list my issues:

1. Zimbabwe has an HIV prevalence of 20 percent. Women and girls aged fifteen to twenty-four are sometimes up to four times more likely to be infected by HIV than boys in the same age group. That is your age group. I have already told you some of the reasons why girls in that group are more vulnerable. But for emphasis, let me reiterate: it is not just your reproductive systems that are immature; your emotional and psychological capacities are also immature, meaning you are more prone to making ill-informed and ill-considered decisions—much like the ones you have been making since you started seeing this boyfriend of yours.

2. Girls in this age group have also been shown to be likely to have sexual relationships with men much older than they. In your case, Jane, this man is more than ten years older than you. It could well be that he is a really decent human being, but it could also be that he is the kind of man who preys on younger girls and engages in sexual relationships in return for money or trinkets or even the illusion of emotional support.

I am not being deliberately cruel. I am raising these issues in the hope that you will see that these are not just statistics about things that happen to other people. Your friend from university whose husband abuses her is already a statistic. She is among the one in three women who are abused by their husbands, boyfriends, or other intimate partners in Zimbabwe annually. So you see, you too can become a statistic. I am trying to help you avoid that.

So now for some action points. Can you promise to think about what I have said? Can you promise to think seriously about terminating this relationship and for the time being concentrating on school? You will be giving yourself some much needed time to mature a bit more, while at the same time saving yourself some serious trouble. It's a lot to ask, I know, but it is something that you need to do. Then I promise I will get out of your hair.

Your loving cousin,
Patience

Dear Jane,

I know that I promised to get out of your hair if you agreed to consider my advice, but I find myself having to talk to you once more. I spoke to my friend Takunda, hoping to get an "outsider's" perspective on this issue. I felt that maybe I was too emotionally close to be objective and that maybe what I was asking of you was unfair. She raised some very interesting issues. She castigated me for making the assumption that you did not know what you were doing. She asked me if I had considered the possibility that you actually knew what you were doing, that the age difference and all the other issues notwithstanding, you actually wanted to be with this man. She was particularly concerned that I was being too judgmental about your choices and decisions. She said that sometimes it is important to let young people make their own decisions about life, for that is the only way they can grow. Even if those decisions turn out to be bad ones, she said, sometimes it is as important in life to make bad decisions as it is to make good ones. She also said that I should respect your right to make decisions about your life, because you are, after all, a young adult and not an adolescent.

I must admit, during the past few weeks when we have been discussing this issue, it has crossed my mind plenty of times that perhaps I should let you make your own decisions. It has crossed my mind that may be this is what you want out of life, but I find myself shrinking from that conclusion. I ask myself whether at twenty-one you can possibly comprehend what it means to be a stepmother to a three-year-old child? Can you possibly be ready for the possibility that you might fall pregnant? Then, at the ripe old age of twenty-two, you will be a parent to a four-year-old toddler and an infant while at the same time managing the demands of a husband and school. I cannot in all honesty conclude that you really understand all this. At the very most, you just think you do.

However, Takunda is right when she says that you are a young adult. I cannot make your decisions for you nor can I shield you from the vagaries of life, much as I would like to. You must make your own way in the world. You must make your own decisions and live by them. If they turn out badly, then you must learn from them and move on. That is life. At this point I believe I have done what I can to give you my advice. It is time for me to exit the scene and let you take center stage.

Your loving cousin,
Patience

Story of Faith

Mamle Kabu

Faith was not the sort of girl most people would have expected to become a prostitute. And she never considered herself to be one either. What exactly is a prostitute anyway? Such an ugly word, full of harsh, accusatory t's. She had never given the word much thought until she heard it directed at herself. After she had recovered from the initial shock and pain, she turned it over in her mind as if hearing it for the first time.

"Prostitute," she thought. "Am I a . . . ?" and pursuing an involuntary grammatical declension, "I am a . . ." No, she could not complete those sentences. Not even in her mind. Not with the first person pronoun in them. She had once heard that at Alcoholics Anonymous meetings the first thing people had to do was stand up in front of everyone and say out loud, "I am an alcoholic." Yes, that must be tough. But then, they *were* alcoholics. She, on the other hand . . .

Apuskeleke. There was another word. Also with hard, repetitive consonants. But the vowels in this one skipped and bounced around the consonants, unapologetically African in their pronunciation, endowing it with five syllables.

Five playful, rhythmical syllables that could be tapped out, sung out, clowned around with. So different from the clipped, contained ones of *prostitute* with its silent *e* at the end. It was hard to believe that the two words had the same number of letters.

It had come from Nigeria they said, this word that had spread like wildfire so that within weeks of its arrival, the young girls swiveling down the streets knew exactly how to react when it was flung out of the windows of male-driven cars. Not a word any "decent" girl could embrace, it was an odd cross between an indictment and a compliment, encapsulating perfectly the disturbing duality of sexiness. Suggestive to the point of onomatopoeia, it evoked the playfulness and license of youth, the pulse and beat of entertainment, and the mischief of sensuality.

Faith had had it directed at her on more than one occasion, but she could admit to herself in private that it had not left a bitter aftertaste. By then it had become a favorite adjective for the type of girl chased after by men with respectable, matronly wives. It might be respectable to be matronly. It might be dubious to be apuskeleke. But at the end of the day, who was being chased after? Showered with attention, money, and favor? When they stared at themselves naked in the mirror, who would cringe and who would strut?

She had never dared think like that before she had met Shika. Shika had been an education all by herself. Someone had once told her, "Education is about a lot more than what you learn in the curriculum." Well, if that was true at the basic level, how much more so at university? Shika had taught her so many things, she could not even count or separate them clearly one from the other. Lesson One had been how to like someone you are programmed to dislike or, in more academic terms, to come face-to-face with your prejudices.

She would never forget meeting her for the first time. "Oh no, I've got some apuskeleke girl for a roommate" was her first, dismal thought. Shika entered in a cloud of perfume, flicking dozens of nylon braids over her bare shoulder. "I've heard about girls like you," thought Faith as she smiled brightly, shook hands, and silently gave thanks that her parents had already departed. She tried to resist the infectiousness of Shika's smile and to divert her eyes from her bouncy bosom, but both proved difficult, for there was fascination in their effrontery. In fact, when she thought about it much later, she could date her liking of Shika to that very moment.

And indeed, that was when the friendship between the apuskeleke girl and the serious—or at least, well-intentioned—student began. In the beginning people commented on the oddity of it, but later on it was forgotten that such a gap had ever existed. Faith was studying economics and wanted to start her own business one day. Shika did not seem altogether sure what she was studying. Since her place at the university had been "fixed" for her by someone, she could not be too choosy about her subject. This did not seem to bother her unduly, however. In fact, she took the first hectic weeks of classes more coolly than Faith despite this unsettling beginning. And she certainly did not let it spoil her enjoyment of all the social events.

She eventually came up with classics. When she broke the news, Faith tried to think of a way to find out more without revealing her own ignorance. But Shika beat her to it with "Faith, what is classics?" Shyness had no place in Shika's life. And its utter redundancy where she was concerned made Faith question its value for the first time. Here was a girl who had got into university with qualifications which were obviously not academic. She did not even know what she was studying. When she found out her subject she asked what it was. Without batting an eyelid. Without worrying what the person she was asking would think of her. And indeed, why worry if you don't care? There was a freedom in that, thought Faith. Another lesson from Shika.

What surprised Faith even more, though, was Shika's utter lack of concern not only over being assigned a subject of whose existence she had hitherto been ignorant, but also over how on earth she was going to get through three years of studying that subject. When Faith realized she was worrying about it far more than Shika herself, she decided to reserve her worries for her own studies. "She knows how she got in and she knows how she will get out" was the only logical conclusion she could draw.

The dawning realization that Shika was just as well, perhaps even better, equipped to get through university than herself, could not but translate into a recognition—it was still too early for the word *appreciation*—of her powers of resourcefulness and strategy. It was not that Faith had never known things could work this way but it was quite another matter to observe it for oneself, especially when one had involuntarily grown to like the person involved and thereby alienated the forces of self-righteous disapproval that could otherwise have so comfortingly come to one's aid.

By the time she went home for Christmas, Faith was able to tell her parents that she had a friendly roommate who was studying classics and that they got on well together. Her early visions of how she would laugh with her mother—and calm her fears—about her apuskeleke roommate had completely evaporated. In fact, that word never even came up.

By the long vacation, Faith's accounts of university life dwelt more on the academic side of things. She would talk about her lecturers and her essays and the stress of exams. It never occurred to her mother that she should be more concerned about what was omitted than what was included because the most comforting thing about making assumptions about people and trusting blindly in the status quo is that you never have to worry about what you don't know.

Among the details Faith omitted to mention was that Shika had presented her with some new clothes (which she had left packed away in her student room). And that she had a boyfriend. And that . . . she had lost her virginity.

She was not worried that her mother would ask about this, being confident not only that she would simply not expect it to happen but also that having prayed about it and left it in God's hands, she would consider the matter covered.

True, Faith herself had not thought it would happen and a year ago might have been shocked by the prospect. But that was then. Indeed, it seemed at least a decade ago since her parents had done their duty in pointing her in the right direction on her new path. For her father this had consisted of a terse warning against "following those so-called apuskeleke girls." For her mother, it was a request for a special blessing after the service on her last Sunday at home. They had all held hands as the pastor launched into prayer.

"Merciful Lord, bless this our daughter as she sets her first foot forward upon the blazing trail of a shining path to a magnificent bastion of academic learning, bringing honor and glory upon us all (say "A-men"). We pray that she will cleave to her books and open wide her mind to the great wisdom, tutelage, and scholarship of the learned scholars of that distinguished and knowledge-able institution (somebody say "A-men"), that she will not fall a prey to the evil temptations, degradations, and corruptions of the fl-e-sh, that she will NOT engage and indulge in premarital SEX and for-ni-*ca*-tion (say "A-men"), but will preserve herself in pure, chaste, rigid, and righteous virtue to the honor of her future husband and master, and the glorifi-*ca*-tion of her heavenly Father (somebody say "I hear you, Lord"). We call down your angels to surround her, like soldiers of righteousness, that she may say no! to drugs, NO!! to sex, *NO!!!* to all the foul, licentious, and deprived temptations of *Satan-n-n-n. . . .*"

He carried on for some time in a similar vein while Faith cringed and fumed. How could he embarrass her like that by referring so openly to her pro-jected sexual activities or lack of them? And in front of her father and younger brothers too? She was quiet on the way home, not daring to criticize their ven-erated pastor but still choking on annoyance and humiliation. She had never discussed sex with her parents and the thought of her sexual activities, albeit imaginary, being brought up in front of them and especially in front of her father—it was beyond embarrassing.

Now when she thought back to it she could not help but smile. Yes, her mother had had good reason to solicit God's vigilance, although she had not appreciated that at the time. After all, what more could a mother do when her daughter was far away, well beyond the reach of her control and influence? What else but pray and have faith?

Had her mother felt like that during the years she had lived with her aunt? Faith wondered. Had she worried about her little girl in the same way she now worried over her teenage daughter? Had she thought about her virginity at that age or only about her basic needs like food and shelter? Or had she just got on with the business of raising her boys and trusted her little daughter to God and her sister-in-law? What would she say if she knew that Faith sometimes wondered how much of her virginity was left after the things her aunt's husband had done to her? Was she even aware that such things were possible? She had wondered more than once if her mother herself might have had such experiences as a girl. But if she had, she would never know. They were no more likely ever to talk about such things than to sprout wings and fly. No one talked about such things. And the only time she ever heard her parents talk about sex was when they commented on topical issues.

A current grumble was that the ABC of AIDS prevention was one letter too many. Teaching single young people to use condoms (and advertising them so openly all over the place) was just promoting promiscuity. As their pastor said, the alphabet of AIDS prevention could only have two letters for true Christians—Abstain if you are single, and Be faithful if you are married. As simple as that. No need for C's or any other complications. Her mother's women's fellowship group had even gone on a march about it. Faith could still see her, decked out in her uniform of printed T-shirt, wrapper cloth, and triangular white head scarf, setting off with her homemade placard proclaiming "Condoms are Manna from Hell."

No, there was no way she could tell her about the changes she had been through in the past year. No way to explain that in that space of time, her parameters had drifted far from the maternal benchmark. What might seem scandalous to her mother—and to her old self—was so unremarkable in her new world that it barely merited a mention. And Shika was not her only yardstick. The truth was that Faith was surrounded by girls who dressed for lectures as for a catwalk. Girls with mobile phones, designer clothes, and more sugar daddies than they could keep track of. Where did a serious student with one boyfriend register in all that?

When she told Shika that she had lost her virginity, she was far more shocked by the admission of its longevity than by the news of its demise. "Oh Faith! You mean, up to now . . . ?" And she put her arm around her, smiling like a mother whose daughter had just announced her first period. Then she took a packet of condoms out of her handbag and ceremoniously transferred them to Faith's handbag. There were no words, just a look that rendered them unnecessary. They both giggled. And then the giggling turned into a laughing fit as Shika gave vent to her affectionate amusement and Faith released her tension over it all.

When they returned from the summer vacation, Shika had more goodies for her. She had shopped generously during her trip to the United States. She always enjoyed giving Faith clothes that were on the daring side and watching her inner conflict as she first protested she could not wear them, then gingerly tried them on to please her, then grew to enjoy the feeling of being trendier and sexier, finally allowing them to supplant former wardrobe staples.

And Shika was not the only one who enjoyed this process. In terms of looks, Faith was the type of girl who could go from "not bad" to "hot" with that little change in styling. She had even facial features that were strikingly enhanced with Shika's extensive cosmetic collection and expertise. Her figure, which was simply slim in conservative clothing, revealed a perfect proportion of "ins and outs" in tight trousers and skimpy tops. The first time Shika had seen her naked, she had stared with undisguised envy. Although her own over-abundant curves were an asset in African society and particularly suited to her lifestyle, she still knew how to appreciate a beautiful figure when she saw one. She had known ever since then that Faith was capable of this transformation.

The new Faith quickly grew accustomed to that sort of admiration. It was even more gratifying from men, and there were quite a few who were prepared to lavish it on her. By the end of her second year, her first boyfriend was a distant memory. In fact, she had finished with student boys altogether and moved on to more glittering pastures. When Shika had first said to her, "Faith, stop wasting your time with those poor students. Don't you know you can do a lot better than that?" she had felt herself in a different category—she liked Shika, but she didn't do that sort of thing.

And she had never made a conscious decision to the contrary, not as such. One weekend Shika had introduced her to some "friends" of the middle-aged, moneyed, male variety. One of them held out his hand and said, "Hello Faith, I'm Chris." She felt herself go hot; his gaze delivered in such a direct manner all the compliments that could sound so fawning from other men. As she extricated her hand from a lingering handshake, she knew that a measure of her self-control had been forfeited in that exchange . . . left behind in his grasp.

She could have analyzed what had happened in logical terms later on and made some sensible decisions about it, but she refused to give it concrete form by acknowledging it. This translated into a failure to fortify herself against the eventuality of any recurrent thoughts or future contact . . . and against the potential impact of any gifts—like the sleek new mobile phone that arrived for her a few days later with a tag saying "Call me! Chris."

It took her breath away. It was the most expensive thing she had ever owned. The very idea of possessing it was intoxicating and oddly empowering. It made her feel like someone who must be worth such extravagance. It made her start thinking about other luxuries and opportunities in more real terms than ever before.

And that was how, before she had ever quite squared up to the task of making a conscious decision about it, Faith found herself involved with a middle-aged, moneyed man of the married variety. The same type commonly shortened to "sugar daddy." It was not the first time she had met Shika's friends, but perhaps it was the first time she had been ready to meet them.

When Chris gave her gifts and money, it did not feel like being paid off. After all, he was her . . . boyfriend. Of sorts. He wanted to give her nice things, make her happy, show his appreciation and admiration. What could be more natural? And this was Africa—there was nothing strange about money flowing in a male to female direction. Even marriage, although more complex, had the same underlying pattern, she mused—man provides woman with financial support, among other rewards, in return for sexual privileges, among other services.

The difference between this deal and marriage, however, was that it would never outlive its customer satisfaction. And Faith enjoyed it while it lasted. Chris made her feel like a queen and gave her the means to dress like one. In her world the existence of his wife was condensed into a gold circle around one of his fingers. It saw no evil, heard no evil, and spoke no evil—she could live with it.

She began to dream big. Like any other girl, Faith liked nice clothes and pocket money, but the serious economics student had not been extinguished, she had merely evolved. And she was thinking beyond the treats and frills of the present to the realities of the future. Things which she had always assumed would take years and years to achieve suddenly seemed within grasp. Moving away from home, getting her own place in Accra, getting a car, going abroad. If she could go to America or Europe during the long vacation, she could look for a temporary job and make some money herself, some hard currency to start saving toward her own business.

She had tried asking her father for money toward a ticket, but his response had been that if she had spied a money tree growing in his bedroom, he would be grateful if she could lead him to it. "Why don't you ask me where I am even getting the money to pay your fees, before you come and ask for a ticket to America?" he finished. Faith had not really expected a contribution from him, but it had also been a way to inform him of her intentions. One of her hallmates had said she could come with her and stay at her aunt's home in Virginia. She had even offered to help get a visa letter for her. All she needed was a ticket.

To her disappointment, Chris did not seem willing to go that far. "Don't worry, Faith," said Shika, whose ticket to America had been bought by a member of parliament. "Don't try to run before you can walk. Just be patient, you will get there sooner or later." It might have been Faith's frustration over the America issue that nudged her toward additional involvements. In any case, fidelity could never reasonably have been an expectation on either side in the kind of relationship she shared with Chris.

Eventually it became more a matter of lifestyle than of relationships. One did not make such a change and then move backward. Impossible. She needed money to maintain her lifestyle and needed to maintain that lifestyle in order to make money. She could no longer conceal her change completely from her parents. She told them she had a student boyfriend from a rich family. This was enough for them, especially for her mother who immediately started dreaming of a big society wedding and a daughter set up for life in grand style. She was keen to meet her 'future in-law' and Faith, grateful as ever that they lived so far away from the university, stalled her with promises. She also bought her mother little gifts, which kept her very happy and even less inclined to question whatever scraps of information her daughter fed her.

Although Faith feared her father's judgment more than her mother's, she was not too concerned about his finding out because he never asked her anything out of the ordinary. Moreover, he approved of the "rich boyfriend" as a step toward marriage, only taking the precaution of asking her mother to warn her against sleeping with the boy before marriage. Her mother often acted as a medium in this way.

In fact, she and her father rarely had exchanges that could truly qualify as conversations. Beyond the standard role of dutiful and respectful daughter—which preserved a safe distance between them—she was never quite sure how to relate to him. Her years away from home had eradicated the chance to get any closer to him, unlikely in any case in a society that demanded total respect for one's elders, gave men complete dominion over their families, and accorded sons more importance than daughters. But despite this gulf, she loved him with the stubborn love that children freely grant their parents regardless of how deserving they are. And she hankered for his approval with every child's craving for parental recognition.

He, for his part, found her something of an anomaly. If only his eldest son could have been the one endowed with her intelligence and ambition . . . or if only she could have *been* that eldest son, he would have counted himself blessed. He was not incapable of appreciating these qualities in a girl, but his own upbringing had been too traditional to show him any great purpose in a girl possessing these things. Women could study and study, get degrees and titles, build careers, and earn more professional prestige than men, but at the end of the day, what gained them the most recognition was marriage and children. There was no getting away from that, as he had pointed out to his sister when she urged him to send Faith to university. "Look, even women with Ph.D.s who have toiled to earn the title 'Dr.'—can they give up their precious 'Mrs.' for that? No, they call themselves 'Dr. Mrs.'"

And it was not just a matter of recognition. There was something not quite right, disconcerting . . . indecent even, about a woman pursuing her individual ambition, independence, and personal gratification at the expense of her natural role. Respectability. That was it. The indispensable accolade bestowed by marriage. He had once had a single woman as a boss. She had been unpopular in the office. "You know she slept her way to the top, don't you?" they whispered behind her back.

No, academic and professional glory was best earned for a family by its sons. A daughter, no matter how intelligent, earned glory mainly by being virtuous and dutiful and conforming to the role laid down for her. It was not that he did not love Faith—he did. And because he did, he sometimes almost empathized with her, deep in a hidden corner of himself—a tiny little truth she would never know. But he could not change the natural order of things. And the potential impact of campus life on a girl's respectability was another thing to worry about. Another thing which would be a nonissue if she were a boy.

And thus, Faith might never even have made it to university without her aunt's intervention. Although all three of her brothers were younger than she, her father was more preoccupied planning and budgeting for their future than for hers. Investing good money educating someone who was ultimately best off with marriage and motherhood did not make sense. But his sister had a soft spot for Faith since she had lived with her for so many years—a fact which also gave her a better appreciation than her brother of how intelligent and academically inclined Faith was. And it was she who finally convinced him that his daughter's talents should not go to waste. Faith, for her part, tried to be accommodating about her father's priorities, but one thing she understood very well was that if she was planning to do anything except get married after university, she would have to find her own resources to do it.

Thus, when her final year began, Faith resolved that this was the time to lay the groundwork for her future, not only by gaining her degree but by building up as solid an economic base as possible in preparation for the leap into the future that would follow graduation. Unfortunately for her, however, the increased academic pressure of the final year made it harder to cultivate and maintain lucrative relationships. So when she heard about the "quick top-up" method, she decided to investigate it.

It consisted of an arrangement with certain hotels in town whereby they provided willing female students with free mobile phones on which they could be summoned whenever they had guests who might enjoy their company. The girls in turn provided photographs for the albums of choice made available to more discerning, less hasty guests. Shika had been "on call" for some time and so had several other girls in their hall of residence. It was a brisk business that provided profits for the hotels, profits for the girls, and pleasure to the clients. A win-win situation. "Mutually beneficial" in economic terms, as all trade should be.

The first time Faith tried it she was nervous. It was not the first time she would be involved in a sexual encounter without sharing the desire for it, but it was the first time she was consenting to such an encounter, and without knowing her partner beforehand. She was not afraid as such because she would be in a hotel where the management was aware of the arrangement and could come to her aid if she were in any real danger. But she had the uneasy feeling that she was crossing a new frontier. When it was time for her to leave, Shika took a tube of lubricating jelly out of her handbag, slipped it into Faith's, zipped it up, and hung it on her shoulder for her. Then she wished her luck and waved her off.

Afterward Faith could not say that she had shared the pleasure of it, but then it had been well understood in advance that her share of gratification from the deal was financial first and foremost. And as an economist, she had no problem operating within the simple principles of demand and supply. As she stashed away her wad of cash, her mind went back to her latest revision on the topic: "A market need not be a physical location. It is any arrangement for bringing buyers and sellers together. On one side stand the buyers whose decisions to purchase serve to influence prices and thereby allocate resources. Demand by buyers in the market refers to the amount of a commodity which they are willing and able to purchase. It is *effective demand* and not mere wishful thinking or desire, that constitutes demand."

Effective demand . . . yes indeed, she mused. Although she had not understood it before, she had just been privileged with a private tutorial. Mischievously, she pictured herself raising her hand in a lecture. "Yes, Prof, I can give you a perfect example . . ." But somehow she suspected her lecturers might not appreciate her primary research and would rather stick to the more traditional commodity and service examples employed in the teaching of economics.

And it was thus, in economic terms, that she preferred to think of what had happened in that dark hotel room. Physically, she could place the experience in the same category as an invasive but unavoidable gynecological procedure. The difference was that the doctor paid the patient for her forbearance, not the other way around. In addition to this, the years of practice she had received at the hands of her uncle made it easier for her to shut off her feelings, shut off everything, and watch her body being used for someone else's pleasure in the knowledge that, this time at least, there would be a reward for it.

And she was pleased with her reward. If there was any part of her that felt upset or degraded, she did not nourish it with recognition. In her young life, she had never had the luxury of being sentimental about her body or her relationships with men. That was reserved for people in the kind of world depicted by her favorite Hollywood movies, in which independent women in control of their lives fell in love with men of similar description and played out beautiful romances untainted by practical necessities and undistorted by demeaning inequities. Their happy endings simultaneously marked the beginning of eternal bliss, or, in the lingo, "living happily ever after." Of course Faith understood that this kind of love did not only happen in the movies, but the levels of real life at which it happened sometimes seemed equally remote to her.

Fortunately, she had discovered early in life that crying over things you could not control did not change anything. Learning hard lessons and finding ways to turn weaknesses into strengths was a more constructive approach, as her studies had confirmed. In fact, as she had learned in her lectures, differences in comparative advantage were the very basis of trade. People sold those goods in which they had a comparative advantage and bought those they had a comparative disadvantage in producing. Underlying the comparative advantage or disadvantage were initial resource disparities, such as endowments of natural resources or possession of a favorable climate. The beauty of trade was that it could enable people to consume more than their productive potential.

She had often wished that Shika could have studied economics too. It all made such perfect sense. Their comparative disadvantage was money. Their comparative advantage was the "resource disparity" of youth and female sex appeal, or, to use its earthy old local nickname, "bottom power"—a literal endowment of natural resources. The beauty of what they were doing was that it enabled them to consume more money than they could otherwise produce.

The equation also worked quite neatly when viewed from the other side, with the men having as a comparative advantage the endowment of money, a resource disparity granted them by the favorable climate of male domination, and thereby as much of a "natural resource" in these parts as any other male endowment.

She tried to explain this personalized interpretation of exchange and trade to Shika and Becky a few days later over lunch. Becky was one of their hall-mates and had offered to buy them lunch in the cafeteria because she was feeling generous after her own latest top-up. She was very receptive to Faith's economics lesson because it gave her the perfect opportunity to boast about the spectacular tip she had received from her client.

"How did you do it?" Faith gasped.

"Easy," bragged Becky, "just do him all the things his wife can't do."

"Or won't do," supplied Shika.

"And make yourself girly-girly, act shy when he talks to you, giggle at everything he says, and make him feel like a king," continued Becky, demonstrating by raising the pitch and affectation of her voice with every word.

"And act like you never knew what pleasure was till you landed in his bed," sniggered Shika.

"Oh Sir! Oh SIR!! *OH SIR!!!*" Becky panted dramatically, fluttering her eyelids and writhing in mock ecstasy.

"Stop that, you look like someone having an epileptic fit," said Faith, trying to control her laughter as she noticed the looks from other tables.

"Well, Lover Boy didn't think so," bragged Becky. "He couldn't get enough of it! He wants to see me again ASAP!" she added, pronouncing "asap" as a word rather than separate letters.

"So Faith," said Shika with a wink, "now you know how to double your money!"

Faith could not help cringing at the idea of staging such a show. She found it degrading not only to herself but to her partner. Already she felt somehow repulsed by the consumers of such "services." She knew she could be considered equally repulsive for providing those services, but she was in it for the money. After all, people who cleaned toilets and collected rubbish didn't do it for pleasure, did they? How many people in this world truly enjoyed the things they did for money?

But to be a client, a buyer, the person who wanted it, enjoyed it, who created the need for the thing in the first place—that was different. And if it was deceitful for her to find that need loathsome even as she satisfied it, then it must be hypocritical for toilet cleaners and rubbish collectors to dislike the odors of their job.

But of course she could see the point of Becky's performance. She was simply adding value to her goods—with excellent results, obviously. Yes, it made economic sense. Despising one's client was not good for business. Unless of course, one could turn it to one's advantage and manipulate him the way Becky had done.

Faith did not quite put on the full show with her next few "hotel guests," but she did manage to effect a gradual improvement in her performance, enjoying the commensurate rewards. And she learned useful lessons not only from the other girls, but from her clients too. By the time the most memorable of them came into her life, she was more than equipped to satisfy him.

The room was in darkness as she entered that night, which was not unusual. Darkness had much to endear it in such situations. For one, it helped to obscure identity, which some clients preferred. It was also a comforting cover for any initial shyness or awkwardness. And then, of course, it had a time-honored role in creating the kind of atmosphere conducive to encounters of that nature. He was lying in bed and hardly looked up as she walked in. He grunted in reply to her greeting and stiffened as she sat next to him, clearly ill at ease.

It was not the first time she had needed to break the ice. There were different ways to do that, but she had learned that the most economical in terms of time and effort was simply to get him in the mood as fast as possible. After all, they both knew what they were there for. And she still had to finish an essay on price elasticity that night. With the boldness of accumulated experience she lifted herself on the bed still fully clothed and straddled him, reaching for his hands and placing them over her hips as she began a provocative gyration.

His response was exactly the opposite of what she had expected. She had only a split second to wonder why this man was so different from all the others before he twisted his body, jerking her off in a convulsive effort to reach the light switch. As light flooded the room, he raised both hands to his head and screamed as if beholding a monster, "My daughter, a prostitute!"

The blow of recognition was even more abrupt for Faith, who, unlike her father, had not suspected anything until that moment of illumination. Only later, when she had time to reflect on it, did she realize that the sickening suspicion must have seized him from the moment she had entered the room. But that was much later. Now they faced each other, caught in the eternity of those agonizing moments.

"You!" he whispered, pointing a trembling finger at her and backing away so that one could have believed the creature on his bed to be a spitting cobra, risen up on its coils, hood spread out, poised to shoot venom.

Faith's heart struck a colossal beat, which reverberated through her entire body and left her shaking uncontrollably. She fell to her knees on the floor, mouthing things she could not later remember, probably calling on Jesus or God, her mouth too dry to formulate proper words and her body prickling all over with a cold sweat.

Before she could attempt to collect herself, her father cried out, clutched at his heart, and collapsed. Faith had seen him suffer a heart attack four years earlier and she recognized it. Any shred of hope that the unspeakable episode might be hushed up was dashed forever as she succumbed to total hysteria. Her screams of "Dada! Dada!" echoed off the walls of the hotel and well beyond the building. Hotel staff burst in to find her wailing with both hands over her head.

Her father survived—in a physiological sense at least. How much of his dignity as a man, a husband, a father . . . a civil servant, a Christian brother, and all those other respectable personae survived, is another question. He spent a few days in the general hospital during which he would not allow his daughter to come near him.

Faith, on the other hand, died a thousand deaths in those few days, trauma-tized by the abominable memory, numb with shame, sick with worry, racked with guilt, and relieved by the very rejection that tore her apart, mercifully postponing the day they must face each other again. His cry haunted her—"My daughter, a . . ." It was the juxtaposition of those two words that made it so un-utterable. *Daughter* on its own was fine. Even *prostitute* on its own, was OK. The problem, the taboo, was in bringing them together.

And yet, even as she shrank from the sting of those words, she wanted to lash back out at them. "My daughter . . . *my* daughter, a . . ." What was so un-thinkable about it? Were prostitutes not all daughters . . . of somebody or other? If her father had done this before—and the chances were he had—didn't he know that the girls he was sleeping with were also people's daughters? Or did he think prostitutes didn't have parents, didn't belong anywhere, just grew on a prostitute tree somewhere? If he did not want his own daughter to be a prosti-tute, why should he accept, enjoy, finance the prostitution of other men's daughters? How quickly pleasure turned into disgust when the watchdogs of knowledge, judgment, and accountability reared their fearsome heads.

She found out from the hospital that he had arranged to be transferred to a clinic back home as fast as possible. Apparently it had indeed been a second minor heart attack. When the story made the rounds later on, however, there were those who questioned the heart attack part of it. After all, what could a man reasonably do who had called for a prostitute and got his own daughter? Cower with shame? Bellow with rage? Rebuke her for shaming . . . him? Or just

escape from the impossibility of it all by collapsing, entering a state of nonfeel-
ing, nonbeing, nonresponsibility—at least temporarily? At least, until there was
more time to think and decide how to handle it? "What would you have done?"
people asked each other.

Yes indeed, the story generated much debate. Hilarity too. "His own daughter?" People choked on kebabs, spluttered and sprayed their beers, coughed and
gasped. "No! What?? This is a joke isn't it? My friend, stop! This one, I don't believe it!" And the teller, enjoying the sensation, would have the delightful task of
assuring them that it was a true story: "I'm telling you! I swear!" And eventually,
when everybody was convinced, then it was time to decry the evils of modern
society, and especially the rottenness of young girls these days.

If any kind of a happy ending could be found to the story, then it must be
that Faith's mother never found out. And indeed, ignorance of the closest stake-
holders was not an uncommon phenomenon in such matters. This fortunate
turn of events might be attributed to various factors. For one, there was the
ever-expedient fact that they lived far from the scene of events, and she was not
one to undertake unnecessary or independent travel. For another, there was the
travel-oriented nature of her husband's work. And then there was the blissful
serenity of an accepting, unquestioning mind and the blessed balm of spiritual
reassurance.

Thus it was that she never had to endure anything but the most sincere and
dutiful concern over her husband's second heart attack. And never had to pack
away the cherished photo in the gilded frame by her bedside. It had been presented to her on her husband's behalf by the church on the occasion of their
marriage blessing the previous year. The church encouraged couples whose
union had not been performed in the sight of the Lord to remedy this no matter
how late, and, to this end, organized mass, wedding-like nuptial blessings every
year.

They even saw to the little details, making available at a competitive
price to each happy couple a matching pair of photo-citations with gender-
differentiated wording and dotted blanks into which the appropriate names
could be penned. Hers read:

> Comfort, my beloved wife, God has chosen you to be my only companion on
> this earth. On this day I pledge to you my everlasting love and fidelity. May the
> joy of our blessed union last forever. Those whom God has joined together, no
> man may put asunder. Your devoted husband, Thomas.

She smiled with perfect fulfillment above the curly writing, secure in the crook
of her husband's arm, resplendent in her white dress and hat.

What she did find out about, however, was the phenomenon of campus call
girls. She was listening absentmindedly to the radio while cooking one day. A

phone-in talk show began on modern forms of prostitution. The discussion became animated when the campus-call-girl issue came up. Clearly it had become quite topical, and who is to say that the story of Faith might not have played some small part in that?

Ma Comfort began to listen more closely when she heard someone mention the word *universities*. The word had become particularly dear to her since her daughter had joined their exalted ranks.

"Look, if you think that these—excuse me to say—*apuskeleke* or *ashawo* or whatever . . . girls are just the ones walking the streets at night, you don't know what is going on in this country! I'm telling you, this problem is rampant, to the point of polluting even our academic institutions—yes, I am talking about universities!" revealed the enlightened caller.

"I blame foreign influences," declared another. "Nowadays we are bombarded with these Western ideas and the young people think they are in America! Look at the films they are showing on TV—anything goes! No wonder prostitution, pornography, homosexuality, and others are now flourishing in our society. I'm telling you, we never had those things here before!"

"Let us not blame our problems on others," countered the next caller. "If women had the power and money in this society, do you think they would be selling themselves to men? Times are hard and opportunities are not equal, so that is their way of also getting something. And if they are brought up with no better ambition than to please men, what can we expect? Even in the very universities we are talking about, they are more interested in campus beauty contests than their studies."

The next speaker choked on indignation: "More Western ideas! Please, that Beijing conference was a long time ago, forget about those things! These are the attitudes that are causing the problem in the first place. Why defend those rotten girls? Tell me, is it poverty and oppression that forces them to wear designer clothes? They just want to indulge in the pleasures of money and sex before their time. Never satisfied with their lot. Like Eve in the Bible. Looking for trouble. Leading others into temptation. Spoiling things for everybody."

Ma Comfort liked the biblical reference and found herself nodding. She was becoming quite fired up and starting to wish she had the courage to call in. She could talk about the alphabet of AIDS prevention and even put her anti-condom slogan on the air! The thought was exciting. But she knew she would never dare. So she continued to participate in the only way she could, nodding her head, muttering and exclaiming at intervals, and trying to commit the highlights to memory so that she could share them with Faith in case she had missed the show.

Yes, she was looking forward to having her graduate daughter back home at last. It was just a few weeks till graduation and she was already bursting with pride. She had ordered a new outfit for the ceremony and spent hours designing it with her seamstress. She was delighted with the style and thought that something similar might even be appropriate for a mother of the bride. She could always return it to the seamstress as a model when the time came, she mused.

She threw away the vegetable peels and washed her hands with a contented little smile. As she set her soup on the fire, she thought back to the horrors she had just heard on the radio and thanked her God that at least, she would never have to worry about anything like that with respect to her dear daughter Faith.

Lovesung for a Father

Zindzi Bedu

For Tamar, for Eula

I.

I love my daddy
I love my daddy
I love my daddy

My daddy comes to the room
He is about to go out
His brilliantly combed hair
Fairly powdered face
      Handsome
He is wearing *sokoto* and *buba*
A dignified African
I love my daddy
I love my daddy I

Love my daddy I Love
My daddy
My daddy the preacher man
My daddy who prays with the authority of raging fire
My daddy the dedicated with his own immigrant's tale
    of fulfilling the American dream
I love my daddy I
      I am sitting at the dining table
I love my daddy I
      I am penning poems in imitation of Langston Hughes
      A mother to my imagined son—
        "Now son,
        Life for me ain't been no crystal stair"
My daddy comes into the room
So brilliant so handsome
I feel pangs of pride so heavy I fall in love in that moment
With this
180 lb 6'2" man
I feel pangs of pride,
I feel falling in love for the first time
Similar to what my mother must have felt
Upon first laying eyes on this man
So brilliant
So handsome
So dark
Seeing him even the ten-year-old daughter quickly conceives love
Yes I love my daddy
Like my mother loved him
Like she would love him still
Were she here in my stepmother's place
My stepmother who must not love him enough
Because every night he visits his love on me.
I love my daddy.

II.

I love my daddy.
From his skillful lips that wake me up from slumber
To his tongue which pierces my mouth
I love this tongue that tells me to push my tongue out
Instructing me in the ways of love
Yes I love my daddy

From his lips to his tongue to his nose
That flat-footed nose which he says is the only is the only part
    of him he sees on my face
The only marker that I am his child
I am his daughter
Every other feature screams my mother's presence
Yes I love my daddy's nose
I love my daddy
I Love
      Love his lips
      Love his tongue
      Love his nose
      Love his hands
His hands that roam the length of my body at night
Crossing over the desert that is my back
I love his hands right down to that finger that illustrious finger that
Dives into the ocean of my vagina
His hands that carry the mountain of my body
Carry it from my bedside to place me on top of him
His hands that roam the length of my body at night
Climbing the mountains
Crossing the deserts
Swimming and diving into the oceans
Making my body his discovery mission
His hands across my back paving the way for his lips and tongue
    to glide through
His lips kissing my armpits
His tongue in my ear
His teeth on my clitoris
He is looking for treasure
The treasure of my hidden spots
Those sensitive spots that when stimulated will arouse in me
    even more love
I love my daddy
From his hair follicles to his toe nails
Right down to that big finger
That's part of his larger hand
My daddy's hands are so big—
One hand can pin down both of mine
While the other roams my body
His hands are so big—
One can grasp my entire head

And slam it down onto the top of our washing machine
One hand can give me a hiding across my entire backside
Wholesome discipline originating from love
My daddy's fingers are so dexterous
They crawl in the tight spaces of my two arms folded across
    my chest on the bed
They crawl in tight spaces to get to my breasts
His nimble prying dexterous fingers
Crawling through tight spaces
Prying open folds
To give his eyes access to my literal inside
Slashing away all boundaries between me and him and love.

III.

My father's eyes have penetrated me
Those brown black oblique circles that peer down on me
As his other flesh rhythmically pushes into me
My world is narrowed down to my daddy's face
His eyes that penetrate, his lips that glide, his tongue that pierces,
    his nose that screams belonging right back to his eyes that tell
    stories in pictures of how I have had my father inside of me
My world is narrowed to my daddy's face
I have held his head down to suckle at my breasts
My world is narrowed to my daddy's face
A face with features that detail how I love my daddy
A face that is standing here in front of me
As I pen poems imitating Langston Hughes
A mother to my imagined son
       "Now son, Life for me ain't been no crystal stair"
I am looking at this handsome figure of a man
His brilliantly combed hair
Fairly powdered face
A standing testimonial to the American dream
Father husband son with his own rags to riches immigrant's tale
I am looking at this handsome figure of a man
I am seeing him with my mother's eyes
I am loving him with my mother's heart
I am proud of this man
So proud it hurts in that beautifully sentimental sort of way
I feel falling in love for the first time.
Between my pen and his face

Echo stories of just how much
I love my daddy.
I love my daddy. I
Love my daddy. I love
My daddy.

Poet's Note

In what follows, I will move back and forth between a first and third person voice. I separate these voices as a strategy of healing. This strategy helps me write honestly about a past that has been confronted and excised, as in Toni Morrison's *Beloved*, for the purpose of greater healing and better living in the present. This strategy helps me write about the resolved past without reviving it. This past claims a different voice; the present claims my strategy. I first encountered this oscillation between voices in bell hooks' memoirs—*Bone Black* and *Wounds of Passion*. Of this strategy, hooks writes:

> The inclusion of the third person narrator who has both critical insight and an almost psychoanalytic power that enables critical reflection on events described is an act of mediation. When we rewrite the past, looking back with our current understanding, a mediation is always taking place. I give that mediation a voice, rather than mask this aspect of any retrospective reflection on our lives. (1997:xxii)

Writing about the past is an act of mediation, the strategy is to highlight this mediation through voice, rather than leave it disguised. In addition, I have to explain that my creative works are usually written under my nom de plume, Zindzi Bedu. I responded to the question, what is Africa to me? with "Lovesung for a Father" because my work on healing and self-recovery gave me the tools to reassess an old wound.

Because her father was Africa to her. His being symbolized the loss of childhood innocence, violation, and humiliation of a forced sexual "awakening." Her father was Africa to her. The memory of what she could never again be. Her broken hymen meant she could never again dream of losing her virginity on her wedding night to a husband who was also a virgin himself. She could never again be daughter to the ones who raised her—a mother and grandmother in Nigeria waiting with pieces of her childhood, memories of when the world consisted of a playground swing taking her higher and higher toward the sky, closer to heaven, all the world crystallizing in eternal joy. Her mother and grandmother were waiting for their little girl who would never return, waiting in an Africa of her childhood that

she would never again reach. In the United States, her father was Africa to her.
Africa pierced her hymen, shattered her innocent dreams; Africa slapped her head
against a washing machine, beat her in a corner by the fridge so that his authority
would always be inscribed in her memory, the weight of a tradition that dictated
daughters always be respectful to their fathers, kneeling down in greeting, carrying
their briefcases when they come home, carrying their bodies atop hers at night. She
died in that Africa. Nobody knew it.

I wrote this poem to retrieve her spirit from the negative weight of words like
rape, incest, and *sexual abuse* because those words do not adequately capture
her experience.

She came to imagine herself as a ruined woman, she imagined herself in a com-
munity of African women ruined. Until she learned to discover another Africa—
an Africa of renewal, an Africa of self-retrieval through ritual.

Memory is like ritual, changing with an ever-shifting present. The healthiest
aspect of memory is that it is not static, but adaptable to present purposes (see
Busia 2006:23; this is also akin to Toni Morrison's concept of rememory).
When words like *rape* and *incest* encode the memory of an African self, however, the adaptability, richness, and benefits of memory are threatened. Words
like *rape* and *incest* fix memory in negativity, rendering it static, cutting short
the imagination it takes to invent and reinvent past selves, to interpret past
events differently for the purpose of healing. I wrote this poem to go back and
retrieve the past—*sankofa*—from the fixity of such terms. I wrote this poem to
resurrect her not into ruin, but into freedom.

My work on healing happened in a space of communion with black women
and in relationship to black men (see Brown 1991). I started reading hooks'
Sisters of the Yam, a book on black women and self-recovery. Reading it, I began
to reflect on the devaluation of black womanhood as a communal problem in
need of communal address. I began to yearn for spaces where black women can
come together on their own terms to connect their individual lives to a larger
community. I began to yearn for black works that presented black love in its
sacred context because I firmly believe that healing a history of sexual violation ought not to involve isolation from or vilification of [black] men. When
sexuality is approached with openness, it proves its potential as a space for self-
recovery. It was hooks who first described Paule Marshall's scene of sacred
union between Jay and Avey to me. What struck me most was that the sanctity
of union was not a solitary endeavor but was created together.

I yearned to read this book and other books in this vein; that was to be my personal project. I was thrilled to discover a course being offered, "In Search of Diaspora Literacy: Black Women Writers," with a reading list that included Paule Marshall's *Praisesong for the Widow*. When I arrived the first day of class to a roomful of black women, I knew the space I had been yearning for had found me.

This poem is responding to many of the insights gained in this course. As such, all the works we read influenced my creative impulse. Most crucial, however, are the insights I gained about the work of memory and the sacredness of black love. In literary representation, black bodies can be objectified; our bodies can also be represented as connected with the sacred within ourselves (see Marshall 1984:126–30; Morrison 1988:87–89). In writing this poem, I tried to connect with the sacred, which is love.

To unmoor memory from its negative fixity, I began with Love, a love I journeyed to get to. When the line, "I love my daddy," came to me, I originally intended to use it ironically; I intended *love* to mean its opposite. I did not want to let go of my bitterness regarding the situation I was about to reveal; I wanted the reader/listener to share this bitterness, until I realized that this was a faithless impulse. As a creative person, I asked myself what would happen if I intended this love genuinely and not sarcastically? Could I truly commit to this love? That was when I realized that for love to disarm the past, I had to believe in and fully commit to it. I could use love to crack open a difficult experience, a love that was not about the victim losing her self and identifying with her abuser. I came to mean love on its own terms, whatever that meant.

She never knew her father, even though she knew him biblically. She wanted to understand, especially afterward. What could explain his acts, that he could come to confuse a daughter for a wife? She was invested in categories of right and wrong but he lived in a world of no boundaries. The world did not end when his eyes, his flesh entered his own daughter's opening. There was no fire raining down from the sky, no thunderous declaration of God's immediate judgment at the breaking of taboo. The world did not end, and the next morning, he arose to say with impunity, "Last night, you opened up to me; it was beautiful," words she did not want to hear. She did not want to be open to him. She did not want to be beautiful. She wanted the clarity of right and wrong that God's pronounced judgment could have reinforced. She did not understand why he did not understand that this was wrong, why he could shamelessly challenge her when she said this was wrong. Her father was Africa to her, he lived in a world of no boundaries. Because he loved her desperately, as he said, he collapsed the sexual boundaries between them. He challenged her to prove he was wrong. Since there was no rain of fire bearing down God's wrath, there was no witness on her side. What she needed was a witness.

I had to believe in Love innocently and openly to let go of embittered judgment. I had to discover the past for myself once I let judgment go. I had to trust. My healing is tied to loving that African man as I wrote in this poem. In every union, including that one, the weight of history lies, a history that goes back to slavery, a history that goes beyond slavery. In the film *Daughters of the Dust*, Julie Dash explores sexual abuse as a legacy of slavery. A number of African American women creatively engage with a cycle of rape and violence that went back to days of African enslavement. One playwright notes, "I wanted to talk about how the violence that happened to my mother was the same violence that had happened to my grandmother, or that had come out of slavery; and that we had passed all that violence and shame on" (Carlos 1994:3). My experience as an African-born woman who migrated as part of a "new diaspora" (Busia 2006:17) questions the origins of sexual abuse, shame, and "ruined" womanhood in slavery. Sexual abuse is not just a legacy of slavery. What is outrageous is the silence and shame. These matters are either too "delicate" or "indelicate" (Morrison 1987:110) to confront publicly both on this side and across the Atlantic.

When she spoke out to her mother's family in Africa, they wanted to ignore her. They asked her to forgive, forget, and silence the past, a request that motivated her to resist. She did not want to forgive him until she had seen him punished. She was still looking for that witness to confirm the breaking of taboo. Her silence became a price for the wholeness of the family, for the sanctity of family image. It made her wonder about secrets, lies, and sacrifice. How many were like her, sacrificing their voices to live out a silent image?

Eula's call in *Daughters* is a refusal to be silenced (Dash 1992:155–57). In her refusal is the refute of ruin. Her call is a call for healing, a call "to live our lives without living in the fold of old wounds" (155). In her confrontation, Eula asks the women to change their ways of thinking, to let go of a negative label that freezes their spirits and their liberty in embrace of a life lived without fear. "Lovesung for a Father" heeds this call. Writing helped me get past labels. I could envision innocence and openness and write it to life. "Lovesung for a Father" was never intended to be simple. I wrote to free my memory from its fixity and open up possibilities for many different interpretations of a complex, complicated, ever-changing life event.

References

Brown, Elsa Barkley. 1991. "Polyrhythms and Improvisation: Lessons for Women's History." *History Workshop* 31 (1): 85–90.

Busia, Abena P. A. 2006. "What Is Africa to Me? Knowledge Possession, Knowledge Production, and the Health of Our Bodies Politic in Africa and the African Diaspora." *African Studies Review* 49 (1): 15–30.

Carlos, Laurie. 1994. "White Chocolate for My Father." In *Moon Marked and Touched by Sun: Plays by African-American Women*, ed. Sydné Mahone. New York: Theatre Communications Group.

Dash, Julie. 1992. *Daughters of the Dust: The Making of an African American Woman's Film*. New York: New Press.

hooks, bell. 1993. *Sisters of the Yam: Black Women and Self-Recovery*. Boston: South End Press.

———. 1997. *Wounds of Passion: A Writing Life*. New York: Henry Holt and Company.

Marshall, Paule. 1984. *Praisesong for the Widow*. New York: E. P. Dutton.

Morrison, Toni. 1987. "The Site of Memory." In *Inventing the Truth: The Art and Craft of Memoir*, ed. William Zinsser. Boston: Houghton Mifflin.

———. 1988. *Beloved*. New York: Plume.

It's Not Rape If . . .

Ann Kithaka

He doesn't tear my pants and hymen ring;
I don't scream and I cream;
I wear a mini-skirt and flirt;
If I am under his authority
In office or matrimony.

To Be or Not to Be a Lesbian

The Dilemma of Cameroon's Women Soccer Players

Sybille Ngo Nyeck

Cameroon is a leading soccer nation in Africa. It is a national passion and the men's national team has performed well in the international arena. However, it has not yet succeeded in building a top women's soccer team at the international level. The following interview helps us to understand why this has not been the case.

The interviewee required anonymity. She will be referred to here as Hoka H.

Hoka H., what kind of experience do you have with women's soccer in Cameroon?

I spent about fifteen years as a Cameroonian soccer player. I was among the best during my career.

Why was your country absent from World Cup 2003?

We took third place at the African Cup of Nations games. Only the first- and the second-place finishers qualified for the World Cup finals.

Did you think your country had a chance to go further? If so, why don't Cameroon-
ian women do as well as the men at the international level?

Firstly, I believe that we need our national championship to be better organized. Secondly, the national team needs more time to prepare. I want to point
out that Cameroon has no soccer-training center for women. If we look carefully at how things evolve, I would say this kind of project has not yet been conceived. However, Cameroon has talented women players just like men—to
come in third place is not bad. But I would also denounce those nations that
host tournaments which try to make sure by any means, sometimes unorthodox, that they remain leaders in Africa.

What do you mean by "unorthodox"?

When I say "unorthodox," I think of how the opposing teams are treated. For
instance, the nutrition of women players is not always controlled. At a techni-
cal level, the referees are chosen in a way that may influence the results of
matches. Sometimes, teams are given accommodations a long distance away
from the stadiums.

Could you tell us how local clubs select female players? How are contracts deter-
mined and what do they say?

The recruitment of girls is done by women players. This means that if in my
neighborhood I meet a girl who is interested in soccer, I may introduce her to a
club and to the championship league. The trainers [managers/coaches] reach
out the same way. They sometimes go to schools, and, with the help of gym
teachers, select their "product." Sometimes women just come to the clubs and
offer their services. We have no standard method of recruitment here.

The contracts are small because clubs have meager incomes. Women who
do receive some money are usually paid between 20,000 and 100,000 F CFA
(Cameroon francs). They are given stipends (between 300 and 300 F CFA) for
each training session, just enough to pay for their transportation. Each signa-
ture binds a player for two years to her club. The contracts do not specify that
she must give an account of her private life.

What about the selections to the national team?

At the national level, there is a preselection process during the championship. . . .
But things are not always easy because there is a category of girls who, sadly,
have been the victims of blackmail. In Cameroon, to be suspected of being a
lesbian is enough to have your place within the national team taken away—this

is not only true for the national team, but also at the club level, as lesbians are threatened. We wonder whether living a homosexual life has any effect on athletic performance.

Are there lesbian women athletes, and, if so, has this created a stereotype?

Lesbians are everywhere in Cameroon. There is no specific place for them in society. They are in all social classes and professions: business, trade, politics, sports, and schools—in sum, everywhere. People just live their lives and try to feel good about who they are. They are not visible activists because our society is far from accepting homosexuals.

How do you think discrimination against suspected lesbians impacts their performance at the local and international levels?

Without hesitation I say that suspected or real lesbians are victims of all sorts of discrimination. The [male soccer] club leaders had even decided to kick them out of the clubs or, by all means, "change" them. Women themselves do not complain about female homosexuality.

There are frequent cases of violence. I would offer as an example the case of the rape of two women soccer players at Mfandena in Yaoundé. I didn't see any club president moved [to response] by this drama. Even the managers of the clubs where they were affiliated didn't react. Neighbors didn't raise a single hand (I wonder if it was planned). It is not rare to see managers of clubs sexually harass women. Sleeping with a manager or publicly hooking up with a man is the way for women to avoid falling victim to blackmail linked to homosexuality. I believe discriminatory policies make us lose many talented players. Some women are abused by either their managers or club members, and when they find themselves pregnant, the same managers force them to have illegal abortions for fear of losing the players.

Also, spies follow girls: after matches; during the training; in night clubs; in school—in sum, everywhere. Some men are sent to date girls, and when it doesn't work, they threaten the women. These threats sometimes reach relatives too, and family life becomes unbearable.

To whom do women complain when they are mistreated?

They cannot complain about being harassed for homosexuality because our legislation criminalizes it. Regarding the abuse of authority and sexual abuse, there is no structure to prevent women soccer players from the arbitrary force of their managers. It also takes a lot of courage, and this is what women players lack in their relationships with managers.

In December 2002 women players denounced for the first time the sexual harassment, violence, discrimination, and public insults by their managers on Radio Siantou. [Recalling this] reminds me that when girls are not accused of being lesbians, they are insulted as being old. This is how the national coach publicly referred to his players after they were defeated in their attempt to get to the World Cup.

You identified women soccer players as "products." What did you mean?

I used the word *product* because this is a frequent word used by managers to refer to women players. Also because some women playing soccer are, in my view, a reflection of those in power who want to make sure that women in sports largely dominated by men do not reflect men. The [belief in] "feminine soccer" treats women as girls who should not expose their legs—they believe this encourages rape. Those who persist [in showing their legs] are suspected of being abnormal. For me, one just needs to have a gift to play this sport, and, of course, this has to be supported by good coaching. In Nigeria they talk about "women's soccer," but here, to the contrary, they insist on calling it "feminine soccer."

In this environment—oppressive toward women in general, and against lesbians in particular—how can women soccer players who love other women survive?

They simply invent themselves. Each person creates her own story. Here women who love women don't call themselves lesbians. They invent themselves by drawing from native languages words that empower them: for instance, the word *mvoye*, which simply means in a local language, "to be good." Good in one's mind and spirit. Good in one's choices. These words evolve and are transmitted from generation to generation.

After your national team was defeated at the African Cup of Nations, the newspaper Le Messager *published an article on women's soccer (September 11, 2002). The following comments were made concerning women and homosexuality: "For the past couple years, this ugly behavior has defiled women's soccer in Cameroon. . . . The biggest plague in women's soccer is without a doubt homosexuality." What is your reaction to these allegations?*

My opinion is that it is unsuitable to call homosexuality an "ugly behavior." One day, I had a conversation with somebody whose attitude surprised me. He said, "I hope that you are not part of what I heard [exists] within soccer." I questioned him about that invisible but outspoken thing he was afraid to mention. He responded, "It seems like all girls in soccer are lesbians." I have to insist that we play soccer with our feet, not with our sex!

The same article accused lesbian soccer players of being sex traffickers who "place" their fellow players with wealthy women, and of being rapists who take advantage of the heterosexual players. Is either of these accusations true?

I'm not aware of prostitution between women. People always want to discredit homosexuals. In our society, homosexuality is not openly practiced, which leaves open ground for speculation. It is also true that newspapers facing a financial crisis will write anything on that subject to sell their papers.

And again, to see women as rapists is to victimize them. It is inaccurate to say that lesbians marginalize heterosexuals; I believe solidarity is what makes a team strong. Heterosexual women have no problem playing with lesbians. This blackmail is orchestrated by the managers and their supporters. They are afraid homosexuals will contaminate others.

The newspaper reported a club chairperson discussing sanctions against lesbian players. What are these sanctions?

It is a very delicate situation because some managers take advantage of their power to abuse girls. Generally they threaten to disclose her personal life to her family because homosexuality is not accepted. That will create a scandal, and usually the girl will be kicked out of the family house or abandoned without any other source of income. Some managers consciously request sexual gratification from women to keep their homosexual lives secret.

Hoka H., are you a lesbian?

I'm good.

Thanks for your openness.

Thanks to you too.

My Name Is Kasha

Kasha N. Jacqueline

My name is Kasha N. Jacqueline. I am a twenty-six-year-old lesbian activist from Uganda. I am the chairperson and a cofounder of the only exclusively lesbian organization in Uganda, Freedom and Roam Uganda (FAR-UG). This is my testimony.

I found out that I was a lesbian in 1987 when I was seven years old, in second grade. My second-grade teacher told me so whenever she was caning me for sleeping with my fellow pupils. She kept telling me that the reason I liked sleeping with girls was because I was possessed by a demon. In primary school I was never suspended or expelled but was often caned.

When I started secondary school, I read about homosexuality and found out that I was born like that and neither did I possess demons nor was I a spoiled child. I was expelled from my first secondary school because of my sexual orientation. When I was asked whether I was a lesbian I said yes, and I was told to go and try my evil behaviors somewhere else. I joined another school but was expelled for writing love letters to other girls in school. Other girls used to receive presents and letters from their boyfriends, but they were never punished.

On April 11, 1995, I received a present from a girlfriend who was not in the same school with me. My present was opened on arrival and my letter was read. They said they couldn't stand my behavior anymore and they expelled me. I joined another school, and in this school I was suspended because of a rumor that I had been kicked out of all my former schools because of my sexual orientation. I was not expelled, because I had already registered for my final exams. But I was not allowed to live at school; I had to sit my final exams while commuting from outside the school, even though it was a boarding school. During my vacation it was the same old harassment of people calling me names, and because I had been to quite a number of schools, I was known in almost every corner of the city. The boys in town hated me, and I lost a good number of girlfriends because they didn't want to be called lesbians.

I enrolled in another school for my advanced education, and this time I decided to join a coed school, thinking it would make me get attracted to boys, just like other girls my age. At this time I still doubted my sexual orientation and thought my attraction to women was because I had only been to girls' schools. But I never was attracted to boys, and instead I fully discovered my homosexual orientation was real. I got worse harassment in the coed school. Boys called me all sorts of bad names, like *musiyazi* (homosexual), which is a very bad word in my local language. It is related to bestiality. Boys started saying that I was a hermaphrodite and they wanted to undress me and find out the truth.

I was really hurt and so upset that I even asked to go home for a while. But instead of finding peace at home, I got more harassment. My uncle couldn't stop calling me all sorts of names, and he even said I was better off dead than staying alive and putting the family to shame.

In 1999 I enrolled in a private university. I expected university to be different from the previous schools I had attended, but instead I found it was hell beyond hell. My picture was pinned up all over the university campus with a big heading reading WANTED. I always thought such headings were for criminals, but here I was being labeled a criminal just for being a lesbian. Any other student who was in the wrong was always called in a proper manner to the administration, but for me it always had to be a poster with my name and picture and that heading, which I hate with a passion.

The first time my poster was put up, it was because the warden said she had seen me kissing a fellow girl in the night. My parents were called to campus, and I was warned and told to report to the administration every day dressed like other girls on campus. All my caps, shirts, trousers, and big shoes were banned from the campus, and I had to report to the registrar every day to show that I was dressed in a dress or skirt like other girls.

The second time my poster was put up, it was for sleeping in the girls' hostel. I always slept off campus, but this night I decided to spend it in the girls' hostel with a friend. The next day my parents were called back to the university and I was suspended. When I returned I was made to sign an agreement barring me from entering the girls' hostels, and also I was not to be within one hundred meters from their location. For God's sake, I was a girl, and here I was being barred from entering girls' hostels! Oddly enough, the boys were allowed in the girls' hostels at any time they wished to go visit.

After that I had to stay in a boys-only compound because that's where I could find a room. What shame. One semester all the new students were told during their orientation week that if any of them were found interacting with me, they would be expelled. This meant that I could not have any friends, and on top of that, the university registrar kept coming to my room to check whether there were any girls there.

One day at about 10:25 a.m., he came around and found a friend in my room, and he said he was going to expel me because he had caught me in the "act," even though he had found my door wide open. This meant that I didn't have the right to privacy or even to interact with any female students. But this time I was not to be intimidated, and I boldly told him that I knew my rights very well and that I would take the university to the courts of law if he didn't stop harassing me. He told me that homosexuality was illegal, thinking I would back down, but I insisted and even told him that I was going to call my lawyer immediately (as if I had any lawyer!).

I waited for him to expel me but he didn't. That time my guts helped me to avoid expulsion, and I finished my bachelor's degree in accounting with some peace.

Cosmo Africa
and Other Poems

Cheshe Dow

1. A Woman I Used to Know

Every now and again
She wakes up to find
That she is bleeding

She wants her body to leave her alone
It's changing before she has had time to know it

Now people she doesn't always know
Want to know her body
Claim to know her body

For six years
She doesn't look at it
Or want anything to do with its powers

Until she meets her first love
He is feverish
He wants to explore it

She lets him

She shouldn't have
It wasn't hers yet to give.

2. My Body and I

He wants to know my body.

Why do these hips and ample bottom
Go everywhere I do and inspire such want?

Because he would stay longer than others have
He thinks his desire is different
But whether confined to one night or one year
In my eyes it is the same thing.

He wants to know my body.

Am I jealous?
I don't think so.
My body wants to be wanted sometimes.
But it is always wanted
Whether I come with it or not.

At least,
For now,
He wants us both.
I suppose that sets him apart.

3. Love

How did she come to believe
That being loved
Was inextricably bound
To the happiness
She could engender,
The food

She could prepare
And the houses she could sweep?

The exhaustion of being loved
Is what keeps her silent.

4. Cosmo Africa

I want to find a man
Who will know I am enough.
A man
Who will celebrate
All of my half circles,
The insides
And the outsides.

The insides,
Whose embrace defines my waist.
The insides,
Revealed by the thoughts I will voice.
The insides,
Nestled between my breasts.

The outsides,
Called to seductive extroversion,
By the wide hips that are my legacy
The outsides,
Brought to tender fullness
By the coming of my child.

Part Three

Challenging
the Institution of Marriage

For African women, as for women across the world, marriage is an institution that can be fraught with ambivalence. The pieces in this section all speak to the challenges African women can face as wives, from the day of their wedding right through to the death of their husbands.

In the poem "Child," Kenyan Ann Kithaka plunges the reader into the violence visited on a wife by her husband that is witnessed by her terrified children. A similar theme is taken up in the short story "Hailstones on Zamfara," as Sefi Atta of Nigeria relates the troubling story of a middle-aged married woman whose abusive husband accuses her of adultery, a crime punishable by death under the Islamic Sharia law that governs many regions in Nigeria and other parts of Africa. The sadness of this tale is redeemed by the solidarity that arises between the uneducated, devout condemned woman and the woman journalist who comes to cover her case and broadcast the injustice of Sharia law toward women and who then takes the older woman's daughter under her wing.

In "The Good Woman," by Patricia Chogugudza of Zimbabwe, and "Ngomwa," by Ellen Mulenga Banda-Aaku of Zambia, well-meaning wives are trapped in loveless marriages from which both eventually escape. When the narrator of "The Good Woman," a mature, successful businesswoman with two college-age sons and a daughter, discovers her husband's long-term infidelity, she goes through a range of emotions, from shock to rage to grief. Eventually, to save her own sanity, she leaves the marriage and the country, seeking more education and a new life abroad. Though it is difficult to leave behind her children and her hard-won assets, it proves to be only a temporary situation; when she regains her strength, she is able to rejoin her children and start her life anew.

The story "Ngomwa" illustrates what can happen to a woman who is unable to conceive children for her husband. Whether the fault is hers or his, she is blamed, and in the case of the narrator of "Ngomwa," an earnest young woman who wants above all to please her husband, the solution is to put his interests and desires above her own. Convinced by a relative to seek the help of a medicine man, the young wife submits to sexual intercourse with him and almost immediately conceives—but the repercussions of this "medicinal rape" are long-lasting and devastating. In the end the narrator finds freedom and happiness, but only by escaping from the confines of her marriage and thereby losing contact with her children.

In "They Came in the Morning," Iheoma Obibi relates the fictional, but all-too-real, story of the situation for widows in her native Nigeria. The protagonist, Chidinma, has been a widow for only a few days when her husband's brothers come banging on her door, demanding that she turn over to the family all his assets, including his successful business and their home. Fortunately for Chidinma, her husband, Paul, had been a forward-thinking man, who made up a will leaving all his possessions to her and counseled her on how to handle his family after his death. Obibi's story shows the positive consequences of marriage as an equal partnership, as well as the potential for some imported customs, such as legal testaments, to work in women's favor.

In "The Battle of the Words: Oratory as Women's Tool of Resistance to the Challenges of Polygamy in Contemporary Wolof Society," anthropologist Marame Gueye of Senegal takes us behind the scenes in a traditional Senegalese marriage ceremony, the "welcome" given by the senior wives of a household to a new junior wife. The husband is conspicuously absent in this story, leaving the women to take out their resentment on each other rather than on him. Although some might read the vicious verbal attacks performed by the senior wives and their surrogates as a form of hazing for the hapless junior wife, Gueye sees the ceremony as a form of women's resistance to the tradition of polygamy, which, she says, shows little sign of changing any time soon.

Taken as a group, the women writers in this section bear witness to some of the ways that the institution of marriage can be confining and oppressive in contemporary African society—in various countries and cultural contexts—as well as to the creative ways women are finding to stretch the boundaries of traditional marital gender roles in order to seek freedom and fulfillment with or without their husbands.

Child

Ann Kithaka

For my daughters Eleanor and Janet,
silent witnesses

Child,
You saw him last night,
Your enraged father,
Half naked, drunk as a skunk,
Tottering into your room,
Poised on your bedroom doorway,
Baying for blood.
My blood.

You saw me too,
Cowering at the corner,
Holding on to your bedpost,
My red nightdress torn in the middle,
Bloody hairpiece hanging askew on my head,
Face puffy and swollen,

Cowering like the coward that I am,
Entreating him to spare me tonight!
I saw the fear in your eyes,
And that of your elder sister,
Who stared around her in a daze,
Wishing the bad dream away.

But the macabre drama
Refused to go away,
And she took refuge beneath
Your double-decker bed.
But you, my brave little soldier,
You stood firm,
Your plaintive voice
Beseeching him to stop:
STOP DADDY! DON'T BEAT MUM!

He did not stop.
He came after me
Like an enraged bull,
Charging relentlessly,
Grabbing my waist,
Jerking me away,
Pulling me this way and that,
Trying to pry me off the bed.
I resisted, loudly shouting
At the maid to come to my rescue;
But she slept on,
Unmoved.
You saw him strike my
Tear-streaked face,
And as I reeled in pain
He dragged me off,
Pulling me toward
Our bedroom,
Shouting obscenities.

I felt you leap off your bed
And follow us,
Enraged like a tigress
In defense of her young one.
I felt him brace himself,

Steadying himself
For the mighty kick that
Knocked you flat onto the cold floor.

Then I saw red!
The adrenaline pumped into my veins
My heart beat wildly,
I started gasping for air,
And in an instant
Reason left me.
I kicked him hard
And swung out against his sweaty face
Blow upon blow,
Shrieking like a woman possessed.
Did you see him crumble
Like David's Goliath
As I knocked the wind out of him?
Within a second he was
Teetering toward oblivion.
Did you feel me
Gather you in my arms,
Whispering my fright into your ears,
Before we took flight into
The dark night?

Hailstones on Zamfara

Sefi Atta

On the day I die I will rise up, arms outstretched, magnificent as the mother of the Holy Prophet, then my executioners will be forced to admit, "We were wrong. We should have revered you more."

I am not guilty. I have always preferred men as I make them up in my head; invisible men. Not the kind some women want, those silly fantasy men in foreign romance books. My men are plain, ugly even, with facial marks, oily skins, dust in their hair. They look like men from Zamfara. They ride motorcycles, take buses and taxis to their places of work. They walk mostly. They never own cars, otherwise they would have to be rich men, the kind who become senators of the Republic of Nigeria, chairmen of federal banks, and such. No, my men have spread-out feet from being barefoot as children. They have palms as brown as tobacco leaves. Under their robes their ribs are prominent. Some have had a hand cut off because they stole to eat. Allah forgives them now that they are cripples. After all, my men pray as Moslems should, five times a day, even though they perform ablution in gutters. Plus they are humble before Him, even if capable of going home to beat their wives to deafness.

Did Our Husband think I was pretending the day I stopped hearing him? Had he forgotten he caused the very condition that made him so angry? I tried to help him understand.

"You call me, I can't hear. You insult me, I can't hear. You tell me to get out of your house. How can I leave when I can't hear?"

"You witch!" he shouted. "I know you're doing this on purpose!"

"It is not my fault," I said. "My left ear is damaged from the beating you gave me. Sometimes I hear, sometimes I don't, even if I face Mecca."

"I divorce thee!"

"Huh?" I said.

"I divorce thee!"

"You must be asking for food again. I'm off to the market."

Where else would I go so early that morning? The trouble with Our Husband was that his anger was like lightning. Lightning from drinking too much *burukutu*, wasting half the profits from his mechanic shop on the brew, and not being accountable for his actions afterward. Lightning loves to show off. "Look at me. See what I do with the night. Let me turn it to day and confuse you." I came home one day, and he was calm. I came home the next, and he behaved as though I'd insulted his father's lineage. Off and on, that was Our Husband, like lightning before thunder comes along and shows who is in control.

He was angry that day because I was not enthusiastic about his announced betrothal, so he boxed my ears. I showed him thunder: of no secondary education; of being married to him at fourteen; motherhood three times over. To prove my endurance, I even chaperoned his new bride, a girl the same age as my eldest daughter, Fatima. I called her Junior Wife, and from then on called him Our Husband.

It pains me," Junior Wife said to me, the morning after her wedding night.

"It will eventually stop," I said.

Her eyes were red with tears. She made me so angry. I did not want another child around the house. I had raised mine already.

"I want to go home," she whined.

"You're lazy," I said. "You did not rise early to make Our Husband's tea. You're supposed to make his tea from now on."

She wrapped her head scarf over her mouth. Under the white chiffon her jaw trembled.

"You see me crying. You don't even take pity on me."

How could I? This was my only home.

"At least you are old," she said. "You should be like a mother to me."

Her kohl appeared like a bruise.

"I'm thirty-two years," I said.

I was orphaned. Mama was long gone. Baba passed away before her, and while he was alive, he had three wives. Mama had only one son. I stopped hearing from him after I left home for marriage, and to be his older sister when he was born was an ousting if ever there was one. My brother, from age two, strutted around with his arms akimbo. If you stared at him, he told Baba. If you ate before him, he told Baba. When I pulled his ears for spitting, he told Baba. Mama gave me a good whipping that one time, so that I would not forget what happened. I loved my brother nevertheless; his ears especially, because they stuck out. And his nose was so long he could pass for a baby elephant. Whenever I bathed him, I poured water over him, picturing him as a little elephant playing in a fountain. That was how I loved him: for what he wasn't, as I loved Baba. I pictured Baba as Allah. Allah, who was capable of anything. He could be furious, enough to use a horsewhip. He could be strict, enough to demand I did not look at his face. Wise. He alone knew why his daughters needed no secondary education. One day he would be caring, I hoped, and I would gobble up his affection like a delicious cup of sour-milk meal, cold as I like it.

Junior Wife ran home that first week. Her parents sent her back with a bundle of kola nuts to appease Our Husband. Her father warned her, before parting, that he would do as Mallam Sanusi did, if she ever came home again. Mallam Sanusi was a legend in Zamfara. His daughter ran away from her husband's house, and Mallam Sanusi returned her. She ran away again, and Mallam Sanusi returned her. The third time she ran home, he cut off her foot so she would never come home again. Mallam Sanusi was a wicked man. Men were not that wicked, which was why Mallam Sanusi became a legend. But that idle threat from her father was enough to make Junior Wife stay put. I asked my daughters not to play with her, Fatima especially, who thought she had found a sister. I told her gently, "You're supposed to respect her. She is your father's new wife." Fatima said, "Then I should marry my father's friend, so that we can play." I laughed. Fatima's mouth was too sharp. "You're going to finish secondary school before you marry," I said. "I will suffer anything for that right."

Junior Wife cried. She said she had always dreamed of finishing secondary school; she was particularly good at multiplication. She was always feeling sorry for herself, and if ever I was like that, I did not care to be reminded by her sad presence. Plus, she was lax with personal hygiene. Sometimes I passed her and I could smell stale urine on her. "Didn't your mother teach you how to douche?" I once asked. That was when she began rolling eyes at me. Did she imagine I was jealous? I was glad her father forced her to stay. From then on Our Husband left me alone at night. I told her to relax when he got on top of her, think of his manhood as a cucumber. I would be fair to her, I promised, so long as she performed her wifely duties and relieved me of mine. Then I gave her extra advice. "Get fat as fast as I did, and he will surely marry someone else."

Our Husband was partial to bones, the bones of girls in particular. To get such bones, he could spend fifty-years' savings on a dowry; a hundred-years' savings even. In Zamfara, men split young bones on their wedding nights. By the time their brides were old as me, their wombs were rotten.

Junior Wife came to me. "I'm pregnant."

"That's very good," I said.

"I vomited all morning."

"It's a girl then."

"Why?" she asked.

"If it's a boy you will vomit all day."

She rolled her eyes. "I don't believe in that."

"Ask your mother. Didn't she teach you anything before you left?"

"It's not a girl, I know."

I had not thought of that. I was so happy Our Husband left me alone at night I was lulled into a stupid state. I was even singing while I cooked. A boy? What would happen to the rest of Fatima's secondary education? I was staring at Junior Wife's face. She had such a haughty expression. Pregnancy had made her stronger, as if she'd found a new companion I could not separate her from.

She actually refused to bed Our Husband. "I have my limits," she said. "You were naive when this happened to you. You didn't know how to trick him. I've told him that if he touches me, his son will be miscarried instantly."

He was dumb enough to swallow that fib? Ah yes, of course, he knew how to find a young girl's passage, but he didn't care what was going on in her passage.

"I should cook you a meal," I said. "To celebrate." I wanted my hands to be busy. I did not want to hear about the possibility of a son.

"Many thanks," Junior Wife said. "But I only eat what I myself have cooked from now on. My mother taught me that, at least." What a cheek for her to assume I would be so malicious as to poison her.

As she grew bigger, the changes began in Zamfara. The state government was building Sharia courts, appointing *alkalis* to preside over them. A contractor laid the foundation for a court in our town center. The earth cracked during the dry season, sandstorms came and went, hailstones followed and dented the finished aluminum roof of the court. I thought it was a divine sign. That was the first time I heard that the Koran forbade women and men from traveling in the same buses and girls and boys from attending the same schools. Fatima and other final-year girls were transferred to an afternoon session. The boys had the morning sessions. By the afternoons, most teachers were tired and went home because the girl students were not many. Fatima's school marks remained high throughout. She even won a trip to a television station, after writing an essay about heaven. She came back with her eyes so big: "Mama, I met Miriam Maliki.

She reads the news on television. She says I could train with the station after I leave school."

I looked at my beautiful daughter, who was jumping up and down. Would anyone care what knowledge she had in her head? And if she ever were on television how would I see her? "We don't own a television," I said, to be the first to disappoint her.

But she would not stop talking about her Miriam Maliki. Oh, Miriam Maliki had such a pretty smile. Oh, Miriam Maliki wore gold bangles and covered her hair to read the news because her husband's family disapproved of her exposing herself. And oh, Miriam Maliki had been on hajj to Mecca.

I thought, what a dimwit for a woman. To care about work when she came from a home with money. She could afford a trip to Mecca? And back? That was typical of the rich; nothing better to worry about. I thought I would tell her off, this Miriam Maliki, if ever I saw her. She had let women like me down.

Then, before the end of school term, Fatima's favorite teacher, her English teacher, was fined for braiding her hair with extensions. Allah—I don't tell a lie. The alkali presiding over the poor woman's case warned her that she would spend time in jail if she didn't stop being fashionable. Hair perms were not allowed anymore. Hair dye was not allowed, except dark brown and black. We heard of a thief in another town who had his hand cut off by a surgeon at the general hospital. The nurses there buried the hand instead of throwing it away. Our Husband came home complaining that people who drank burukutu were being flogged publicly. We got word of the student in another school far from Fatima's. She too was to be flogged because she was pregnant. Thirteen years old, and she said a mad man had raped her. Unfortunately, the alkali told her, as she was a woman her testimony was not so important.

Our Husband came to my room at night. His breath reeked of burukutu. He fell over me and I gasped in the dark. "Spread," he said, fumbling between my thighs.

"I have no juices."

"I'll use my spit," he said. I struggled under him.

"Please, I'm not supposed to lie with you. It's not my turn today. I'm not supposed to."

That was the night Junior Wife gave birth to a baby boy. Our Husband named him Abu. He announced that Abu was going to university and the rest of us would have to make sacrifices. I wandered around the whole day after Abu's naming ceremony, thinking of Fatima. I went to the tailors to order a dress for her. I passed the Koranic lessons where young boys chanted verses. I stopped for cattle rearers. I smelled fresh blood in the abattoir. It made me sick.

I heaved by the wood-carvers' sheds, and there he was. He had the facial marks of a peasant, my invisible man.

"What happened to your hand?" I asked.

"It got cut off," he said.

"What did you do to get it cut off?"

"I stole."

"Did you ask for penance?"

"This is my penance." He waved his stump at me. His extra skin was folded neatly at his wrist like a belly button. He was smiling.

"How do you carve?" I asked.

"With my one arm."

"How do you pray?"

"With my one arm."

"How do you love?" It could have been that I found my partial hearing in his missing hand. You know how people find others in life to compensate, especially in difficult times? Why else would I ask? He pointed his available index to his temple. "Love is here."

"I'm a married woman," I said, in case he suspected me of flirting.

"You have a rather sad face," he said. He laughed and it scared me. If a man laughed in Zamfara these days, a woman could be in trouble. I drew closer to my invisible man, and he smelled of wood dust and cracked earth. The mixture cured my nausea instantly.

"Let me see your carvings." I took the one with the biggest head and traced her broad nostrils, then behind her neck. Then her lips. I was thinking of Miriam Maliki.

"I like you," I heard my invisible man murmur.

"What do you like about me?"

"Your breasts. I would like to suck them hard."

"Let me feel," I said, meaning his carving. We were standing in his shed, among the carvings and wood dust.

"When did you become a bad woman?" he asked, as I unzipped his trousers.

"Today, I am not so well," I said. He was like a rod of warm iron. He said he didn't mean to insult me, he just wanted to know. Women in Zamfara could consent and then act as if they were raped. I let him suck my nipples. I felt fear for Fatima's education like a tremor between my legs. He said I reminded him of his first cousin, one he'd almost married. He said this was not an abomination. In his village, people married within their families, but most of them were deformed people, so he refused, because he never thought he would be one himself. He stole a transistor radio. It belonged to another cousin who died, but a half-brother claimed it. It was a property dispute. He just wanted to listen to the news, he said. The whole world could be explained by listening to the news.

"You see what is happening in Zamfara? It has nothing to do with Sharia law—you are exciting me—It has nothing to do with Islam. It has nothing to do with the Koran. It doesn't even have anything to do with Arabs . . . who come here to preach against infidels—you're making me excited! Slow down!"

It was a property dispute, he said. All the madness and the sadness in the world, from war to starvation, came down to property disputes.

"Except my ear," I said, fastening my brassiere. My hands were wet.

"That too," he said, zipping up his trousers. "Your husband believes he owns you."

"Not his drinking," I said. "That is no property dispute."

"That too. He drinks to appease himself. If a rich man drinks, who flogs him? Ah, you are like sweet mango to taste. I could lick you all over."

"I feel sick," I said. Truly, to think Our Husband and I were part of the same sorry group. Who forced his hand in marriage twice? Who led him to his beloved burukutu? I pulled my panties up.

"You are going?" my invisible man asked. His nose was as broad as his carvings, and his eyes were a shade of light brown.

"It seems unreasonable," I said, "to cut off a hand for stealing a transistor radio. For the sin of drinking, they really should cut a throat."

He frowned at that. "You are quite a harsh woman."

I was pregnant by the end of that month. I had not been as sick as I normally was. I was sicker; sick all day. It made me thin. I was worrying about Fatima's schooling. I was running around for Junior Wife's newborn, Abu. She was refusing to touch him. She said he might as well have been born a stone. She cursed her parents who gave her to Our Husband in exchange for a dowry. She said marriage was like slavery.

"But you're a miserable one," I told her. Everyone was quick to compare themselves to slaves. What slave had the power to tell Our Husband to let her sleep separately? I had to fake typhoid so that he would not come to me at night. My temperatures were easy; I was making his morning teas again. My nausea was convenient.

Junior Wife told me one evening. "You're hiding something from me. You seem one way while you are the other. You say one thing and mean the other. Our Husband says you do this to drive people to madness." Her eyes were red, not from crying but from lack of sleep.

"Have you fed your son?" I asked.

"See?" she said. "You're doing it again."

"Your son needs to be fed," I said, sharply. Doing what?

"My son is like you," she said. "A snake hidden in the grass. He does not cry, so that I will worry about him. That is why I no longer sleep at night."

"He's an innocent child."

"No, he isn't. His big head almost killed me." She turned her face away from me. I moved to check her head for fever. She slapped it. "Don't touch!"

By the end of the week she was rocking herself. Her hair was falling out, her breath stank, she'd stopped douching. Her baby was shrieking now, and it was I who was acting like his mother. I who was carrying him and attending to his mess. Our husband was furious. "This household is cursed from top to bottom. One really has to be sure where one picks one's brides. Everything is falling apart since she arrived. If she doesn't take heed, I will send her back to that father of hers, so that he can do as Mallam Sanusi did and cut off her foot."

Threats. He was trying to outshriek his own son.

"What will happen to the baby?"

"He will stay here. My son will not be deserted. If his own mother won't care for him, I will accept the next best mother."

"Who?"

"Who else? You, of course. And he will attend university. And he will become a doctor. And he will be rich. Then he can be president of Nigeria . . ."

"*Bismillah*," I said. "I'm sure he will, since he resembles you."

"Oh, shut up."

To him that was an invitation to come to my bed again. Not because we'd exchanged pleasantries, mind you. He said that since I was up to my usual tricky ways, my typhoid must have cleared. This time I was prepared for his entry.

"I'm pregnant," I said.

"How?"

"By the grace of Allah as usual, and it is a boy, and if you lie with me, your son will instantly be miscarried."

"Spread your legs," he said. He was rubbing spit inside me. I was writhing not from pain, but from the thought of burukutu in my passage.

"I'm—" I said. He collapsed on top of me.

"Will you shut up! Now see what you've done. Only you are capable of doing this to me. Never, ever, has this happened . . ." His manhood was like water on my belly. His chest hairs were in my nostrils.

"I can't breathe," I said. Junior Wife had strayed into the room without a knock. She stood there with her hair looking like a mongrel's, her eyes were redder than ever.

"Something terrible has come to pass," she said in a soft voice.

"What?" It was I who asked. A mother knows. She senses danger. She senses it in silence, a silence that is connected to her womb.

"Have I married a couple of witches or what?" Our Husband asked, staggering out of my bed. "Why do you barge in like this?"

"Unfortunately he is dead," Junior Wife said.

"Who?"

"Abu." I heard the ceiling collapse. You know how coincidences happen? A whole section of the ceiling just caved in behind me. It made such a noise I was sure it had pounded the floor to pieces. I turned to check. The ceiling was intact. It was Our Husband lying on the floor. He had fallen down in grief.

I could have pitied him the way he mourned. He embalmed the body. He wrapped the body in white cloth. He dug a hole and placed the body gently in. He covered the hole up. He even ordered a tombstone. One morning I heard him weeping like a woman, "Abu, Abu."

I asked, "Would you like some tea?" His eyes widened as if he'd seen a witch. He ran away from me.

That same week he sent Junior Wife packing, back to her parents. He said she should be prepared for her foot to be cut off, after the way she had neglected his son. Neglected? I was happy to see that murderer out of the house. To kill her own child, there was no excuse, not even motherly madness. When Fatima started lamenting how two losses in one week were impossible to bear, I told her, "Save your upsets. Save them for times that are worth it. They will come."

Our Husband was drinking burukutu like water now. He'd stopped going to work at his shop. He would leave home early in the mornings to do the work of drunkards. Meanwhile, his mechanics were pilfering from him. I was thinking, how did they dare in this new climate? The situation was so tense that Christians and Moslems were coming to blows on the streets, burning each other's houses, taking daggers to each other's throats. One Christian in the marketplace had a cross pendant ripped from his neck by a Moslem. It wasn't even real gold. They fought until the Moslem died, and then a group of Moslems retaliated with bows and arrows on a Christian settlement. These were the stories we were hearing, yet Our Husband's mechanics were pilfering? That was some poverty. I would rather beg knowing I had two hands to show for myself.

We did not hear a word from Junior Wife, who had returned to her father's house. We never even asked, so we did not know her father finally begged her forgiveness for abandoning her. He said he did it to make her strong, so that she would not be homesick and run away. She told him of the threat Our Husband made. Her father said, "Come on, I'm not as wicked as Mallam Sanusi." She told him also of Our Husband's drinking, and her father exclaimed, "He drinks! You never said!"

That was it. They came for Our Husband while he was doing the work of drunkards. They dragged him out of the shack. They took him to court. The alkali presiding over his case ordered fifty strokes. I did not know any of this until his friends brought him home, whimpering like a baby. They could find no trousers soft enough to cover his buttocks, so he was naked except for a dirty shirt. Fatima cried the most of my daughters as we laid him face down on his bed.

"There must be a reasonable explanation for this," I said. He cursed Junior Wife and her father and told me what happened.

"I am so forlorn!" he wailed, louder than a muezzin. "Heaven awaits me! I've always been humble. Leave me to die. Let my sores fester. . . ."

"I've heard alcohol helps," I said.

He wept silently now, into his mattress, gibbering something about my never changing my tricky ways and his friends coming back to save him. I used warm water and a boiled towel to cleanse his skin. The job took a long time. His buttocks looked like shredded cloth and he had urinated on himself. Shit was hanging out of him. I took Vaseline and slid it over each of the fifty welts while he sobbed on. He cursed the day this and that. He really was like a baby with all that complaining, and as I reached his anus with the Vaseline, he farted.

"Hm," I said, holding my nose. "Men really should douche."

"You can't even say sorry!" he shrieked. I was laughing. Not because of what he said or what I saw, but because of what I'd said: men really should douche. It came out of my mouth like a bullet, without my thinking. I laughed so hard that tears poured from my eyes and burned them. This house of ours, what else could go wrong?

"You evil woman," Our Husband said. "You will pay for this. You think it's funny? You will pay. Just wait. I will get better, and I will do something that will make you want to die."

I stopped immediately and held my chest. "Fatima?"

His voice became shaky. He'd reached the stage of uncontrollable lips with his crying. "W-what did Fatima ever do to me? It was you. Y-you and this horrible behavior of yours since you lost your hearing. P-punishing me, punishing me, for what was m-merely an accident. Did you think I made you h-half deaf on purpose? C-curse you. . . ."

I nodded. So long as it was me.

The day Our Husband was able to walk straight he went straight back to court and told them he had an accusation to make. The alkali, knowing his face, asked him to make it concise. Our Husband declared that it was his wife. She was pregnant by another man. She had committed adultery and that was why he'd been drinking burukutu: his wife was a very loose woman.

They came for me in the afternoon. What was I doing at the time? Dyeing my hair? My real hairs were so white for a woman who had turned thirty-three years. They told me of Our Husband's accusation in court. They took me in custody. "Who will look after my children?" I asked.

One of them answered, "Why are you bothering to ask?"

I said, "I shall be away several days."

He said, "Your pregnant belly is evidence, if ever I saw any. I warrant you will be away longer than that."

That was when I met Miriam Maliki. She came to visit me in custody. I'll never forget the way she commanded the guards, "Let her out of there. She's pregnant and she's no danger to anyone." The doors miraculously opened for me. Allah. In all my life, I'd not seen such a delicate woman with power. She was as tiny as Fatima. Her head was covered with a black scarf and her eyes were big and sparkly. I saw her thin wrists and fingers without knuckles. I thought, this one, she hasn't suffered a second in her life.

"I'm Miriam Maliki. Have you heard of me?"

"My daughter said she met you."

"Your daughter?"

"Fatima."

"Fat?"

"Ima."

"What?"

"That is her name. Fatima. You said you would train her, and she would be on the news. She was jumping up and down, and she even said—"

She nodded. "Listen, it's you I'm worried about. Do you know I heard your story and immediately came out here? I could not believe what they were telling me. You were taken from your home? Like a mere criminal? To this mud dungeon with nothing but a bucket? And your own husband accused you? What did you tell them when they came for you?"

"Who will look after my daughters?"

"Did you tell them you were innocent?"

"Did they ask?"

For the first time she seemed to see my face. "I'm sorry," she said. "I am so angry about this. Forgive me. I heard your trial is tomorrow. I'm disgusted by the prospects of such a case in Zamfara. I will be there at your side."

"My side?"

"Do not be afraid. Look at me. I know you're innocent. You will not be put to death."

"Death?" I said. "For what?"

She said, "Don't you know? Don't you know how these courts intend to punish married women who have committed adultery?"

How? I asked. "Death by stoning," she said. "Have you not heard? You are the first."

Indeed, she was with me during my trial. Not by my side, but she was sitting with others who were allowed in the court. If she had been by my side, I may have been able to answer the questions better. "Why didn't you tell your husband earlier that you were pregnant?" "I just didn't." "How do you lie with a man who doesn't exist?" "I just did."

Miriam came to spend time with me after my sentencing. She said that in all her life she never imagined this would happen in a place she lived, that a woman would be stoned to death for adultery. She said I was maligned, or raped. I told her imagination was a dangerous exploit.

"You're brave," she said. "You're like a mountain."

"See me as I am instead."

"The court was unfair to you."

"You can't fault Islam."

Her voice rose. "It has nothing to do with Islam!"

"A property dispute?" I asked.

She began to pace. "The state cannot sanction such courts. It won't be allowed by the federal government. You know this is what it's really about? People wanting to break our country apart? Not about declaring Zamfara an Islamic state. Not even about the Islamic fundamentalism that people say is sweeping the world."

People said that?

"I've fought for the rights of women...."

What about children? What about men who had one hand cut off?

"I'm against under-aged marriages. The psychological effects alone are bad enough. Some women develop cancer of the cervix...."

My mother died of a rotten womb.

"And God only knows why when Moslem men want to get closer to Him, they look for Moslem women to pick on."

"I'm going to die," I said.

She took my hand. "I will make sure. I will make sure people hear of you. Others have taken interest, not just me. Elsewhere in the country they are writing about you in newspapers, calling this a barbaric injustice. Foreign papers are hearing about your case as we speak. Once they carry your story, there will activists involved. They will petition our president. Very soon our little court in Zamfara will be the focus of the world. A world that is worried about the spread of Islamic fundamentalism. You understand? It is very likely that your life will be saved because of this. Have hope. You are a symbol."

Fatima came to visit while Miriam was still with me. She brought me sour-milk meal and mangoes. She hardly spoke when Miriam said to her, "I remember your lovely face." And the way Fatima could not meet her eyes, I knew my daughter had found a love on which to base all others. She would love women, and her love would be unrequited. She told me her sisters were doing well, considering. She told me Our Husband was fasting and growing a beard for religious purposes. I told her, "Tell your father Allah has his reward." Was he allowing her to continue her secondary education nevertheless? She said he was.

"Make sure you get your education," I said. "Make sure it's in your hands, then you can frame it and hang it on the wall, and when you go to your husband's house, carry it with you."

"I don't think that's what education is," she said, "something to hang on a wall."

"Listen," I said, "I know what I'm saying. What is in your head might not save you. Hang your education on the wall of your husband's house, so that whatever happens you can say to yourself, 'This is my education', and no one can take it away from you."

She left only after I ordered her. She wanted to stay, but I did not like her seeing me in custody. "Did you include me in your essay of heaven?" I asked. She said no. I said, "Therefore don't worry about my going there."

Are you being sarcastic most times?" Miriam asked, after Fatima left.

"Me?" I answered.

"I notice," she said. "The way you talk. You say one thing and mean the other. I don't mean to be rude, but it's like I hardly know you."

She hardly didn't.

"Sometimes, I wonder if, forgive me, you are crazy."

I was thinking of Junior Wife. Could I be if I saw madness in others?

She rubbed her pretty lips. "You and I, I feel for you so strongly, as though you matter more than my mother. Can I be bold? There is nothing to lose. I want to show you something."She unwrapped her scarf from her head. Underneath was a rainbow. Red, orange, yellow, green, blue, indigo, stripes all over. Her hidden hair.

"It's prettier in the sky," I said.

"My husband says it's ugly. He says I've lost my head. He calls it my lost head, but he says it as a joke, mind you. I have two girls by him, you know. He loves them as boys. You will call me lucky to have such a man, but really, he should love them as girls. He also thinks he was my first. I married him when I was twenty-three, after I graduated from university. He was not my first. I lied that I was stretched by riding horses. I hope I'm not overwhelming you."

"A little." Why would she tell me this now that I was about to die? Would she tell me if I were not about to die?

"What are you thinking?" she asked. I was looking at her gold bangles.

"Does your husband have a lot of money?" I asked.

"No. We are what you call comfortable. A lot? Not at all. Do you consider me spoiled?" I thought hard about that. In our country, Sharia was a poor person's law.

"Yes," I said.

"Are you scared to die?"

"Yes."

She drew closer. "You're carrying a child. That will give you time. They will not stone you until your child is born."

"It's a nothing," I said. "It is nothingness within me."

"Why didn't you answer the questions you were asked in court?"

"I just didn't."

"What really happened to make you pregnant?"

"What difference will it have made?"

I didn't have to think a moment about this. Sometimes I was confused, often afraid. To answer correctly was to give in most days. But so what if my reason was one or the other? I had a lover; a man who became invisible in court. There was no evidence against him, the alkali said. I needed three independent witnesses to prove his guilt. Our Husband's testimony, anyway, was greater than mine.

Miriam was crying. "You shall not be forsaken."

When stones were hurled at me, they would be hailstones on my head; hailstones over Zamfara.

"In the name of Allah," I said. "The Beneficent, the Merciful."

The Good Woman

Patricia Chogugudza

One

When Zimbabwe achieved its independence in 1980, Paida listened with pride as the leader of the women's wing of the ruling party, in her first address to the nation, announced that in the new Zimbabwe, women were no longer going to be mere bedroom fixtures aimed at producing children. They were now going to assume new responsibilities in high-ranking posts.

"Women," the president of the woman's organization said fiercely, "are now equal to men."

But even as Paida laughed and embraced her sisters, she had a disturbing sense that they were breaking some important rule. She could sense something subversive in all this talk, and she had a sinking feeling that the euphoria would end badly. Was this new woman, who was now equal to men, a *good* woman?

From her youth, Paida had endeavored to be a *good* woman. She had struggled to be a *good* daughter, a *good* sister, a *good* student, a *good* mother, a *good* wife, and now she was determined to be something else: a *good* strong, independent woman.

But for Paida and most women, the new independent woman could not be reconciled with the *good* woman. Despite the declarations by the ruling party, the reality was that in postcolonial Zimbabwe, a *good* woman was one who showed obligation, duty, allegiance, loyalty, faithfulness, and commitment to her marriage, to her in-laws, to her children, and to her husband. She also knew that to most Zimbabweans, both men and women, a *good* woman negated herself. A *good* woman was docile, passive, tame, meek, compliant, and obedient. Just as a young girl is subservient to her parents, Paida knew that a *good* woman must be submissive to her husband and her husband's family. A *good* woman gave and gave and gave. A *good* woman was the flower whose petals must never fade. A *good* woman made the world beautiful; her role was to decorate the world. The image of the new woman posed a dilemma to Paida and to the rest of the women of Zimbabwe. Women began to question how they could be independent and yet also expected to remain under the control of husbands who had no regard for their interests.

Men, too, were disgruntled at the image of the new woman. "I know women fought in the war, but who cares? The war is over. My wife is my wife and ought to behave like a wife," was the reaction of most men.

Paida, worried about the conflicting expectations, decided to confide her anxiety to her mother. But Paida's mother was not sympathetic, and she complained to Paida's brothers, who, fearing their wives would start becoming unruly as well, were critical of their sister.

Paida found it difficult to convince her family that her marriage to Paul was making her unhappy. She could not make them see that while Paul pretended to be a good husband in their presence, he was not committed to her equality. For her mother, her brothers, and even her sisters, no woman had ever been equal to a man. So instead of supporting her, Paida's brothers began to withdraw their love, respect, and protection from her, scorning what they termed their sister's wayward behavior. The only one who seemed to understand was her older sister Julia, but she too was a woman and could not do much to help.

Two

After some time, Paida, desperate to save her marriage and her image, devised a plan to confront Paul. One evening, she came home primed to seduce her husband. Her grandmother had always told her that the ways to a man's heart are good food and irresistible sex. After she was sure Paul was sated with both,

Paida turned to Paul, nestled close to him, and asked him softly to register her as the co-owner of their house.

Paul had known that Paida was up to something, but he had never expected his wife to be this unreasonable. How could he ever explain to his family that Paida's name was on their house? Paul was the first son, and his house belonged to his family. Paul felt that Paida surely ought to understand that.

"If you want your name on the house, then pay the mortgage. I will sit here and do the groceries instead," he grunted.

Then he turned his back on Paida and pretended to sleep. That was the end of the discussion.

Paida could see that this was a lost cause. She did not earn as much as Paul, so there was no way she could pay the mortgage. She felt beaten down, but she knew she could not give up. She was determined to get something for herself, something to her name. So she applied herself to her work even more vigorously. She set out to get further education and to create supplementary income. She laid her hands on anything that could generate money. But the more she brought money into the house, the more challenging she became for Paul. To annoy her, Paul began to make less and less of a contribution toward the family's upkeep. Paida began to complain about Paul's attitude, and in resentment, Paul began staying out more and more often, to the extent of even taking holiday trips without her.

It was not just Paul, and the antagonism was not just against Paida. It seemed as if there was a general social anger toward all women who were perceived as refusing to be traditional African women. The attack was aimed at women in rural areas, in the market place, as well as in the professions. Men were using all they had to demean the new woman, whom they saw as a threat to their masculinity. To spite their wives, some men slept with their wives' maids, friends and sisters, doing whatever they could to physically, emotionally, economically, or psychologically break the tenacity of the new woman.

Three

One Tuesday evening, Paida received a phone call from one of her best friends, Ropafadzo. It was a very cold evening. Mashava has that kind of piercing weather, a weather that can make one very depressed. Paida had been feeling the freeze long before the evening had started. The strain between her and Paul had been getting worse by the day. Paul was now always in a bad mood. If he was not out in his garage, he was reading the paper or away at one of his sisters' or brothers' homes.

When the call from Ropa came, Paida knew immediately that it was bad news, and when Ropa told her where to go, all Paida muttered was "thank you."

One part of her told her to forget it, to hide away. "A good woman does not spy on her husband," Paida tried to tell herself. But then immediately she thought, "What would Paul do if I were cheating on him? Throw me out, of course." At that she became very angry, mostly at the thought of how hard she had been trying to make the marriage work. It was the anger that pushed her to action.

She hurried out of the house, keys in hand—no money, no driver's license, no weapon except her anger. Hers was not a big car, just a small battered BMW she had saved up her own money to buy. She got into the car, sniffling a little, and started the engine, but nothing happened. The car was dead. She checked the battery. It was fine. Then it hit her that someone had tampered with her car, immobilizing it. When she had parked the car earlier, the engine was fine. She was sure Paul had disabled her car so she could not follow him. The shock of that callous act sobered her. She stopped crying, determined to fight it out.

She walked over to her sons' bedroom and asked one of the twins to come and fix the car for her. Ted, the one who was good with cars, came out complaining that he needed to go to sleep early for a test the next day. The truth was that Ted did not want to be disturbed from his movie. But he came out anyway, knowing he would never hear the end of it if he didn't.

As soon as Ted looked at the engine, he knew what had happened. Ted and Nel, the other twin, knew that their dad always checked their mother's mileage every time she left home and every time she came back. The boys, especially Nel, were bitter toward their father for doing this and had been almost tempted to tell their mother. But, unsure how she would react, they kept their mouths shut. They did tell Mbuya Maggie, the lady who helped with the housework. Maggie, in turn, found a way to inform Paida to be careful. Maggie knew what Paida was going through with her marriage and tried to be a big sister to her.

Ted fixed the car easily. Sensing that something was wrong, he offered to go along with his mother instead of going back to watch his movie. Reluctantly, Paida accepted his offer.

Mother and son drove off in silence toward Simon Avenue. The night was quiet and the town of Mashava was almost dead. Soon Paida veered into Simon Avenue, and as soon she negotiated the curve, she saw her husband's Mercedes Benz parked in a small backyard. Because it could not fit in the garage, the car had most of its back end right in the driveway.

Paida's heart somersaulted. As she pulled in, she could see everything going on in the little living room through the thin curtain that covered the window. Paul was sitting inside the dimly lit room, on a broken love seat, holding a baby in his arms. A woman sat squeezed against his hip, both of them smiling at the baby. It was obviously his child. From the plates still lying on the table, Paida could tell that the couple had just finished dinner.

Four

Paul heard the sound of the small BMW long before it pulled to a stop. He always recognized the sounds of his cars and often boasted about his good ear.

At the sound of the car, Paul and the woman exchanged glances, then a few words, but instead of Paul coming out, Paul's girlfriend came bouncing out toward Paida. The woman was in her early thirties, very tall and thick. She was a giant. There was no way Paida could have confronted that kind of opponent.

Paida had never in her thirty-six years fought with anybody. Her father had always warned her against fighting, calling it unwomanly. The Roman Catholic Church, in which she had been baptized, called it a sin, and the missionary school she had attended had reinforced this message, telling the girls, "ladies do not run."

As Paida saw this woman marching toward her, she suddenly realized that in the real world there is no room for stylish pseudo-Victorian/Anglican women or naive, traditional African girls. Her sophisticated middle-class values were working against her.

Paida hoped against hope that Paul would come out. But he did not even look outside to see what was happening. He just sat there, his baby in his arms, waiting for his girlfriend and his wife to fight it out. Paida's fear of embarrassment was her worst enemy. It gave the other woman the confidence she needed to be sure she could thrash Paida.

Then insults started raining on her.

"Who are you? And what do you want in my backyard, whore?"

Paida tried to stammer something to the effect that the man whose car was parked in the backyard was her husband and that she and the children needed him home for some emergency. But before she could finish, the woman grabbed Paida's car keys and then grabbed Paida by the shoulder.

Pressing her down, the woman said slowly, but with terrible heat—each word pronounced with fierce intensity: "Listen, bitch, and listen well. You don't burst into people's places and demand your husband. Husbands are not owned. You left your husband for college. You needed a degree. I needed a man. I looked after your husband all those years you were getting educated. I cooked for him. I warmed his bed at night, and now I have his baby. Your husband does not need you, and yet you have the audacity to come and claim him. How do you think he was faring all those years while you were bitching with your university professors for grades? Ha? Paul needs a wife, a woman like me who can cook and feed him, a woman who respects him and stands by his side while he makes progress. I am not just his girlfriend. Your so-called husband married me too. He paid bride price for me. You didn't need a husband; you made your choice. Now get out of my backyard, bitch."

That speech opened Paida's eyes to so many truths. First off, she realized how people lie to themselves about love and being loved. She realized that love is about the choices people make to respect and to protect, and she realized that those choices cannot be forced on the other. She realized too that all the years she thought she knew her husband, she did not. What had made her think, she asked herself bitterly, that she owned her husband any more than any other woman he wanted to give himself to? A marriage ring, the children he had given her, or the vows he had made? Paul had not shown respect for any of these tokens.

Paida turned to leave, acknowledging that she had lost, but Paul's girlfriend was set on humiliating her. Stretching out her muscular hand, she again pulled Paida toward her.

"I am going to thrash the hell out of you and throw you over the fence so you can pick your way from there," she snarled, grabbing Paida's headgear.

Paida was paralyzed. She knew that her only weapon was common sense and thought fleetingly of trying reason it out with this woman. But any attempt at reason would probably just get the woman even more excited.

Fortunately, before the woman could pull Paida off her feet, the car door opened and Ted got out. In the husky voice of a fifteen-year-old just breaking into manhood, Paida's son told his father's girlfriend to take her hands off his mother.

The woman was taken aback. At the command in that voice and the height of the young man, she thought at first that Paida had hired a gangster. But when she realized that Ted was just a boy, she started to threaten again.

At this Ted pulled himself up, told the woman in the same steady voice that he was not a gangster but Paul's son, and that if she would excuse them, he and his mother would like to leave.

The woman paled. Paul had never told her that he had children with his wife. But then again, she doubted that Paida could be the mother of such a big boy, since she looked so young. How could she find out the truth?

Ted, sensing the woman's confusion, gave a short laugh. He felt sorry for this woman, just as he felt sorry for his mother, but he could not help seeing the irony of their situation. It was clear that his father had lied to both women. The whole incident was embarrassing to him, yet without bitterness, he pulled Paida's car keys out of his father's girlfriend's hand and opened the car door for his mother. He took his mother by her drooping shoulders and sat her gently but firmly down into the driver's seat, closed the door, got into the other side of the car, and handed her the keys.

Paida did not say anything. She could not. They drove back home, and all the way Paida was quiet. All she could think of was how she had put her son through hell. Ted too was in deep thought, and clearly very angry. They got home and parked the car, both still too shocked to talk. Paida simply hugged her son and went into her side of the house. Ted retired to the children's quarters.

Five

When Paida got back home, she wanted to lock the door, but she knew she could not. Locking the door meant demonstrating her anger, and knowing Paul, she could not do that. In his mind, she had overstepped her limits by following him to his girlfriend's place, and that meant she was already in deep trouble.

Paida looked at herself in the big mirrors on her bedroom walls and saw a spooked image of herself. Something had broken in her. She felt small, fat, undesirable, and pathetic in what she had always thought was a plush, beautifully furnished home. All its luxury meant nothing. Paul had chosen a hovel over their home, choosing to dine in that wretched house when her food and her heart had waited here for him, getting cold.

Paida tried to think of what could have gone wrong. She knew that she had kept her promise to love her husband. She was polite to Paul when he came home after work, even when she had had a bad day herself. She had been taught that it was her duty to welcome her husband with a smile and to tend to his needs. Her tradition and her church had taught her that. If Paul wanted tea, even in the middle of the night, Paida would get up and make him a cup.

At one point, Paul had asked Paida to wear the traditional beads women wear on their waists for love play, and though Paida had thought it rather old-fashioned, she had worn them to just please her husband. She had wanted to be both the traditional and the sophisticated wife for Paul. Thinking about it now, Paida felt for the beads around her waist and tried to remember when Paul had last toyed with them. She couldn't. Deliberately, she ripped them off her tired body. She was through with trying to please.

Six

The whole night, Paida kept replaying what the woman had said: "You left your husband for college. You needed a degree. I needed a man. I looked after your husband all those years you were getting educated." Yet it was Paul who had virtually pushed her to go back to university. As any good African woman would, Paida had asked for Paul's permission to take up her studies again.

"Of course, Paida, you have the brains and the energy. You go ahead. I'll support your efforts," Paul had urged her.

But Paida knew now that Paul had wanted her to go because it would allow him more freedom with his girlfriends. His reply had been too quick. Trustingly, Paida had gone back to university and had worked hard so that she could make her husband and children proud of her. After she graduated and returned home, she went on to win another scholarship to do graduate studies. All her friends thought Paul would say no. Paida thought so too, and for days she had not told him about it, until one day she gathered the courage.

To everyone's surprise Paul had not objected. He was his charming self and told Paida once more that she had the intelligence to do it and he did not want to block her. Paida was a little disappointed because deep down, she did not want to leave him again.

As Paida thought about it now, she realized that that had been the beginning of their problems. Paul had never been the same. Paida had kept thinking it was her fault that Paul was pulling away, and so she was set on making up for whatever disappointments she was causing him. Yet Paul never seemed satisfied. He did not seem to care, nor did he see a problem in how things were going.

Paida had wondered whether the best way to win him back was to have another child. Yet Paul had not wanted another child. He had been angry when she became pregnant with their daughter, five years before. The twins were enough, he kept saying. The only reason she had had Theo was because of the pressure from his parents and from her family. During her pregnancy Paul did not touch her but instead sent her home to her parents, claiming that he could not stand the sight of her pregnant.

But now Paul was making babies indiscriminately. Paida was angry. Paul had made some other woman pregnant, which meant that he had been having extramarital sex without a condom. Paul had deliberately exposed her to diseases. Paida felt filthy and violated.

Seven

Feeling vulnerable, Paida got up and went to the study to check their savings account books. Paul kept all the other accounts that were exclusively in his name somewhere else. The only book that was in the house was the business-account savings booklet, which was a joint savings account, the closest Paida and Paul had come to owning anything in both their names. Paida opened the booklet and almost buckled. The savings account had a zero balance. It was empty. That devil of a husband had pulled all the money out of that account. Paida fell down, feeling physically sick.

She sat there on the floor staring at nothing for a long time. Paul had cleaned out their one joint account. How had he done that? Why? She became panicky. Should she go back and have a showdown? But the thought dissipated as quickly as it had formed. She was scared; she couldn't face that woman again, and besides, Paul did not care.

Then the crying started. The sounds she made were deep violent ones. She went to her bed and sobbed into her pillow, shaking. She tried to sleep but could not doze off for even a moment.

Morning came. Paida had hoped somehow that Paul would come home and take her in his arms and apologize. Now she told herself that she just wanted him to come home so that at least she would be able to retain some dignity.

But Paul did not come home, not until seven thirty the following morning.

He came in, took a quick shower and changed. He spoke to no one in his family as they all dressed and got ready for the day. Paul left for work and took the children with him. He did not even acknowledge Paida's presence.

Paida cried after he left. But in her bitterness she knew one thing: the marriage was over. That morning took away all the love she had left for her husband. Even though it took her another two years to leave him, the snapping point came that morning.

The following weekend Paul went to Harare in Paida's car, and when he came back, he announced to the children that he had found a buyer and had disposed of the old BMW. That was Paida's punishment for misbehaving.

But even then Paida did not leave. She vowed she would stay in this marriage until her boys had finished high school, until the twins were old enough to fend for themselves and their sister. Paida kept that promise to herself, while she endured the embarrassing, humiliating, degrading marriage. When she was sure her children would be fine, she would leave.

Eight

Paida came home from church one Sunday to find Paul and his brother Del at the house ranting and raving. Paida was not surprised. Paul had always called his family to sit in on any problems they were having. Sometimes it would be a kangaroo court on how indecently Paida was behaving. Other times it was to read letters to the family that Paida had allegedly written or received from lovers, or some such nonsense Paul had made up just to demean Paida's growing reputation as a professional and as a strong woman, and of course to counter the attitude Paida had developed in the two years since the incident with the girlfriend.

On this day it was a case of negligence. Del was accusing Paida of refusing to pay her contributions to the upkeep of Paul's mother in the village. Paida tried to explain that it was Paul who had told her to never go to the village again. (The truth was that Paul was taking another woman to the village, and his refusal to let Paida visit his parents was a gimmick to buy himself more freedom.) But as Paida was trying to put her case across, Del lost his temper and slapped her. Paida could not believe this man had slapped her in front of her husband, and Paul was not going to do anything about it.

Paida decided enough was enough. A primal instinct to defend herself got hold of her, and without warning Paida went for Del with all her strength, aiming at his private parts. This was the only way she knew how to defend herself.

Paida had used this approach on Paul once, and since that day, Paul had never tried to physically assault her again.

Paul, sensing the danger to his brother, quickly came to his brother's aid. They both started punching Paida. A man cycling past the house heard Paida's cries and rushed to her rescue. Breaking up the fight, he chided Paul and Del for hitting a woman. The brothers got into Paul's car and drove away, warning Paida to be gone by the time they came back.

Paida's sons arrived home soon after, and the man who had witnessed the brutal attack on their mother told the boys everything.

Finding Paida lying on her bed numbly, Nel told her that she had suffered enough and that if she was doing it for them, it was not worth it. They were grown up, he argued, so they would manage. He urged his mother to go and make a new life for herself.

At first Paida had told her son that he had no business interfering with adult people's affairs, but as she listened to him talk, she realized that her children had a right to tell her how they felt, since the decisions she was making also involved them and were affecting their lives. Later that day, Paida called the twins and sat them down to find out what they felt. She was stunned at the misery, the pain, and the horror she had put them through. From their description, every tear she had shed had made them bleed. Paida began to realize that in a way she had been selfish. She had wanted to be a martyr, but her martyrdom had been a burden she was putting onto her children. It was a great relief to her sons when Paida finally agreed with them that she should leave.

Nine

But two years after Paida left Paul, she still had not gotten her divorce. Paul was making it difficult for her. At every court meeting, he kept pleading that the two of them were still compatible, a ploy he used to keep the courts from dividing their property. When Paida tried to force her way back to collect a few personal belongings, Paul had the house locks changed. Thus Paida had to start over again from scratch while for Paul it was as if nothing had ever happened.

At first Paida had hoped that the Matrimonial Causes Act, which had just been signed into law, would protect her. But despite public declarations by the government, the majority of the people in the country had no respect for, or knowledge of, these laws. Even her own lawyers, most of them men, had no regard for the new laws; deep down they felt no woman was entitled to a share of the matrimonial property. Paida found out that in reality, women were receiving mixed messages. On the one hand, laws, policies, and constitutions had been developed to guarantee women their rights and ensure equality with men. But when women appealed to these provisions, they were accused of being antinationalist, Westernized, or elitist.

Paul had begun with mudslinging. He sought every opportunity to prove that Paida had not been a good wife. Then there had been the threats from relatives and friends. Paida's mother-in-law openly told her to leave her son alone or face the consequences. Paul's brother Del constantly sent warning threats through his wife or girlfriends. Del had been using Paul's house as security for his business and was afraid that if the divorce were granted, Paul's house would be sold and he would automatically lose his business. Finally, things had become even more complicated and painful as the rest of the world began to learn about Paida's situation with Paul. People started to take sides, and Paul's friends started blocking Paida's professional success.

"We could give you this position, but since the divorce you no longer belong to this province," one man said to Paida when she was applying for a promotion.

At another point, Paida was investigating the possibility of moving away from the small town, but word had already gone ahead of her. "You are still clearing out family issues, and your moving here would jeopardize your chances of making up with your husband," the interviewer had said to Paida in a patronizing way. It was as if the men had formed a conspiracy against her.

Ten

One morning, she was sitting with her sister Julie in her sister's kitchen, talking about her situation with Paul. A flash of anger grabbed Paida every time she thought of how much she had suffered, but on this one morning she did not let her anger engulf her. Instead she spoke to her sister in a calm, controlled tone of voice.

"By the way, Sis Julie, I have been accepted into a graduate program in the U.S.A. in women's studies. I will be leaving in two weeks. I think I need to give my life a break."

Her sister was taken aback.

"What about your studies here, Paida? You are in the middle of a master's program—are you giving it up? What about your job? What about your children?"

Julie could not imagine Paida living without her children, especially her little girl. "Do you realize how difficult it is to be a woman on your own, away from your family?" she asked her sister.

"I don't have my children now, Sis Julie," Paida replied quietly.

Paul was keeping Paida's children away from her so that the courts would not take the house from him. But Paida's boys understood. They promised their mother they would hold on until she was ready to get them. Paida had found a boarding school for her daughter and asked her sister to pick her up during the holidays.

"Of course I'll watch out for your children, Paida. But are you sure you know what you're doing?" Julie asked with concern.

Paida nodded her head. She could not trust herself to speak. She knew that as long as she was around, the anger between her and Paul would suffocate the children. She assured her sister that after she was settled, she would come for her children. She would take them away from the anger, the pain, and the bitterness and try to give them another chance at life, at trust, at love.

Paida had come to realize that in Zimbabwe the problems between men and women are cultural, not individual, and one's own society would betray the individual, or even testify against the individual, especially when that individual is a woman. According to Zimbabwean culture, Paul had a right to everything she owned, including her children. Paida was ashamed to fight for what belonged to her; she knew she would be labeled feminist, Westernized, elitist, or unpatriotic. She was leaving the country because she was ashamed to expose her greed to her friends, to her family, to her children, and even to her students. Paida felt that in her own country, among her friends and family, she was becoming the enemy. A divorcing woman was a bad influence on her brothers' wives, on married women, and on young women in general.

Julie saw her sister's pain, and her heart was torn apart. She wished she could take away all the hurt her sister was going through. At that moment Julie wished she could tell Paida to stay, that all would be well. But it would not. Julie understood she had to let Paida go.

Taking leave of her sister, Paida smiled and told her in a lighthearted manner that perhaps if she went overseas she would find the man of her dreams.

Eleven

True to her word, six months after Paida had settled in the United States, she sent for her daughter and Ted, who wanted to take up a business management degree there. The other twin, Nel, decided he would stay at the university in Zimbabwe and finish his degree program, but he joined Paida the day after he completed his studies. How Paida managed to put together money for tickets for her children to join her was another miracle. She kept telling herself that if she could survive Paul, she could survive anything. She worked as a graduate assistant, waited tables, and cleaned offices, holding two, or even three, jobs at a time. She cashed in her pensions back in Zimbabwe, and in the end, she put together enough money to be with her children.

Her daughter was now at college, proving to be a lot more focused than her mother. At eighteen years old, Theo had no boyfriend. Paida would sometimes try to sweet-talk her daughter into dating. But Theo would simply tell her mother that she was not in a hurry and that men were not necessary. "I'll get my degree first, and then I'll see," she always told her mother.

Whenever Theo said this, Paida could not help wondering whether the failure of her marriage was affecting the decisions and choices her daughter was making. But there was not much Paida could do except to hope that her daughter would have the courage to survive whatever ghosts haunted her.

Twelve

Although she had not found the man of her dreams, Paida was happy. In the United States she had been too busy bringing up her children and forwarding her dreams to concentrate on relationships. Instead, she had discovered within herself a passion for writing. She had begun to write a memoir—the passages flowing out of her over long stretches of nonstop typing. The more she wrote, the more she realized that she was telling a story that would be of interest to other women. She became consumed with wanting to write and publish her story.

Through her writing, Paida found the courage to be who she was and who she wanted to be. Her writing, her imagination, and her self-knowledge were the weapons she chose to face the future, to revisit her past, to mend broken dreams, to repair relationships, and above all to fight for her rights, the rights of all Zimbabwean women, and the rights of women everywhere.

Ngomwa

Ellen Mulenga Banda-Aaku

Overwhelmed by hysterical relief, I had to stop myself from bursting into laughter when I heard that my Auntie Malita, who had raised me as her own, had died. I caught myself, swallowed my chuckle, and breathed a sigh I hoped would be mistaken for grief. My two distant relations, who had traveled ten hours to deliver the bad tidings to me personally, caught my smile and exchanged a quizzical look. I sobered fast and was suddenly overcome with grief.

A few minutes later, it hit me: I was euphoric over Auntie Malita's passing because for a split second, with naive wishful thinking, I believed that by dying she had set me free from an experience in the past that had left me physically and emotionally shackled. It had changed me. My smile had become tight and my laughter a pitch too high. The twinkle in my eyes had faded, taking my spirit and agility with it. My movements became hesitant and furtive. I trod carefully, frightened that if I let go and lost my guard, the truth, looming persistently over my shoulder, would jump out and expose me.

I excused myself from my guests, on the pretext of getting ready for the long trip to the village to bury Auntie Malita. In solitude, for the first time in years, I allowed my mind to consciously wander back.

Auntie Malita was my late mother's elder sister. When I was twelve, she rescued me from the life of lovelessness I lived with my father, my stepmother, and the six daughters they had between them. Love was just as scarce at the missionary boarding school in which Auntie Malita placed me. The missionaries preached love and kindness yet seemed incapable of possessing or demonstrating it. I lived for the holidays, which I spent with Auntie Malita in her thatched roof mud-brick house, surrounded with a dry-grass fence. It was just the two of us, with chickens, a couple of goats, and a pig or two when times were good, for companionship. Auntie Malita was black, tall, and so strong I was convinced she was born a woman by mistake. She tottered violently from side to side as she walked, using her polio-ridden right leg to balance her big frame.

"God took away my leg but gave me extra strength in my arms," she would joke, hoisting a sack of dried, shelled, groundnuts onto her back. Then she would carry it all the way home from the market, with me tagging behind, watching the sack jolt from left to right with each disjointed step she took.

I entertained Auntie Malita just by listening to her. She loved to talk. Quiet by nature—a trait I apparently inherited from my mother—it suited me to listen and often laugh at Auntie Malita's constant banter.

"If you want to be a good wife . . ." were the words that preceded most of the advice she heaped on me. It was obvious that she was very proud of having produced twelve children before she was widowed.

"I've served my purpose as a woman on this earth. I was a good wife and produced many children. You will also make a good wife one day," she would add with determination that left me in no doubt that it was her mission to make me a good wife.

In 1958 I sat for my junior secondary-school-leaving certificate. My father, a stout, successful maize miller with a severe stammer, sent for me right away. He offended Auntie Malita by sending her an unnecessarily provocative message that implied she was trying to rob him of his daughter. Auntie Malita had never liked him, holding him responsible for my mother's dying of a broken heart. Why else would an otherwise healthy, twenty-year-old woman just wither away and die? In retaliation, she sent me back to him without giving me the time to get used to the idea of living with my father and his family again.

Behind my father's back, my stepmother turned the edges of her mouth down whenever she looked at or spoke to me. Desperate to get rid of me from the day I resurfaced in her house, my stepmother nagged my father to find me a suitor. "I . . . I if any m . . . m ma . . . man out there wants any of my daughters; h . . . he should approach me. I am not going out there to find him," my father would stammer in response.

"She will never find a husband," my stepmother would protest.

"The . . . then so be it," my father would end the conversation.

It was a regular conversation in our household, and it took place as if I weren't there. It became even more regular when my father started looking to send me to a teacher training college in the city.

"She doesn't need further education, what she needs is a good husband," my stepmother complained, trying to dissuade my father from spending money on me. To her relief, before my father enrolled me in the college, he came home one day and announced that a family had approached him for my hand in marriage.

When my stepmother discovered that my suitor was from a well-known family of renowned origins, she backtracked.

"Kamba is an intelligent girl. These days women are furthering their education. Let her do her teacher training, she can always get married in two years' time when she finishes," she said.

"W . . . W . . . wo . . . woman!" my father roared. "You have kept me up all night talking about how she should get married before she's too old. Now the best suitor a parent would ask for has approached us, and you say it's better she goes back to school! Gi . . . gi . . . give me peace!"

Two years later, I was married. My house was a four-bedroom bungalow in an area previously reserved for the white colonialists only. My husband was Sam Meya, a tall, well-built, educated African who carried himself with the confidence of a handsome man. He was Westernized: even in the privacy of his home, he ate with a fork and knife. He spoke English like a white man. Few doubted that Sam Meya was an unfolding success story. To me, he was God. I was indescribably happy, I felt like I was floating. Auntie Malita floated beside me.

"I always said you would make a good wife," she would exclaim proudly whenever she visited me in my new home.

I was a good wife. I applied all the cultural rules of marriage that had been drummed into my head with the zeal of a trainee on probation. I listened, never questioned or asked, obeyed, and waited patiently to produce many children.

They labeled me *ngomwa* before I felt I was one. It started with innocent questions. When is the baby coming? Are you with child? What are you waiting for? After the first six months of my marriage, the questions were replaced by furtive glances in my direction, glances that suggested something was wrong. Auntie Malita sent messages from the village now and again to ask if there was any good news for her. There was none.

A month after my first wedding anniversary, Auntie Malita lost patience with nature. She dragged me around the country in search of answers. The diagnoses were abundant: a jealous relative was holding my womb in her hand, preventing me from taking child; my hips were not broad enough; there was nothing wrong with me, I should be patient and relax. Auntie Malita hated this last response.

"These western doctors are just too lazy to work, that's why they say nothing is wrong," she said. She would throw her arms about and complain whenever patience was recommended. She seemed less offended at the more bizarre pre-scriptions. I bathed on my mother's grave at midnight under a full moon. I was lashed fifty times on the back by a frenzied witch doctor to release the evil spirit inside me. I was asked to produce an elephant tooth, the heart of an ant, a tuft of hair from a white man's head. The list was endless. Auntie Malita obliged and delivered promptly whenever possible, ensuring that I observed every ritual. She became a regular visitor to my home, sneaking in and out, most times without Sam's knowledge.

"If I come around too often he'll get suspicious," she explained one evening when we returned later than expected from visiting a medicine man and I asked her to stay the night.

"We can't have him suspect we are seeking help because he might think you are an ngomwa." When she said that word, she wore an expression on her face like she had just sucked on a lemon. It was the first time I had heard it, but I knew instinctively what it meant.

Auntie Malita stayed the night. After I helped her settle into bed, I sat up as usual and waited for Sam to come home so I could serve him his dinner.

I must have fallen asleep in my chair. There was a loud banging at the door; I jumped out of my chair and stumbled to open it. As soon as I unlocked the door, Sam shoved it open. He was drenched and only then did I realize it was raining.

"Are you going to keep me waiting outside my own house?" He was shaking and his eyes goggled. I knew better than to answer. Instead I turned and hurried out toward the kitchen.

"Are you turning your back to me?"

I reeled around and rushed back to the living room, my heart pounding violently against my chest and sweat rolling from my armpits into the waist-band of my skirt.

"I'm wet! Soaking wet because I'm kept waiting outside my own door!"

"I'm sorry, I fell asleep, I felt a bit tired."

"Tired! What work do you do to make you tired?"

I kept quiet. He wasn't expecting a reply.

"Where is my food?"

His question made me turn back toward the kitchen. I spun back and forth a few times as he ranted, unsure of whether he wanted me to get his food or stand and listen to him. Deciding on the food, I rushed to the kitchen. In my haste, I reached for the hot metal plate in the oven without a cloth. Pain seared through my palm; I dropped the plate and it clattered to the ground, splattering chicken stew everywhere.

Sam stormed into the kitchen; he caught the side of my face with the open palm of his hand. A ball of light exploded in my head and set a siren ringing piercingly through my ears. I hit the floor, bounced back up again, and reached for the oven. Groping around blindly, I tried to retrieve the remaining dishes from the oven, not wanting to delay his dinner. My quick reaction seemed to annoy him. He lunged forward, gripped my shoulders, and shook me hard, then let go of me abruptly. I slipped and plummeted into the puddle of stew. This time I stayed down, clamped my mouth shut to stop any sound escaping. He spat. His spittle smacked my forehead and slid down the bridge of my nose.

"Ngomwa!" He spoke low and slow, the edges of his mouth turned down as if I were a piece of dirt, then turned and left the room.

Kamba, time is not on our side," Auntie Malita declared the following morning, as if I didn't know.

Sam had left early for a week's trip to the city. As soon as his car drove out of the yard, Auntie Malita surfaced. We sat on a straw-woven swing chair on the verandah. Although the sun had broken through, the cool morning breeze felt icy. I shuddered, my stomach churned with anxiety and fear. Why me? Ngomwa. I couldn't get the word out of my head.

"You heard?" I finally spoke.

She nodded, pinched some snuff from a crumpled newspaper, crushed it into her palm, and sniffed.

After a long pause she spoke.

"He is getting impatient. We have to act fast. I have something in mind but you have to be very strong and be prepared to persevere."

I wondered what she meant. Had I not shown enough perseverance? Auntie Malita sighed thoughtfully, then continued.

"Carry on with Sam as if you have not noticed anything amiss. Even if he calls you ngomwa, you keep your mouth shut!"

I nodded.

"We have to produce a child before he sends you back home for failing to fulfill your obligation as a wife. He has fulfilled his obligation by providing all this." She waved her arms around, encompassing my house and garden. "We charged too high a dowry to let him down. He is a wealthy, respected man, but without children, all he has means nothing. In our culture, a man without children is not considered a man."

"But if I can't produce—"

"Shhhh!" Auntie Malita hushed me and lowered her voice. "Have you stopped to think that the problem might not be with you?"

I looked up at her to see if she was serious. I knew it was me. It had to be! Hadn't Sam called me ngomwa?

"What do you mean?" Her insinuation startled me.

"It takes two to produce a child, but as a woman it is your responsibility to ensure there are children in the marriage. If you don't, there's a queue of women out there waiting to fill your shoes. His family is aware of that; they won't hesitate to find him a woman to give him children. We can't allow that to happen."

As I tried to make sense of what Auntie Malita was saying, she softened her tone and said, "My dear, sometimes you as the woman have to help the man along. You have to spare him the embarrassment of a childless marriage and bring honor to him and his home."

"I still don't understand."

"You do." Auntie Malita reached for my hand and held it tight.

"Think about it. Isn't a child born in a man's house, from between his wife's legs, his child?" Her voice was so low I strained to hear her.

"I can't do that to my husband!"

"You won't be doing it to him, you will be doing it *for* him," Auntie Malita hissed.

"Remember, all those women waiting to fill your place have eyes too. As soon as you are kicked out, they will come in, and then they will go out and bring children from out there into this home to avoid the same fate as yours. When the next woman brings children to the marriage, you will be certified ngomwa."

I cringed at the word.

"Now tell me, when you retired to bed last night what happened? Did he come to you?"

I nodded, recalling my relief when he had pinned me down. Despite the fact that he thought I was dirt, I took comfort in the fact that I was still of use to him.

Something still bothered me. "What if he finds out I betrayed him?"

Auntie Malita replied, "Kamba, what man will not look the other way, to salvage his ego?"

We set off early the following day, travelling eight hours in a hired Land Rover with driver. At sunset, we descended upon a cluster of huts huddled together under the shade of big baobab trees. As soon as we arrived we were met by an old man, who led us to a hut and asked us to wait inside. Auntie Malita seemed to know her way around. Children played, and the few adults scattered around the compound paid us no attention, as if they were used to strangers descending on them.

I sat in stupefied fear as Auntie Malita wandered in and out of the hut. I visualized Sam's expression when he called me ngomwa. Then I saw the rare look of pride on my father's face, the day Sam Meya married me. I imagined my stepmother's smirk if Sam kicked me out for being ngomwa. Deep inside I knew that I had to do whatever it took to have a child.

Auntie Malita brought me some local wine and forced me to drink it. It was very sweet and burned my throat and chest, but I gulped it down to loosen the tight knot in my stomach. My head began to spin and I began to feel nauseous. The knot in my stomach stayed put.

Later that evening Auntie Malita led me, inebriated more from fear than wine, into another hut and laid me on a straw mattress. As soon as she left the hut, I felt a presence. A tall shadow loomed over me, and I was overwhelmed by the smell of soap, a strong distinct antiseptic scent that caught in my throat. A heavy weight clamped me down, shutting my air out. I gasped and tried to struggle but I couldn't move. Pain shot through me and I let out a scream that turned into an inaudible muffle. My insides, dry and unyielding, burned from the friction. To distract myself from the pain, I sank my teeth hard into my bottom lip. I tasted blood but dug my teeth in further. The mattress beneath me squeaked rhythmically for what seemed forever.

The scent of soap followed me everywhere. It came to me in waves, starting off distant, gradually building to a strong vivid scent bringing me the physical sensation of the hut and the presence that lurked there. Each time I smelled the soap, I was reduced to a quivering, sweat-drenched wreck.

"She's having a difficult pregnancy," Auntie Malita would explain to friends and relatives. She said I was lucky to have taken seed the first time.

"It doesn't often happen first time."

Her words offered no comfort. I had lost control of my mind and my body felt alien to me.

After I gave birth, Auntie Malita justified my odd behavior. "That's why her pregnancy was so difficult—twins are always difficult to carry."

My behavior improved with time. The images, scents, and feelings that haunted me were replaced by the gentle tugging at my breasts as my twin boys suckled, the feel and smell of their smooth skin against mine, and the sounds of baby talk and pattering feet. I embraced motherhood, allowing it to consume me. Shamelessly, in my newfound refuge, I abandoned Auntie Malita. She reminded me too much of something I craved to forget.

Grieving and shame-ridden, I traveled with my two distant relations to bury Auntie Malita. The depth of my grief surprised me. I had never experienced such pain, but then I had never before lost someone I loved, and I loved her.

As I tried to come to terms with Auntie Malita's passing, I wondered whether she had realized that the goods and fat envelopes I sent her monthly were meant to compensate for my not making time to visit her, and my reluctance to have her in my home. Had she been aware of the conflicting emotions that wrestled within me? Fear, anxiety, and my selfish need to protect my secret, on the one side, versus the love I had for her and the guilt I felt at abandoning her. The relentless guilt led me to indulge her with gifts and ultimately to rejoice—albeit momentarily—at her passing.

At Auntie Malita's funeral, I howled, loud and long, like a wild animal caught in a trap, to release the pain embedded deep within me. My pain was intensified by the realization that I would never have the opportunity to let her know how much I loved her, never be able to ask for her forgiveness. I resigned myself to living with my guilt, accepting my retribution.

Two weeks after I returned from the funeral, the Meya family came home to pass on their condolences for the woman they had all recognized as my mother. Just before they left, they sat me down and told me that Sam was taking a second wife. The distinct scent of soap engulfed me and I felt myself start to shake.

I was labeled a mad woman, a title I earned after being referred, by my doctor, to a psychoanalyst who worked in the only mental institution in the country. The Meyas waved the label at my family. I was rendered unfit to look after children, too fragile for the role expected of me as a first wife, and thus I was undeserving of the honor of being Mrs. Sam Meya.

My family had no defense against madness—they were acquiescent, apologetic. Too embarrassed to attend the meeting, my father sent the family elders, who, after the brief meeting, ushered me hurriedly out of my marital home for good. They were eager to bury an unwelcome issue that linked our family name to a dreaded adjective: *mad.*

No one understood that I was not mad; that momentarily the conflicting emotions that had raged within me had clashed: relief, guilt, and grief had reverberated in my mind with such intense force that I couldn't hold out. My body had shut down mentally and physically for a time, but now that the storm within me had calmed, I was myself again.

I couldn't contemplate telling them the unbelievable truth, the true source of my breakdown. Besides, if the truth did come out, what would it make me?

So I let my boys go gracefully, taking solace in my belief that a child never forgets its mother.

Broken and defeated, I retreated to the only place that had ever felt like home. The familiarity and pleasant memories of Malita's hut and its surroundings conjured up in me an inner peace that I was unaccustomed to.

I kept the hut the way Auntie Malita had: a few chickens, goats, and a couple of dogs for company. I grew flowers and vegetables in her garden. Somehow, I felt she was with me, and I hoped she would be pleased with how I was looking after her home.

I found work as a matron at the missionary school I had once attended, and I took two little girls from the local orphanage into my care, their innocence and laughter soothing my soul.

I mended. Gradually, unconsciously, I threw my head back and opened my mouth fully when I laughed. Slowly, my eyes began to express my happiness, and my stride became firm and purposeful. For the first time since I was a child living with Auntie Malita, I was free.

I am no heroine. I did not stand up and walk away from an abusive situation. I was ejected from my marriage by circumstances beyond my control, and not until I was out did it dawn on me that I had been unhappy. If Sam had not kicked me out, would I have left? Probably not. Would I have ever questioned my feelings or my circumstances while I was Mrs. Sam Meya? Most definitely not. My culture taught me that the strength and pride of a woman lies in staying and persevering in a marriage, irrespective of the challenges that come with it. I didn't withstand the challenges. I wasn't strong enough to persevere. I failed my culture. But I am free now, and I am happy.

Sam's second wife has no children. I guess that makes her an ngomwa.

They Came in the Morning

Iheoma Obibi

"Bang, bang, bang!" This continued for some time, until Chidinma realized it was happening downstairs and it was at their door.

The voice shouted again, "Open this door, eh! Rubbish, are you people deaf?"

Slowly and with extreme hesitancy Chidinma tried to lift her head from the tear-stained pillow, but she couldn't move. She blanked out the racket and dozed off again.

The commotion continued, far noisier now. Almost as if she were dreaming, she heard Mama Ike saying, "It's okay, ah, what is wrong with you people? Eh, should the door come off as well?"

Chidinma heard Mama Ike remove the padlock, slide the bolt, and open the door, and then she heard footsteps shuffling in. The house was locked up tight like a prison. Let's face it, nobody lived like this, only those of us in downtrodden Lagos, bustling with armed robbers and touts, known locally as area boys, all struggling to make ends meet and along the way making life a little bit difficult for the rest of us.

A deep voice Chidinma did not immediately recognize asked, "Who are *you*, and who invited you here?" Mama Ike did not have time to respond before another voice added, "Where is the so-called widow? Where is she? After all, is her husband not dead?"

"She should come out and tell us what happened again; last time she told us, her story did not make sense," continued the deep voice.

Mama Ike sighed and folded her arms. "She's been up all night and is sleeping now," she said, legs and arms akimbo, bra straps exposed under the thin spaghetti straps of her blouse.

"Sleeping? What do you mean, is her husband not dead? Now she has all the time in the world to sleep. She should be here, where we can look at her with pity," the same voice added.

Another chorused, "At this time of the day, go and wake her up, jo!"

Mama Ike had noticed that they had already invited themselves to the comfortable settee in the living room and started looking past her through the kitchen door, in the direction of the fridge. Greedy bastards, let them wait, she thought. They were five in number, but not all were as vocal as the leader. She had experienced such scrounging relatives before, and they were all the same. Had she not seen them do the same to her, all those years ago, after her husband died? Their spots did not change; they just got a little better at it, and now they spoke a little English. Not very well, but enough to get by in Lagos. As she too was a guest, she offered a conciliatory gesture. "So, what can I offer you? We have Fanta, Coke, mineral water."

"Eh, I want a beer. Let me go and see the fridge for myself," said the most vocal, who happened to be the infamous Nda Paul.

"No, there's no need," Mama Ike answered coolly. "We don't have any beer. There's only Coke," she said, sending a cursory glance in their direction and walking toward the kitchen herself. By the time she got there, she changed her mind about the Coke, offering them only the Fanta. She picked up five Fanta bottles and glasses, placed them on a fruit-colored plastic tray, added some groundnuts from one of the cabinets, and carried it all out into the well-appointed parlor. Swiftly, Mama Ike laid out everything on the carved mahogany table and placed a bottle of Fanta and a glass besides each visitor. She opened each bottle as she did so.

One of the men had the nerve to ask, "Is there nothing to eat?"

Mama Ike quickly retorted, "We are in mourning. No one has had time to cook. Where is your wife to help?" she finished, letting out an undignified hiss. With that, she brought the traditional Igbo kola nut with accompanying peanut butter and garden eggs, placed them on the table and left the parlor as she did so.

Mama Ike had been on a visit to Lagos when she'd heard that her son's former classmate, Chidinma, whose own mother had died while they were still at university, had just lost her husband to the cold hands of death. Death had come and stolen him in the night, just like that, pinched him off the shelves leaving an empty space in his place. Her son, Ikenna, had always had a soft spot for Chidinma and was worried about her, just as he had been when her mother had died all those years ago. He had begged Mama Ike to come and stay with Chidinma, reminding her that she had invaluable experience to share at a time like this, being a widow as well.

Mama Ike was a thick-set, ocher-colored Igbo woman with an ample bosom that heaved up and down as she spoke and jingle-jangled when she moved about. She found Lagos too hot and humid, causing her to sweat all the time. She sought solace in bathing three times a day and in wearing flowery cotton tops with loose-fitting equally flowery cotton trousers that she'd had the tailor make for her in a rush the first week she'd arrived in Lagos. Mama Ike's light coloring was the honey that had brought her good fortune; she was never short of suitors of all persuasions. Quite a few were not well in the head, others had more money than sense, and she could count many others that had bad breath. In Lagos, where everything is fake, even a light complexion can be achieved through the bleaching bottle, but Mama Ike's complexion was locally called "original flavor." Nice bright ocher, not fake. She'd learned how to take advantage of her good fortune and had decided early on not to remarry again after the death of her husband. She was discreet with her friendships with men, and her children never knew that she had continued to be sexually active for a very long time. Her casual but important friendships, as she chose to call them, had given her a fair sense of independence. Even now, with menopause creeping in, she was still sexually active. The only problem was that her friend was also aging, so they did not do it as often as she would like.

Chidinma wanted and needed to sleep. Her body hurt in places she never knew could feel pain, and her head ached from the racket of the air conditioner, which had completely broken down and was now more of a hot fan than a cool breeze, recycling the fine brown dust pouring out of the open vents. Chibueze, her husband, had always promised to fix it, but she realized she'd have to take care of it now. The pain began in her toes and inched slowly upward along her solid thighs, into her stomach, and then lodged itself in her chest, where it hurt the most. The pain was suffocating, unbearable.

On the night after his death, Chidinma had dreamt she was with Chibueze in a brightly lit room, begging him to come home and sobbing uncontrollably. She was roused by Mama Ike, who was shaking her with a passion and calling on her to wake up. That night, and for several nights afterward, Mama Ike had brought in a synthetic floor mat and had slept right next to her bed, covered only in her famously flowery wrapper. Chidinma did not say so at the time, but she was pleased that Mama Ike recognized how hard it was for her to sleep at night.

The commotion downstairs continued, and she knew that if she did not go down, it would be another mark against her that she would have to deal with at a later date. Chidinma pulled herself up from the bed and straightened her clothes, deciding to ignore the pain in her body. She would head downstairs and confront them.

Good afternoon, Nda Paul. Ah, Nonso, you're here as well. How now, long time no see, *abi.*"

Silence engulfed the room suddenly at Chidinma's unexpected appearance. Nonso spoke at last. "Ah, our wife, how are you now, eh?"

Paul, the eldest of the brothers and the most obnoxious, burst out, "They said you were sleeping! It's a bit early for that now, don't you think!"

Chidinma did not respond immediately. It was too early to fight, and she needed to know why they had come so soon.

Nonso came to her aid once again and she was grateful, but also wary. She did not yet know the real intention behind his apparent friendliness. "Paul, she looks tired, she too needs to sleep, *aba!*"

An uncomfortable silence settled in the parlor. Clearly, the family had had a meeting, and she would soon know what the visit was all about. Everyone was waiting for Nda Paul to speak.

Chidinma focused on her fingers, realizing that they too were suffering. Her cuticles were split at the sides and her nails were chipped, without their usual coat of polish. Chibueze had always insisted that she take care of herself and loved looking at her painted nails. He liked the color red, especially on her toes. From a faraway place she heard a slight coughing sound and realized that Paul had started addressing her.

"Eh, Chidinma, our wife, you know why we are here. It is a sad time for the family and we have to see how we will bury our brother Chibueze."

Chidinma kept quiet. She continued looking at her fingers, and now stretched out her feet, lifting them slightly to look at her toes. No one paid attention to her. Paul continued.

"We think the body should be taken home on Tuesday for burial in the village later. We will let you know once we have set a date. Your concern now is to bring out some money for these arrangements."

She heard "bring out some money . . ." and knew that the struggle for Chibueze's assets had started. She said nothing, waiting for Paul to indicate if he had finished.

"I have seen Chibueze with a stocktaking book for the provision shop in Simpson Street," Paul continued. "Bring it for me and also the keys to the shop. We don't think you can manage all the shops now, can you? Anyway, that is not your duty anymore."

Chibueze had already told her what to expect. She had the strange feeling that he was speaking to her from the mortuary, advising her as he used to when they had shared the same study group at university. She'd gone to do her master's against the wishes of her mother but with the blessing of her dad, who had agreed to pay all the fees and had been happy when she had come home after the fifteen-month program with a well-educated suitor. Chibueze was different from her other suitors. It seemed that he had benefited immensely from being educated.

Very slowly, Chidinma asked Paul, "But where will I get the money? Chibu never left money in the house, not a lot anyway." She was willing herself not to cry; she did not want to be seen as weak.

Paul responded immediately. "What are you saying, that you want to eat it all? Eh, you see what I said about her is true, she is a very greedy woman." Chidinma noticed that he had shifted a little to the edge of the settee.

"No, just that we have to sign at the bank and it might take a while," she said, realizing that Chibueze had not informed Nda Paul of the recent change to his accounts. A bank consolidation had forced them to switch banks, and she had been added as a signatory to the accounts with no limit to her spending. In reality, with the death of her husband, she was now the sole signatory. Chidinma kept this knowledge to herself.

"Hmm, my dear, let me tell you now. You are just a wife and you only have a girl for our brother. You better know how to bring that money now, you hear." Paul was now leaning forward on the long settee, his eyes wide, his neck rigid. He jutted a finger at her aggressively.

"But—" Chidinma began.

"No buts, Chidinma, what nonsense," Paul interrupted. "Who do you think you are, eh?" Paul raised his voice angrily. "It's my brother's money, not yours, eh, you hear?"

She shrank back into her chair, conscious of everyone's eyes upon her. "*Shebi*, we have to pay the hospital and mortuary people," she said quietly, struggling to keep focused on her fingers and not stare directly at Nda Paul.

"Bring the money now!" Paul raged. "Remember we need to pay the ambulance that will carry the body and buy tickets for the relatives from Lagos to travel with the body. And then we need some extra, for food. Do you have ears to hear?" he finished, tugging his own right earlobe for good measure.

As Chibueze prepared himself to die, he had told Chidinma, "If they come asking for money, give it to them, but a small amount at a time. Do not give them plenty, or they will waste it and still come back for more." She had cried as he gave these instructions, but she remembered them now, as she climbed the stairs one at a time, holding the banister tightly in case she fell. She made her way to Chibueze's slim-line, brown leather briefcase with the initials that matched hers. It contained 340,000 naira. She carefully counted out 45,000 naira and closed the briefcase, placing it back under the mattress. She did not wrap the cash in a black nylon bag, as was the custom. Leaving the room, she locked the door behind her. Chibueze had tried as much as he could to arrange his affairs before he died, but he knew that he could not protect her from the greed of his relatives and the archaic traditions they followed.

She held out the cash to Nda Paul. "Here, this is the remaining money left in the house. I had wanted to use it for the market."

Paul grabbed the slim bundle and started counting the Naira notes. "How much is this exactly?" he asked scornfully.

"Why don't you check, I'm not sure. I didn't count it," she replied.

"Chidinma," Nda Paul said venomously, "surely this is not all the money my brother has! You mean to tell me you are giving me only 45,000 naira? Hmm, my dear, you'd better go and get his money, you hear. Need I remind you that the money is no longer yours? We are not even sure that this baby girl you claim is Chibueze's is actually his." Paul spoke with authority as the eldest of the brothers. None of the men in her parlor disagreed with him or came to her aid now, not even Nonso, who had earlier been so kind.

Nda Paul was holding out his hand now, asking, "Where are the keys for the shop, Chidinma? Where is his inventory book?"

Chidinma went and found the keys in the kitchen but returned without the inventory book. She didn't know where it was kept. She'd have to ask the boys in the shop, she said, and excused herself, leaving the parlor. Lying back down on her bed, she heard them leave. She knew it was not over. For the first time she was not sure that she would have the willpower to go through with the strategy Chibueze had laid out for her.

Throughout the visit, Mama Ike had not uttered a word. She listened quietly, and her presence ensured that Chidinma had at least one supporter, one woman looking out for her. Mama Ike had sized up Paul, realizing he was not too educated and had clearly been jealous of his younger brother's success and beautiful wife. Mama Ike had heard the latest rumors about Chidinma's in-laws—that Paul's wife had left for the village, taking the children with her, as things had been hard for them in Lagos. She had reportedly told anyone who'd cared to listen, "Marriage is not for suffering; after all, these other husbands who are doing well, do they have two heads?" This had angered Paul, who blamed his younger brother Chibueze for bringing this shame upon him by not supporting his latest request for financial assistance. But this was the fourth time Paul had come to Chibueze for start-up money, and this was the first time his brother had turned him down. He had done so because he realized his time was limited, and he had started to put his affairs in order.

Mama Ike had learned that Paul had first been given money to start a spare-parts business dealing in recycled Peugeot parts and had started off rather well, but once the profits came in, he had lavished the money on young girls and good times and had not reinvested the money in the business as he was supposed to do. One day, the landlord from whom he had rented the shop came and evicted him, while his apprentices, who had not been paid in months, sold off the remaining stock to make up the salaries owed to them. This had been Paul's consistent pattern of behavior, until by the fourth time he had requested assistance from his brother, he had received an emphatic no. Paul immediately blamed Chidinma for poisoning his brother's mind against him and had been lying in wait for her ever since.

When Mama Ike saw that it was the very same Paul in the parlor that morning, she was worried for Chidinma and decided to sit in the parlor too and hear with her own ears what he had to say. She knew from experience that desperate people like Paul will go to any lengths to get what they want, including a visit to the local witch doctor.

The confusion surrounding the preparation for the funeral continued. Chidinma did not argue about the amount of money she was asked to fork out every two days but kept a meticulous record of how much was given to Nda Paul, for what purposes, and in whose presence. She had gone to check on the shop and had become visibly upset when she learned that Paul, now master of the shop keys, had taken to collecting the profit each day from the shop boys. The shop was now empty of stock, as none had been replenished since he collected the keys. Paul had not bothered to pay the shop boys and had made it clear that the shop was now his and he did not want them there. Chidinma expected more to happen on the day of the burial and after, but she was not sure what.

As the day of the funeral grew closer, Mama Ike suggested that Chidinma should cut her hair. Chidinma had wept, but Mama Ike had a plan. She figured that at least they would have to work very hard to cut her hair any shorter. So the barber had come to the house and had left Chidinma with one inch on her head, which she dyed a brilliant brown to make herself happy.

Early one morning two days before Chidinma was to leave for the village, in the midst of the oppressive heat and all the fat, wailing aunts occupying too much space, a lawyer named Mr. Igbokwe came to the house. He said he had been given instructions to act as Chidinma's lawyer. He apologized for getting to her late, saying that he had not been notified of Chibueze's death and had only just seen the big obituary placed by a committee of friends in the daily newspaper that morning. "The probate will be easy to complete," he said briskly, "as all the paperwork was in order." Chidinma was too embarrassed to ask what a probate was and resolved to question Mama Ike about it later.

Mr. Igbokwe was a very short Igbo man with a shiny head that squeezed out sweat as words tumbled from his mouth. He spoke too fast, shaking his head from side to side, saliva collecting at the corners of his mouth. His lime-green linen suit had been created for a much taller and much better-looking man. Mama Ike, sensing that he had more to say, ushered him upstairs away from the prying ears and eyes of the in-laws, who had all stopped wailing when they heard the word *lawyer*. She sat him down in the only free space available, the main bedroom. Since he was a man Chidinma did not know, it was necessary for Mama Ike to stay with her to hear what he had to say. Mr. Igbokwe had a lot to say, and before he left, Chidinma had signed several papers, with Mama Ike acting as a witness. She signed all of them, even though she understood little to nothing of what he was saying. Mr. Igbokwe used big words.

The funeral came and went. Chidinma returned from the village, bruised but alive, and her hair no shorter than when she'd left. She was glad it was over. Mama Ike had followed her to the village and some of her own relatives had come as well, but that still did not stop her in-laws from inflicting bodily harm on her. She had refused to drink the water in which Chibueze had been washed when they prepared his body for the wake. For this indiscretion, she had received a resounding slap from a female in-law she had never met before but who was a member of the *Umuada*. This had added more confusion to the highly charged atmosphere, and it had taken the diplomatic intervention of Mama Ike, her relatives, and Chibueze's friends to keep the situation under control. Chidinma knew her husband would have stood by her, so she ignored the whispering, "Stupid girl, eh. Why are you so stubborn? Ha, the life of a widow is hard!"

After the funeral, a family meeting was called to discuss her and her daughter, and she was summoned to attend. Nda Paul was at the meeting and insisted that she list all of Chibueze's assets. In the same breath she was informed that as she had only a girl, she was not entitled to her husband's share of the family land.

It was not until after Mama Ike had left Lagos and returned to her home that the final surprise came from Chibueze. Even though he was now six feet under and in the arms of the Lord, he'd always been a fanatic chess and card player.

He'd known what was going to happen after his death, and he had played his strategy to the end by employing a lawyer to write up his last will and testament, going into careful detail about everything he wanted done.

No one could remember the time an Igbo man had written a will like the one Chibueze wrote while he was still alive. A meeting of the elders and relatives was called to discuss it. News of the will was whispered in hushed tones at community gatherings the length and breadth of Lagos, lest the women get ideas. Chidinma was called to several meetings, asking her to explain how such a thing could have happened. They did not like her response.

When Mama Ike heard about the will, she danced so hard her breasts jingle-jangled while her buttocks did a dance on their own. She only hoped her own son, whom she had struggled to educate, was able to display such protection for his wife and children. After all, had he not experienced the harshness of being brought up by a poor widow?

Well, Nda Paul had it coming to him. Chibueze had left the ace for last.

The Battle of the Words

Oratory as Women's Tool of Resistance to the Challenges of Polygamy in Contemporary Wolof Society

Marame Gueye

Song 1: "The Bride Has Bad Karma"*

The bride has bad karma, God has refused.
The bride has bad karma, God has refused.

Since this morning, since they have started the wedding,
Only disasters have happened in the house.

Look, the cow they bought has died,
The sheep they bought has died,
The groceries are rotten,
The tent they built has fallen,

*Songs recorded and translated from the Wolof by Marame Gueye.

The person who went to get the bride has died.
The bride has bad karma, God has refused.

Hey, the bride has bad karma, God has refused.
The bride, the cow they bought has died,
The sheep they bought has died,
The tent they built has fallen,
The groceries went rotten,
The bride's mother has gone crazy,
The bride's father has gone crazy,
The groom's mother has gone crazy,
The groom's father has gone crazy,
The cow they bought has died,
The tent they built has fallen,
The bride's room has collapsed,
The bed they bought has broken,
The bride has bad karma, God has refused.

The bride herself, the bad karma has been with her for a long time.
When she was a baby, when her mother was giving birth to her,
Her father's older brother died.
During the naming ceremony, her mother's younger sister died.

The bad karma has been with her for a long time.
Any man who marries her, the day he slept with her for the first time,
Was the day he became impotent for good.
They were trying to be loyal by saying that a spell was cast on him.
The bride has bad karma, God has refused.

When the bride was coming,
They bought a cow,
The cow died.
They then bought a sheep,
The sheep died.
They bought the groceries,
The sheep ate it rotten.
They built a tent until it was done,
It collapsed.
They brought the musical material,
The thieves stole it.
The owner of the musical material took them to the police.
Look, the bride has bad karma, God has refused.

The marriage will not last.
The man is very quick to say "I don't care,"
The woman is very quick to say "fuck your mother,"
This is why the marriage will not last.

I swear the marriage will not last.
There is no need to be afraid,
The marriage will not last.
You do know that it will not last.
The man is quick to say, "I don't care,"
The woman is quick to say, "fuck your mother,"
This is why it will not last.

The marriage will not last,
You know it will not last.
The man is quick to say, "fuck your mother,"
The woman is quick to say, "I don't care,"
She goes out too much,
And she gives away her pussy.
You know the marriage will not last.

The marriage will not last.
The woman has a husband, and she has a lover,
She goes out too much,
She gives away her pussy,
And she was not a virgin,
This is why the marriage will not last.
I swear it will not last.

Song 2: "There Is a Monster in the House"

Next time one has a donkey, plait its hair,
The bride has plaited her hair.

Next time one has a donkey, plait its hair,
The bride has plaited her hair.

I have a rake, I will no longer borrow a rake,
Her teeth are out like a rake's.

Next time one has a donkey, plait its hair,
The bride has plaited her hair.

Look in this house, we will no longer borrow a rake.
I have a rake, I will no longer borrow a rake,
Her teeth are out like a rake's.

In this house, during the rainy season
When the grass grows in the yard,
We will not borrow a rake,
The leaves in the yard,
Have you seen her teeth?
They're out like a rake's.
I have a rake, I will no longer borrow a rake,
Her teeth are out like a rake's.

Next time one has a donkey, plait its hair,
Or make it wear very tight clothes,
The bride has worn very tight clothes.
Next time one has a donkey, plait its hair,
The bride has plaited her hair.

Make it wear very tight clothes,
Next time one has a donkey,
Make it wear pants, shoes, and a tie,
Make it wear a big "boubou,"
Or have it wear a décolleté.
Next time one has a donkey, plait its hair,
The bride has plaited her hair.

Look at the bride's hair, she says she has a weave,
Look at her eyes, she is wearing false eyelashes,
There goes a monster.
She says she is wearing false eyelashes,
There is a monster in the house.

The man goes around marrying all kinds of women,
This time he has brought a monster into the house.

The man goes around marrying all kinds of women,
There is a monster in the house.

So next time one has a donkey, plait its hair,
The bride has plaited her hair.

Next time one has a donkey, make it wear foundation,
The bride has worn foundation.

Next time one has a donkey, make it wear eyeliner,
The bride has worn eyeliner.

Next time one has a donkey, get it pregnant,
The bride has come with pregnancy.

They were married on Friday,
They slept together for the first time on Saturday,
On Sunday she gave birth to a baby,
The baby was so ashamed, it died.

Next time one has a donkey, get it pregnant,
The bride has come with pregnancy.

Song 3: "To the Sister-in-Law"

Dedicated sister-in-law
You travel so much to the point that you are no longer charged
    for travel fees.
Did they build the genitals of drivers for you?

Sister-in-law, you travel so much to the point that you no longer
    pay for travel fees.
Did they build the genitals of drivers for you?

Hey I say, you stop taxi men,
You say stop to truck drivers,
You say stop to minivans,
You say stop to motorcycles,
You say stop to buses,
You say stop to taxis,
You say stop to minivans,
You say stop to trucks,
You say stop to those going to Ndar,
You say stop to those going to Kaolack,
You say stop to those going to Dakar,
You even say stop to those going to Louga,
You say stop to planes.

You travel so much to the point that you are no longer charged
    for travel fees.
Did they create the penises of drivers for you?
I say did they build the penises of drivers for you?

I say a truck driver will come over, you stop him,
He goes with you.
The taxi man, you stop him, he goes with you.
The motorcyclist, you stop him, he goes with you.
The minivan driver, you stop him, he goes with you.
How are you going to pay for that?
From your pussy,
Did they build the genitals of drivers for you?

I say stop welcoming guests,
Sister-in-law, stop welcoming guests.
Any guest you welcomed you have kicked out later,
Stop welcoming guests.

I say stop welcoming brides,
Sister-in-law, stop welcoming brides.
Any bride you welcomed, you have kicked out later,
Stop welcoming brides.
The youngest sister-in-law is the one who is going to fight you first.
I say stop welcoming brides.
Any bride you welcomed, you have kicked out,
Stop welcoming brides.

You the friend in the neighborhood,
You are the one she sends.
Friend, stop going to get brides,
Any bride you went to get, you have slept with,
Stop going to going to get brides.

Friend, stop going to get brides,
Any bride you went to get, you have slept with,
Your penis looks like a duck's.

Song 4: "Our Beautiful House"

Because you heard of our beautiful house, you want to join us,
This house has been built by the vaginas, the penises have done nothing.

Because you have seen our beautiful house, you want to join us,
Because you have seen our gold jewelry, you want to join us,
Because you have seen our beautiful clothes, you want to join us,
Because you have seen our furniture, you want to join us,
Because you have seen our bedroom set, you want to join us,
Because you have seen our multiple-story house, you want to join us,
This house has been built by the vaginas, the penises have done nothing.

Because of our beautiful house, you want to join us,
Because of our gold jewelry, you want to join us,
Because of the diamonds, you want to join us,
Because of the bedroom set, you want to join us,
Because of the gas stove, you want to join us,
Because of the soda we bathe ourselves with, you want to join us,
The vaginas have accomplished all this, the penises are capable of nothing.

Look, in our time, "marry me and I will take care of myself" is the fashion.
I say "marry me and I will take care of myself" is the fashion.

You say "marry me" "marry me,"
You do not know what's in marriage,
Wait until you've spent years here,
When the man goes to the market and comes back empty-handed,
You will know he has no money for the daily expenses, he only has his penis.

I swear you say "marry me" "marry me"
You do not know what is in marriage,
Wait until you stay here for two years,
I say wait until he goes to market and nothing sells,
You will know he has no money, he only has his penis.

Look, because of our beautiful house, you want to join us,
I walk past you wearing gold, you want to join us,
I park a car, you want to join us,
I wear diamonds, you don't where they came from, you want to join us,
This has been accomplished by vaginas, penises are capable of nothing.

This house has been built by vaginas, penises have done nothing.
This multiple-story house has been built by vaginas, penises
    have done nothing.

This house has been built by the vaginas, men have done nothing.

The *Xaxar* Tradition

These songs were performed during a ceremony called *xaxar*, which is practiced among the Wolof of Senegal and the Gambia. When a bride joins a co-wife or co-wives in her husband's home, a xaxar ceremony is organized by the co-wife or wives. Xaxar is a verbal fight between the senior wives and the new-comer, who is seen as disrupting the harmony of the household. It is performed before the new bride enters her room. Xaxar is very similar to the *marchande* organized by Songho-Zarma women from Niger during their husband's remar-riage. As explained by Aissata Sidikou-Norton in *Recreating Words, Reshaping Worlds,* "The *marchande* is a mock ceremony which is organized by a first wife with the help of her family and friends in order to ridicule her husband and her new co-wife" (46). In the case of the xaxar, the new wife and her friends participate in the singing by responding to the first wife's verbal attacks. Also, whereas the marchande songs are usually short, xaxar can be very long because, depending on the events that unfold during the ceremony, women can impro-vise and add lyrics to their songs. Also, while xaxar sometimes ends in a fight, the marchande is purely play. (It is important to mention that the original xaxar was also play. It is only nowadays that it has changed into eventual physi-cal fights between the two camps of women. Even then, women who fight are scorned for not being good sports.)

Xaxar can also be organized by the wives of a groom's brothers, who are literally the bride's co-wives, especially if they also live in the same household. This second case is less brutal and more ceremonial. To avoid the confrontation with their co-wives in the ceremony of xaxar, most brides disguise their looks and enter their room without the other women knowing. In such cases, the senior wives get frustrated and call her a coward who does not have the guts to face them in a verbal fight; they still perform their insulting songs and might be harsher on her than they would have been in an official ceremony.

During xaxar, women compose songs that denigrate and sometimes insult the other party. The senior wives' intention is to discourage the new bride from joining them. The new bride must show that she can stand up to the challenge by responding to their verbal attacks. Usually each party has a griotte who leads the singing. While the songs are central to the ceremony, the dancing and body movement of the participants also play an important role. Because sex is cen-tral in women's fights in polygamous relationships, they test the sexual prowess of each other through very graphic movements and props. The women often make up mean stories to upset the other party. There have been instances where women have asked for divorce due to the results of a xaxar ceremony, because the other party had unveiled a shameful family secret or had proven to be too tough to share a household with.

This ceremony, which is perceived as brutal to women, is gradually vanishing among the Wolof for many reasons. For one thing, most women no longer want to share a house with their co-wives. Also, because of the fights and insults that might occur, husbands often offer a gift in exchange for a promise by their first wife or wives to halt the ceremony. This gift by the husband, called *takku dënn*, serves to break the verbal fight during the xaxar. Its literal meaning is "something to tie the chest with," and it emphasizes the impact of the new bride on the old one's life. The "tying of the chest" implies that the news of her husband's marriage to the bride has dislocated the chest of the first wife. It creates a shock in her household, which she has to share with another woman from then on.

Traditionally, xaxar had a purging function for the woman whose husband was taking a new wife. It was organized to let women, especially the first wives, pour out their anxieties and frustrations about sharing the same man. It relieved tension and allowed women to accept each other after all was said and done. One can say that it served as an icebreaker. Though some women continued their conflict well after the ceremony, the traditional xaxar was less aggressive and no physical fight was allowed. Women set boundaries on what could be said in the songs. Those who got angry or engaged in fights were ridiculed and perceived as fearful because they could not bear the idea of sharing a man. In more organized women's communities, they were even fined.

In Wolof society, a woman who is afraid of a co-wife is a bad woman — *jigeen ju bon rekay bañ wujj* (only a bad woman fears a co-wife) — because if one has been a good wife, one should not care about having another woman with whom to share the "job." Nevertheless, the very fact that the xaxar ceremony is organized confirms that the society is aware of the disruptive and traumatizing impact of polygamy in women's lives, especially for first wives.

The shifts that have occurred in the practice of polygamy are apparent in the xaxar ceremony. Today this ceremony is more serious: women engage in very harsh name-calling, and fights are often inevitable. Women take the opportunity to test each other's weaknesses. While they seem to be having a lot of fun during the ceremony, the lyrics of their songs suggest an antagonism that makes one suspect that their lives together will not be easy.

Xaxar in Action

The songs presented here are versions I collected in the summer of 2005, when I went to Senegal with the intention of having a well-deserved vacation after defending my dissertation. I just wanted to spend time with my family. However, after one week at home, I decided to call Adji, one of my research informants, just to catch up with her and tell her I was home. Adji was the best xaxar singer in the whole region. She was excited to know I was home and asked if I had come to collect more wedding songs. I replied that I was on vacation. Adji told me that she had a xaxar program the next Saturday and invited me to go with her. And because I would never miss an opportunity to see her perform, I accepted. Before we parted, she advised me to dress nicely and borrow all the gold I could find in my household to impress the new bride and her friends because we were going to be siding with the first wife, who had hired her.

On Saturday she came to pick me up around 10 p.m. (most brides join the marital home late at night). When we arrived at the house, there were already about twenty women in the living room. They were all relatives and friends of the first wife. They cheered at Adji's arrival, and I could see the excitement in their eyes. Many congratulated us on our attire and asked who I was. The first wife was also dressed to kill, and she was a beautiful, imposing woman. Adji did the introduction and told them I was her apprentice from America.

"But isn't she Mère Ami Diouf's daughter?" one woman asked.

"Yes, but she lives in America," Adji quickly responded.

As if she didn't hear her response, the woman continued, "So, you are the one who lives in America?"

I nodded.

"When are you going to take us with you?"

"Soon," I replied, smiling.

"The day I arrive in New York, Bill Clinton will notice he never had a real guest before!" she said, laughing. Everyone laughed.

"You should take Adji. I am sure she will make a lot of money singing xaxar," she continued.

"They don't have polygamy in America," Adji cut in.

The woman looked at me, surprised.

"Is it true?"

"It's true, they don't," I responded.

"What about the men there? They must be doing something; they cannot stay with only one woman. It's just not their nature. Besides, how is every woman going to find a husband if men marry only one woman?"

"I don't believe the world has more women than men," another woman replied. "I think Allah made just as many women as men. He created Adama and Awa, not Adama, Awa, and Coumba."

The first wife was looking at them smiling. "Well, all I know is that those American men all have *deuxième beaux*," she said.

In a corner, two women were giggling while wrapping a rope around a big stick. When they finished, one of them took the stick and tied it around her waist. I realized that they were making a fake male genital. The woman started swinging her newly acquired manhood, and the other women screamed with laughter.

"If you do her with that, she will not be able to walk for weeks," one woman said, talking about the new bride.

"That will serve her right," another replied. They all laughed.

We heard a knock at the door, and a young man entered. He must have been in his mid-twenties. I was later told that he was the groom's younger brother. He politely stood in the middle of the room. I could sense he was nervous.

"Listen, can I beg you not to do this?" he finally said.

One woman got up and almost yelled at him. "Leave us alone! You worthless man, you could not do better than an old witch who has been prostituting herself all her life? Her other lovers left her there, but you, you could not resist her. You just had to marry her!"

Embarrassed, the young man took off.

"Yes, you'd better go before I pull down your pants; I am sure you have a tiny thing in there!" Adji retorted. We all laughed.

Right at that moment, someone came in running. "She is here, she is here, she is here!!!"

We all charged for the door, except for the first wife who ran to her room with two other ladies (it is bad luck for her to see the bride enter the house). Head ties had turned into waist ties, and one could tell that these first wives were up for some blood. Adji was at the front, and those who had volunteered to drum grabbed their aluminum bowls and started playing. Outside we could hear singing and a bus approaching.

"We are going to start with 'The Bride Has Bad Karma,'" Adji ordered. "But wait until she comes out of the bus." The other women agreed.

There were a few minutes of suspense that seemed to me like hours. Finally, a woman came off the bus and walked toward the doorstep. She had a bottle in her left hand and was reciting prayers while pouring the liquid from the bottle at the entrance. Our camp started booing her.

"You are the witches! We should be the ones who are afraid of you. Your witchcraft brought you to our lovely home. You cast a spell on our husband, and now you want to make us believe that you are the victims." The words were coming from everywhere. The lady continued her activity without a word.

Meanwhile, other women had come from the bus and started answering back. "Don't mind them. All they have left now are words. They are desperate old wives whose husband has found a young girl. He loves us and we love him back. If they had been good wives, he wouldn't be drooling at us. We are here and we're staying for good. Wrinkled witches!"

Out of nowhere, Adji's voice rose.

> The bride has bad karma, God has refused!
> The cow they bought has died!
> The sheep they bought has died!

The tent they built has fallen!
The groceries they bought went rotten!
The bride has bad karma, God has refused!

"We will see about that!" a woman from the other camp declared, trying to respond to Adji's lyrics. Clearly, the second wives had decided not to respond through songs. They continued performing their rituals. The bride was covered in a white veil, and we could see her face. Someone was guiding her, and they entered the living room. We followed with Adji singing very loudly. The bride's accompanists seemed to be very bothered by the song. They were talking back, but Adji's voice and our drumming drowned them out. Even though our lyrics were not true, they had an effect on the newcomers.

Polygamy and Women's Powerlessness

Among the Wolof, it is believed that people have both positive and negative energies. Those who have too much negative energy are said to carry bad luck or bad karma. In the selection of mates, a man's luck or success depends a lot on the woman he is with. If a man marries a woman and becomes successful, his wife is congratulated for bringing him good luck. On the other hand, a woman is blamed for the bad luck of her husband. For example, young women who have lost more than one husband are said to be carrying bad karma. Consequently, in the context of polygamy, a first wife is always told that she should be happy that her husband is wealthy enough to get a new wife, thanks to the first wife's good karma.

Unlike the traditional pattern of polygamy, where the first wife had a say in her husband's remarriage, women in contemporary Wolof society are left out of the loop and often do not know about the coming of a co-wife until a few days before. Some husbands are married for a long time before letting the first wife know. This creates a feeling of betrayal on the part of many women. In the song "The Bride Has Bad Karma," the bride's arrival is inevitable, and the first wives look to a higher power to prevent it. They communicate their unwillingness to share, but at the same time they emphasize their lack of power.

Contemporary Wolof women are expected to accept polygamy on the surface. For example, a husband's remarriage is not considered grounds for divorce, as long as he accomplishes his duties toward his first wife, such as clothing her, feeding her, sheltering her, and paying her the takku dënn. A woman whose husband has met the requirements is not expected to complain. Even when he literally abandons her, as long as he is financially taking care of her, she is advised to be patient. This creates a situation where women are silenced and their right to voice their concerns is undermined. For this reason, the xaxar songs create a space where women can articulate their frustrations and offer their opinion about the institution of polygamy and how they wish things could go.

Adji's first song emphasizes a woman's wishful thinking about the ceremony celebrating her co-wife's arrival. Though she is accusing her co-wife of carrying bad karma, she wishes the karma worked so that the wedding ceremony would not take place. The repetition of natural disasters not only shows the first wives' wish that the ceremony, hence the entire marriage, never happened, but it also highlights their helplessness. Their prayer for disaster demonstrates their disapproval of the marriage and shows an extreme desire to stop it. This is proof that women do not really favor polygamy; if they had to choose, few would agree to share a husband. Even when polygamy is favorable to women, such as in rural areas, many of them prefer to have their husband to themselves because of the unreliability of most men when it comes to the equal treatment of their wives. Women welcome co-wives only because they do not have a choice. The xaxar songs are an essential space for them to voice their true opinions about the institution of polygamy.

Adji continued:

> I swear the marriage will not last
> There is no need to be afraid,
> The marriage will not last.

> The man is very quick to say "I don't care,"
> The woman is very quick to say "fuck your mother,"
> This marriage will not last.

This time, although they are reverting to the traditional bashing of the bride, the first wives also suggest that the husband is not perfect and that only they can handle his temper. Faced with their helplessness as far as sharing their husband is concerned, the first wives blame everything on the bride, whom they see as the architect of their predicament.

Because of men's deceitful actions in modern polygamy, first wives feel betrayed and outsmarted when their husband takes a new wife. Instead of blaming him, they usually accuse the bride of being the conniving one who lured him into the union. For example, songs 3 and 4 are lengthy direct attacks on the new bride. Her beauty and birth are questioned, and she is accused of being less than a human being. This negative representation speaks to the care taken by co-wives to distance themselves from each other. The "other" becomes the antithesis in the creation of oppositional identities such as pretty/ugly, civilized/uncivilized, good/bad, chaste/loose, human/subhuman.

> Next time one has a donkey, plait its hair
> The bride has plaited her hair.
> She goes out too much
> And she gives away her pussy.

The man goes around marrying and marrying and marrying
This time he has brought a monster into the house.

As the ceremony continued that day, the husband's sisters entered the living room. As dictated by custom, they are the ones to first welcome the bride. Adji shifted her song suddenly to the song dedicated to the sister-in-law.

You say "stop," "stop" to all drivers
To a point that you no longer
Pay travel fees
Did they build the genitals of drivers for you?
Taxi men,
You say "stop,"
Truck drivers,
You say "stop,"
Motorcycle drivers,
You say "stop,"
Bus drivers
You say "stop,"
Did they build the penises of drivers for you?

While women's songs often highlight their submission to the husband, xaxar songs do not spare him and his family. For example, most sisters-in-law are very manipulative and exercise some control over their brothers' wives. They are also often the ones who talk their brothers into remarrying, especially when they are not on good terms with the first wife. Thus, if a woman is in conflict with her husband's sisters, she may seize the moment of the xaxar to relieve herself of the frustrations regarding the latter.

This situation is a good indication of the ways in which society pits women against each other. The oppressive factors do not always come from men; there is a lot of woman-on-woman violence in Wolof households. Many women who join their husband's home find other women, such as the mother-in-law, holding positions of authority within the household. Mothers-in-law sometimes make life very difficult for their daughters-in-law. Wives are expected to accept abuses from their husband's mother and sisters without complaint. The xaxar ceremony thus provides women with an opportunity to take care of some "old business" that in normal circumstances they would not have the space or the temerity to talk about.

With song 3, the first wife and her friends attack the sisters-in-law and accuse them of being prostitutes. The song points to the sister-in-law's looseness and her preference for drivers, although instead of openly saying the kinds of men the sister-in-law sleeps with, Adji emphasizes the kinds of vehicles they drive. Conscious of a sister-in-law's typical habit of siding with the new bride to fight the first wives, women seize the occasion of the xaxar to chastise her and show her that they understand her game. As the song continues, the attack shifts to the husband and his friends.

> Stop going to get brides
> Any bride you go to get you have slept with
> Stop going to get brides
> With your penis that looks like a duck's!

At this ceremony, one of the sisters seemed very annoyed by Adji's accusations. She searched in her purse and handed some banknotes to her. Adji took the notes and gave them to one of the ladies and continued singing about the husband's friends.

All the while, the men, friends and relations of the groom, were locked up in his brother's room and didn't dare come out, even though giving Adji a gift of money would have stopped her insulting lyrics.

The Empowerment of Women in Polygamy

When she was sure that no man was coming out, Adji turned against the bride again.

> Because you have heard of our beautiful house
> You want to join us,
> This house has been built by the vaginas
> The penises have done nothing.
> Look, during our times,
> "Marry me and I will take care of myself" is the fashion.
> You say "marry me, marry me,"
> You do not know what is in marriage,
> Wait until you spend years here,
> When the man goes to the market and comes back empty-handed,
> You will know he has no money for the daily expenses,
> He has nothing,
> He has only his penis.

The woman with the fake male genitalia was going around dancing and humping other women to back up Adji's lyrics. Even some women among the bride's procession were laughing. This song announces that sexuality is central to women's lives and during the xaxar ceremony Wolof women are empowered to overcome the taboo and speak about it. It also sketches out a new reading of polygamy that puts procreation at the center of women's participation in the system.

It might appear odd to state that there is power to be gained by women within polygamy. However, if one considers that women in polygamy do not always rely on the man for happiness, it is understandable why there is some demystification of the male. This pattern was prominent in the past because women did not see the man as the center of their lives. Rather, their children were the reason they stayed married. This is also a pattern that existed in pre-Islamic Wolof society, where women agreed to polygamy to provide a father and security for their children.

This tendency continues to exist among Wolof women despite the material-ism of many who want to be married to rich men, even if it means becoming the second or third wife. I call this return to traditional values a postmodern approach to polygamy. Women turn a disadvantageous situation to their own benefit. It is crucial for a woman to have children in order for her to be at the apex of womanhood. Many women get married to have children. These women are not interested in romantic love or in whether their husbands can materially take care of them and their children. They rely on themselves economically; all that matters to them is a biological father for their children.

According to Islam, women should not have children outside wedlock. Con-sequently, in order to procreate, one obviously has to get married. Because dem-ographically there are more women than men in most societies and because in Wolof culture men marry mostly younger women, unmarried women who pass the age of thirty generally must choose from men who are already married. For these women, having a child becomes the most urgent and crucial reason for marriage. They do not see men as material providers but only as procreators.

Younger women may agree to marry already-wedded men for material rea-sons. Because of the rise of unemployment among young men, young women turn to older men who are already established in their careers and are often very generous with younger women, giving them handsome gifts during courtship. Once married, such women end up finding that the wealth the husband showed them when they were dating was only superficial and that his wives actually rely on themselves.

Song 4 brings another perspective on polygamy as perceived by women. It enables the first wives to show their experience and tell the new woman secrets of marriage that are not often known by the outsider, and it emphasizes facts that are often overlooked, such as women's material contributions to their households. The first wives emphasize that they have created the wealth of the household; the husband is good only for his sexual services. This philosophy empowers women in various ways. When women do not have to compete for material attention from the husband and see in him only a sexual procreator, there is less reason for conflict among them. They are able to assert their rights because their husband cannot control them by refusing them food or clothing.

If problems arise, he is quite likely the one to lose because he has no material power. This situation also enables women to get divorced more easily in the case of abuse since they do not have to worry about material support for themselves and their children.

> I walk past you wearing gold
> You want to join us,
> I park a car
> You want to join us,
> I wear diamonds, you don't know where they came from
> You want to join us,
> This has been accomplished by the vaginas
> The penises are capable of nothing!

This part of the song emasculates the male. Having incapacitated him, women gain power and take ownership of a space (the building) that has long represented male success. By taking responsibility for the material well-being of the family, the women confirm that their place is not the private sphere only. This also shows that the Wolof woman has a passive-aggressive articulation of her feminism and agency. She does not go around showing off her power in the household (she is in reality the provider), but when she is challenged, the husband's secrets are out in the open, and there is no bigger offense to a woman than bringing her a younger co-wife, especially when she has been the sole provider for the household. The young bride is reminded that all that glitters is not gold.

Clearly, polygamy cannot be seen as an institution that always subjugates women. In fact, one can say that women find can find agency within polygamy if they are able to shift the focus from the man to their own interests. Such women do not fear the arrival of a new wife.

Sharing a Man

Just as Adji was starting another song, the new wife's griotte handed us a considerable amount of money. This marked the end of our performance. The bride was taken to the first wife's room in order to announce her official arrival. We followed. Her griotte was singing and praising her. The first wife was seated on her bed with a very dignified look. The new wife's aunt spoke through her griotte, saying that they came in peace. The first wife was an older sister, they continued; the new wife would follow her and take her advice, for she was not coming to disrupt the household.

The first wife also spoke through Adji. She welcomed the bride as a sister and told her that she could rely on her for advice and friendship. As long as the new bride behaved like a sister, she said, there would never be problems between them. After going back and forth exchanging words of welcome and peace, the bride left for her room where she would meet her groom and continue her rituals.

The first wife gave Adji money and pieces of cloth for her performance. When we got into the taxi that was taking us home, Adji gave me my share of the money and cloth. I came home late, wondering what was next for the two wives.

The wedding songs are definitely a way of asserting women's resistance to the institution of polygamy, but are they enough to establish a consistent and practical female response to the numerous oppressive factors that come with sharing a man?

Part Four

Focusing on Survival
Women's Health Issues

This section explores some of the most debilitating health issues facing African women today: the health repercussions of female genital cutting, which is prevalent in many cultures throughout Africa; the effects of the HIV/AIDS epidemic and other serious diseases such as cancer; and the ongoing effects of the trauma visited on women by protracted violence and civil war.

Four pieces in this section focus on the highly contested topic of female genital cutting (FGC), referred to by opponents of the practice as female genital mutilation. Descriptions of the practice and its aftereffects are described in harrowing detail in two poems by Ann Kithaka of Kenya; a hard-hitting denunciation of the practice for both boys and girls by one of the most outspoken human rights activists on this issue in North Africa, Dr. Nawal El Saadawi of Egypt; and "Surviving Me," a theater script by South African performance artist Janine Lewis.

The performance artist and playwright Janine Lewis presents a vivid allegorical enactment, created collaboratively with a theater group of young South Africans, of the long-term effects of female genital cutting on girls and young women. The character of the Girl in the play feels lost and unloved by her culture, unsure of which traditions to follow or when to follow her own heart. Eventually she learns that the only way past the trauma that haunts her is to go right through it, and she emerges on the other side of her trials stronger, wiser, and ready to take her first steps toward freedom and autonomy.

The medical doctor and internationally respected human rights advocate Nawal El Saadawi was one of the first in her home country of Egypt to sound the alarm on the health damages that can be caused by the practice of circumcision, both of girls and boys. Forty years after her groundbreaking volume *The Hidden Face of Eve: Women in the Arab World*, she is still one of the most ardent and effective advocates for human rights, as the essay included here demonstrates. Dr. Saadawi takes a hard line against the practice of female genital mutilation (which she herself underwent as a child), calling it a human rights violation and a health threat of the gravest nature that should be totally banned—but she equally condemns the widely accepted practice of male circumcision, which she calls male genital mutilation (MGM).

Other pieces in this section discuss the tremendous health effects on women of the HIV/AIDS epidemic in Africa. In her short story "Slow Poison," Juliana Makuchi Nfah-Abbenyi of Cameroon describes a young man's death from AIDS from the point of view of his mother, who laments that while she uses up her entire savings futilely seeking a cure for him, she is also treated as a pariah by her relatives and culture. Her only support comes from the Presbyterian nuns who run an AIDS community outreach program in her village. The grim march of HIV infection to full-blown AIDS and death is recounted in poems by Ann Kithaka and Cheshe Dow, who write of the struggle to maintain dignity and community in the face of widespread sickness and death.

Pauline Dongala of Congo-Brazzaville, in her essay "Prayers and Meditation Heal Despair," describes the impact of the violent civil war in her country, which forced her and most of her family to leave their homes and seek shelter in the forest, becoming prey to hunger, disease, and uncertainty. Though Dongala and her immediate family were able to escape to the United States, she lost many friends and relatives to the conflict, and, like so many other women who live through such traumatic experiences, she became depressed and ill. Dongala offers her own experience of the power of prayer and meditation to heal individual despair (which might in psychiatric terms be referred to as post-traumatic stress disorder) as well as to effect social healing on a society-wide level.

Taken together, these pieces show the remarkable resilience of African women in the face of tremendous pain and suffering. The authors offer multiple lifelines of resistance to other women coming behind them on the journey to personal and societal recovery and strength.

Tell Me Why

Two Poems

Ann Kithaka

I Wonder

Clansmen, come,
Enlighten me.
Where did you dispose of
The severed bit of
My despised anatomy after
The unkind cut?

Did the toothless hag,
The self-professed bush surgeon,
Fling it into some mysterious
African pot
To concoct that rejuvenating soup,
Consumed so gleefully by the *rika*?

Or perhaps the council of
Elders roasted
The delicacy over some
Ritualistic fire
Amidst ribald rhetoric
After the event?

Maybe the old hag
Threw it into the
Chilly morning sky where
Some ravenous bird
Intercepted and devoured it
Mid-flight to nowhere.

Or maybe still . . . God forbid
My father's prized cockerel
(Slaughtered that same day
To make the herbal chicken soup
Fed to me by Auntie
To heal the circumcision wound)
Sought it where it lay
Slithery
On the ant-infested ground
And swallowed it in one
Triumphant gulp.

Mother, Why?

Exalted mother,
I shall extend you no reprieve
For your blatant silence
When they spilt my virginal blood
On the altar of tribal misogyny.

Had your indomitable maternal instinct
Taken a compulsory leave of absence?
Were you a manacled captive,
Your leap, thrust, and heave
Insufficient to stop the sacrilege
So callously wrought on me?

Show me the gag, then,
That stopped you from condemning
Or even cursing this macabre rite.

Where was the spirited female fraternity?
Could their ingenuity not conjure
A conspiracy to cut only a small bit
Instead of this sadistic butchering
Of all that is soft and best in me,
Leaving my womanhood a gaping scar?

This jagged relic of primitivism
Has eroded my self-esteem,
Leaving me vulnerable and insecure.

Could not the council of elders
Be appeased with a surface job?
Could they not, mother?

Surviving Me

Janine Lewis

I am a lecturer at the Tshwane University of Technology Department of Drama, Gauteng, South Africa. The young adults I teach come from diverse traditional African cultures, but they are heavily influenced by Western culture, as evident in their fashion, speech, and entertainment choices. Although young people today are bombarded from various sides regarding self-improvement and self-empowerment, demands that they focus on their (Westernized) education are juxtaposed with the insistence that cultural traditions be upheld. Often, little or no explanation or justification is given: it is simply tradition.

The confusion borne out of the clash between tradition and modernity is dealt with in various ways. Young black educated men and women, when faced with traditional circumcision and traditional menstrual rites, often choose to forego their knowledge of Western teachings about human rights and doggedly follow tradition, regardless of any questions they may have. White African youth brought up in strict Calvinist cultures often function blithely within narrow boundaries regardless of questions they too have. The tradition versus modernity struggle persists for all.

174

I was brought up in a white English South African environment where I was fortunate to be able to ask questions and get answers that were as honest as they were revealing. This background has taught me to voice my opinion or ask questions of various cultures, not to pass judgment (and fortunately it has never been perceived in this way) but instead to find answers to my questions or allow others to voice their answers, so that we learn together about our cultures and our differences. We may agree to differ on various viewpoints, but I think it is important to at least have the opportunity to volunteer our opinions and discover where the points of agreement and disagreement actually lie.

In facilitating a course I designed, "Theatre for Empowerment," I strive to provide an environment for voicing the "forbidden" questions and opinions, as well as a platform for the open discussion of the forbidden. The course has brought me into various places, cultures, and situations within the rural, semi-urban, and urban sectors of South Africa. Through the course I have learned to appreciate and embrace differences between the peoples of South Africa. Eventually, this desire to embrace difference led to the devising of the play *Surviving Me*.

In this play, a young African girl confronts her archetypes through her dreams in an effort to make sense of her reality. She is grappling with the issue of facing her past in her pursuit of finding herself.

> Which one are you now?
> Rural or real?
> Whose rules do you follow?
> Which traditions do you follow?
> Which culture?
> Are you real?
> Where do you fit in?

A script was created in collaboration with Marianthie van der Walt, an alumna of my course. This concept script was then further elaborated with the multicultural, multilingual cast. Eight of the eleven official languages of South Africa were represented in the cast: Tswana, Zulu, Xhosa, Pedi, Seswati, Afrikaans, Sotho, and English. Identity questions within the South African context were shared and explored through the performance process. I would like to believe that, although we may not have found concrete answers, by asking or voicing the questions we have grown as individuals in pursuit of a new unified culture.

The play was presented under my direction at the Tshwane University of Technology, Department of Drama in March 2006, with an original video montage created for the show by Katty Vandenberghe and vernacular text in Xhosa by Sibongile Ngele. Verbal exchanges take the form of abstract prose compiled to create an eccentric tale. The play uses a variety of performance techniques, including masks, physical theater, and puppetry, where the mask is used as an extension of the performer.

A pivotal moment in the play describes a young girl's journey of self-discovery and her present-day exposure to virginity testing, a sensitive and hotly debated practice still performed in South Africa. This section is told by intertwining two stories in three juxtaposed voices: the young girl's story, describing her first virginity test at age seven; her mother, who defends the cultural tradition of virginity testing by saying that it is far less gruesome than female genital mutilation and tells her own story in Xhosa; and the young child echoing the mother's story of being genitally mutilated (as if remembering) told simultaneously in English.

Although confronting her demons gives the young girl some insight, no answers are provided. The audience is left to draw their own conclusions and to face their own responses to the issues posed. The play was well received when we performed it. Audience members from various cultures engaged with the cast and crew afterward, sharing their responses to the theme of finding oneself and one's role in life.

Characters

GIRL	Figure of reality—or is she?
WISE MAN	Authority figure. Own wisdom within
DIVINE CHILD	True, pure self
SHADOW	Representation of what we wish not to be
ANIMA/ANIMUS	Mind and intellect (male) / Soul and breath (female)
WISE WOMAN	Source of fertility and nature; Mother figure
PERSONA	Mask of self presented to the world
CHORUS/ENTOURAGE	Chorus when neutral; entourage when masked, as required

Outside—Meeting Herself

The GIRL *clambers up onto a chair that is suspended from a tree. It starts to rain on her. Music begins—she opens an umbrella and sits in the rain. After a short pause, enter the* WISE MAN *in a Santa suit with a bag of presents slung over his shoulder. The music is interrupted.*

GIRL: What are you doing here?

Frustrated because he ignores her.

Excuse me, I—

WISE MAN: Penny for your thoughts?

GIRL: What are you doing here?
>> *Closes umbrella.*
WISE MAN: What does it look like I am doing here?
>> *Starts rummaging through gifts.*
GIRL: Is there anything I can do for you?
WISE MAN: No, thanks, I'm good.
GIRL: See the thing is . . . I'm not. You're kind of interrupting something here.
WISE MAN: Really, like what?
GIRL: I am waiting for someone.
WISE MAN: Guess I should be going then.
>> *Gets up to leave.*
GIRL: Wait a minute, what are you doing here?
WISE MAN: A particular little Girl has been very good this year, and I am delivering the gifts she ordered.
GIRL: Sorry Santa, wrong dream, wrong Girl, wrong time.
WISE MAN: Don't be too sure.
GIRL: Look, I really don't have time for this! I don't have a lot of time, so what do you want? 'Cause I really need to move on.
WISE MAN: It's me, silly!
>> *Taking off Santa suit.*
GIRL: Me, who?
WISE MAN: Me, you!
GIRL: You, me?
WISE MAN: Me.
GIRL: You?
WISE MAN: Disappointed?
GIRL: A little.
WISE MAN: How much is a little?
GIRL: Less than a lot.
WISE MAN: How much is less than a lot?
GIRL: A little.
WISE MAN: I see.
GIRL: There's no way you're me.
WISE MAN: I'm not all of you, no.
GIRL: I have to find me!
WISE MAN: Stop looking.
GIRL: I need me!
WISE MAN: That's why we're here.
GIRL: I have to find me!
WISE MAN: All good things come to those who wait.
GIRL: Where am I?

WISE MAN: None so deaf as those who won't hear.

GIRL: Where am I?

WISE MAN: None so blind as those who won't see.

> The WISE MAN moves to open the theater door . . . and disappears inside. From within the Santa bag, the DIVINE CHILD emerges and helps the GIRL down.
>
> The DIVINE CHILD hands her a gift box from the bag, but as she moves to hand the GIRL the gift, she hesitates, places the box down, and opens it to reveal a smaller box. This too she offers to the GIRL. This ritual is repeated three times, with the DIVINE CHILD placing the boxes in a circle around the GIRL. Inside the final smallest one, she finds a key; this she hands to the GIRL, who opens the theater door and enters, followed by the DIVINE CHILD and the audience.

Door 1—Entrance to Theater

> As the GIRL and the audience enter the theater, the WISE MAN is no longer seen, but he does however make certain announcements throughout the following scenes, like a puppet master. The DIVINE CHILD carries Santa's bag of goodies (also representative of SHADOW, built up of issues over years); she is also handing out cocktail umbrellas to the audience.

WISE MAN: The clock ticks, but only in time.

Undress.

Take off your clothes. Take off your body.

Hang them up behind the door.

Tonight we can go deeper than most disguises.

GIRL: What is it that I have to keep telling myself again and again?

That there is always a new beginning, a different end.

I can change the story. I am the story.

Begin.

> Doors standing within doorframes on wheels are brought on by members of the ENTOURAGE. The GIRL enters through one. She sits and watches what is revealed to her.

Door 2—Headlines of Life

> Four headless people enter and sit on preset chairs. They unfold the newspapers from under their arms and begin "reading," placing the newspapers where their heads should be. The newspaper gets manipulated as "mouths"/faces speaking/ reading the headlines of her life. The doorframes become picture fames, framing the headless people.

ENTOURAGE: There is no way out of the mind.
    One desperate woman's search for the truth.
    Substantial decrease in breathing space worries experts.
    Girl forgot to take care of her inner being.
    The highs and lows of losing grip.
    Fear of rejection climbs its way to the top of the charts.
    Absence of a small tissue becomes big issue.
    Frustrated female fails the test of forgiving herself.
    Self-acceptance reaches an all-time low.
    Social life found decapitated in downtown apartment.
    Emotional well-being takes a turn for the worst.
    Self-pity runs for parliament.
    Pile-up of regrets causes major crash.
    Pressure drives good Girl in bad direction.
    The good news is your level of self-esteem is up to you.
    The bad news is your level of self-esteem is up to you.
        Dragging Santa's bag, the DIVINE CHILD *moves over to the* GIRL.
        The DIVINE CHILD *removes newspapers from the bag and through-*
        out the next dialogue stuffs the paper into the GIRL's *costume, hangs it*
        around her head, creates shoes from it, and finally shoves a wad of
        paper into the GIRL's *mouth.*
GIRL: Will you always follow me?
DIVINE CHILD: Who's following whom?
GIRL: That's what I'm beginning to wonder.
DIVINE CHILD: There are two marks on a circle. Which is ahead? Which
   is behind?
GIRL: Neither.
DIVINE CHILD: Then we're tailing one another.
        The DIVINE CHILD *puts down the box and opens it to reveal a*
        flowerpot. As she pours water into the pot from a preset watering can,
        the image enlarges (depicted either in video or still images). This reflects
        on the water and against the white dress she is wearing.
        Doors change. The GIRL *enters "another" door.*

Door 3—Shadow and Entourage

SHADOW: *a serpent-like creature with the "evil"* ENTOURAGE
pointing out negativity and hopelessness in her life, emphasizing un-
fulfilled dreams and desires.
    The SHADOW *appears from one of the stage doors. The* GIRL
stands transfixed with the newspaper in her mouth. The SHADOW
talks to the GIRL, *and even though she wants to reply, she is unable to;*

she keeps on trying, but she just can't communicate with him. The masked ENTOURAGE *appears from out of the other stage doors and enters through the doorframe on stage just behind the* GIRL, *closing in on her.*

SHADOW: I heard you were looking for me, so we came as soon as we could.

GIRL *tries to reply.*

SHADOW: Speak when you are spoken to!

GIRL *tries to reply.*

SHADOW: Tut tut, poor little princess stuck in a rut. Such a shame, she should have known better.

ENTOURAGE: Never trouble trouble, till trouble troubles you.

SHADOW: But she did, didn't she?

GIRL *tries to reply.*

SHADOW: Hush. To talk without thinking is to shoot without aiming.

ENTOURAGE: What cannot be cured, must be endured.

SHADOW: Silence! Let's see what we're dealing with here . . . she seems sane enough, but underneath it all . . .

ENTOURAGE: Complexity, chasing, conscience, claustrophobia, confusion, conflict, craving, crashing . . .

SHADOW: So much, too much.

GIRL *tries to reply.*

SHADOW: But wait, there's more!

ENTOURAGE: Sulking, seeking, suffering, scared, scarred, sinking, shivering, suffocating.

SHADOW *Screaming!*

GIRL *tries to reply.*

SHADOW: I know. Aching for . . .

ENTOURAGE: A chance, safety, security, conciliation, charm, sympathy, clarity, salvation.

SHADOW: But it never comes.

What do you do, what do you do?

ENTOURAGE: There is a screw loose somewhere.

ENTOURAGE *exits.*

GIRL *tries to reply.*

SHADOW: No use screaming, Princess, I can hear you. Unfortunately nobody else can, or cares. You're playing solitaire, remember.

Exits laughing.

WISE MAN: I'll keep telling this story—different people, different places, different time—but always you, always me, always this story, because this story is a tightrope between two worlds.

A traditional song is heard, sung by a solo female voice. The WISE WOMAN *appears dressed in traditional garb, with an enamel basin filled with water on her head. She walks slowly across the back of the stage. She is not the one singing, but one of the* CHORUS *members is, dressed in neutral and rolling a small box across the stage. Another* CHORUS *member in neutral fits a door into the frame on stage and pushes it in mime into position, where he locks the wheels. The rest of the* CHORUS *(changed from being the* ENTOURAGE*) spills onto stage moving slowly, low, mist-like; they join in the singing, harmonizing with the* CHORUS*. The box is placed behind the door, where the* WISE WOMAN *arrives and assumes a position on the box.*

The GIRL *opens the door to reveal the* WISE WOMAN *(singing volume increases). The* GIRL *slams the door shut (the singing ends abruptly). The* GIRL *begins to run (away from the parts of herself that she is unable to deal with) followed by the* DIVINE CHILD*. She continues to run in circles around the entire stage. The* CHORUS *moves over, up, and around the door, and eventually shoves the* WISE WOMAN *through the door and disappears behind it.*

Door 4—Archetype of the Wise Woman

The GIRL *eventually runs into the* WISE WOMAN *(mother figure) and backs up to resume running as a puppet manipulated by four* CHORUS *members, ultimately being lifted up to run in the air. She is trying to run from things in her life and ultimately from herself, but she isn't getting anywhere. She is confronted with the fact that things seem to change, but they actually stay the same—moving forward, keeping still.*

The WISE WOMAN *is standing still.*

The WISE MAN *moves the door around the* GIRL *as he confronts her.*

WISE MAN: Nice weather for jogging.

GIRL: I'm not jogging.

WISE MAN: Oh, I see.

Long silence.

WISE MAN: What are you doing?

GIRL: I'm running.

WISE MAN: Where to?

GIRL: Away.

Long silence.

WISE MAN: But you're not going anywhere?

GIRL: I'll get there.

WISE MAN: How?

GIRL: I'm running.

WISE MAN: Moving forward, standing still?

GIRL: I'm running as fast as I can!

WISE MAN: More haste, less speed.

GIRL: I'll get there!

WISE MAN: Where?

GIRL: There!

WISE MAN: The more things change, the more they stay the same.

GIRL: I have to get there!

WISE MAN: You're so busy trying to get there that you forget to *BE THERE*!

> *Suddenly the* CHORUS *stops manipulating the* GIRL *and she col-lapses to the floor. Like the* DIVINE CHILD, *the* WISE WOMAN *now remains with her on stage always and is a silent witness/instigator of what is to come. Her presence is always felt. The* GIRL *is noticeably more upset by her presence.*

GIRL: How do you seem to convey me to myself?

Why does nothing matter as much as this?

WISE MAN: I am a message. You change the meaning. We are the map that you redraw.

Door 5—Trickster and the Entourage (Revisit)

> *The* TRICKSTER *can change shape—the neutral* CHORUS *is used to represent different aspects of him/her. He/she is represented by four or five people—each with a stick extension, one with a mask, the other four on each corner of a cloth, manipulating it together like a puppet-like creature against the back wall, on the floor, etc. His/her changing is split up between them—the ensemble is both a protagonist and an antagonist at the same time.*

GIRL: Hello? Anyone there? Here? Hello! Anyone?!

> *She is overwhelmed, confused, and unable to process everything that has happened.*

TRICKSTER: Illogical emotions, untamed—yet not quite free. Unsatisfied destiny—screaming in silence . . . just to be. Questions without answers calling your name. Voices without faces urging the flames. Passions without freedom begging for gain. Fear without love fighting the pain.

GIRL: What now? Who are you?

TRICKSTER: Those who do not wish to know, ask those who cannot tell.

GIRL: Whatever, I don't think I really want to know anyway.

TRICKSTER: Oh, but you do know, you know exactly who I am, who we all are. But the truth hurts, doesn't it?

Truth seems to be the cry of all, but the game of few.

GIRL: You're not making sense.

TRICKSTER: Careful what you wish, careful what you say . . .

GIRL: You don't know what you're talking about.

TRICKSTER: Careful what you wish, you might regret it. Careful what you wish, you might just get it . . .

GIRL: Just leave me alone! I just wish . . .

TRICKSTER: Wish you might,
　　　Wish you may,
　　　You wish your life away.
　　　Are you satisfied?

GIRL: I want myself
　　　I want *me* now
　　　I want it all
　　　And I don't care how!

TRICKSTER: All the wants you waste,
　　　All the things you chase
　　　And it all crashes down
　　　And you break your crown
　　　And you point your finger
　　　But there's no one around.

GIRL: This is not my fault!

TRICKSTER: I watched in silence as your feet turned to clay.

GIRL: I have lost me! I'm not responsible for all this!

TRICKSTER: Those thorns in your inside, for the tree you planted. It tears you and you bleed.

GIRL: I'm bleeding, me?

TRICKSTER: You bleed.
　　　You know how.
　　　Only you can save you.
　　　She runs into the silence of the "naked" people.

Door 6—Animus + Anima

The TRICKSTER *remains* (ANIMUS) *and the naked characters (representing the* ANIMA) *in the background represent parts of herself that the* GIRL *won't acknowledge and tries to keep hidden.*

　　　Naked ENTOURAGE *members play with masks attached to backs of their heads.*

ALL: Where are the stains now?
　　　Turn away.
　　　The stains stay.
　　　Ignore the stains,
　　　But they don't go away.
　　　Let me out.

You continue to confine me/you.

Set me free.

Free me.

Set me free.

Free me. . . .

> *The rest of the* ENTOURAGE *enters from the back, playing with the masks on tops of their heads. Percussive sequence. Fast, ominous scene, which the* GIRL *joins into. All leave as the frenzy dies down, leaving the* GIRL *in an exhausted heap.*

Door 7—Revelation to Herself

> *A door slams. She sits up as if awakened from a bad dream. The* ENTOURAGE *continues to leave one by one, unnoticed. Projections of daisies in a symbolic montage on the back wall.*
>
> *The following piece comprises two stories told in three voices:*
>
> —*The* GIRL *talks accusingly at the* WISE WOMAN *as her mother—telling her story of virginity testing.*
>
> —*The* WISE WOMAN *tells her story of Female Genital Mutilation.*
>
> —*The* DIVINE CHILD *echoes the* WISE WOMAN's *story as if remembering, in English.*
>
> *(The* WISE WOMAN/DIVINE CHILD *text should be interspersed as the performance flows, sometimes overlapping, sometimes repeating after one sentence as if in translation, and others as whole chunks of the story).*
>
> *Each female in her own space on the stage.*

GIRL: My body is my own, I thought.

You said it would be fine. You said it was the right thing to do. That according to the culture you feel very much proud of yourself if you are a virgin and your parents are proud of you too. You had already given my permission.

WISE WOMAN: Uyayazi ikuba izinyanya zethu ziphuma kude emantla Zidluliswe kwizizukulwana. Izithethe zibalulekile. Izithethe zakho zibalulekile. Zizithethe zam ezi. Zizithethe zakho ezi. Izithethe zam zizithethe zakho.

DIVINE CHILD: You know our ancestors come from far up north. It has been passed down through generations.

The culture is important. Your culture is important.

This is my culture. This culture is your culture. My culture is your culture.

GIRL: I was seven. And glad I didn't yet have breasts to flaunt with my bare chest like most of the other girls at the Nomkhubulwane Festival—honoring a goddess of rain, nature, and fertility.

There was an uncomfortable hollow feeling in the pit of my stomach—but the frenzied excitement, dancing, and singing helped silence the nonstop questions in my head.

WISE WOMAN: Ndaxelelwa ukuba ndisiwa emazantsi omlambo, apho kuyokwenziwa isiko elithile, emva koko ndakunikwa ukutya okuninzi kakhulu. Nje ngomntwana ngungekho nto ndiyaziyo ndaqhutwa njengegusha eyokuxhelwa.

DIVINE CHILD: I was told that they were taking me down to the river to perform a certain ceremony, and afterward I would be given a lot of food to eat. As an innocent child, I was led like a sheep to be slaughtered.

GIRL: There, girls between the ages of seven and twenty-six were all waiting anxiously for their turn.

Then, it was my turn.

All stood and watched—everyone from the community. And you, you were chanting the loudest in my ears.

I lay down on the mat in front of the woman doing the test, my modest bead skirt hardly covering what in moments would be flaunted wide open to the world.

WISE WOMAN: Ndithe ndakungena kwelihlathi labucala, apho kwakukho igumbi elimnyama kakhulu, ndaye ndakhululwa yonke impahla endandiyinxibile. Ndagqunywa amehlo ndahanjiswa ze. Ndaye ndathathwa ngabafazi ababini abanamandla, ndasiwa kwindawo yoqhaqho. Abafazi abane abanamandla bandinyanzelisa ukuba ndilale ngomqolo, ababini bandibamba imilenze yomibini. Omnye umfazi waya wahlala phezu kwesifuba sam ukuqanda ukuba ndingashukumi ngasentla. Isiqwenga selaphu sahlohlwa emlonyeni wan ikuze ndingaviwa xa ndilila. Baye bandicheba ngezantsi.

DIVINE CHILD: Once I entered the secret bush, I was taken to a very dark room and undressed. I was blindfolded and stripped naked. I was then carried by two strong women to the site for the operation. I was forced to lie flat on my back by four strong women, two holding tight to each leg. Another woman sat on my chest to prevent my upper body from moving. A piece of cloth was forced into my mouth to stop me screaming. I was then shaved.

GIRL: I squeezed my eyes shut . . . wishing they were my legs. This is all right. It is tradition. All good girls are doing it. It is what remains of our way, our culture . . .

It only takes a few seconds.

Her bare hands were warm and moist . . . the tester seldom washes them.

WISE WOMAN: Luthe lakuqala uqhaqho, ndalwa kakhulu. Iintlungu zazingaphaya kwam, zinganyamezeleki. Kulomlo ndasikeka kakhulu ndalahlekelwa ligazi elininzi. Bonke aba besebenza oluqhaqho babenxilile.

DIVINE CHILD: When the operation began, I put up a big fight. The pain was terrible and unbearable. During this fight, I was badly cut and lost blood. All those who took part in the operation were half-drunk with alcohol. Others were dancing and singing, and worst of all, had stripped naked.

> The GIRL moves over to the DIVINE CHILD, who is sitting on the floor, and cradles her in her lap.

WISE WOMAN: Abanye babedanisa becula, into eyayimbi kakhulu, abanye babehamba ze.

DIVINE CHILD: I was genitally mutilated with a blunt penknife.

WISE WOMAN: Bandisika ubufazi bam ngemela ebuthuntu. Emva koluqhaqho kwakungekho namnye owandincedisa ukuba ndihambe. Into abazifakayo kwisilonda sam zazinuka kwaye zibuhlungu. Yayingamaxesha amabi la kum. Qho xa ndifuna ukuchama kwakufuneka ndime ngenyawo. Umchamo wam wawuye uvuze, ufikelele nasenxebeni, lonto ibangele ubuhlungu kwakhona. Ngamanye amaxesha ndandizinqanda ukuba ndingachami kuba ndisoyika intlungu. Zange ndinikwe mayeza okupholisa intlungu zam okanye ipilisi zokubulala intsholongwane. Emva koko ndaphathwa nguthyafa ndalahlekelwa ligazi elininzi.

DIVINE CHILD: After the operation, no one was allowed to aid me to walk. The stuff they put on my wound stank and was painful. These were terrible times for me. Each time I wanted to urinate, I was forced to stand upright. The urine would spread over the wound and would cause fresh pain all over again. Sometimes I had to force myself not to urinate for fear of the terrible pain. I was not given any anesthetic during the operation to reduce my pain, nor any antibiotics to fight against infection. Afterward, I hemorrhaged and became anemic.

WISE WOMAN: Kodwa ngoku, apha, kuba thina saziva intlungu kulula kuwe . . . ndize apha ukuze kube lula kuwe . . . ukuhlolwa qha.

DIVINE CHILD: But here, now, because we suffered you have it easier . . . I came here so that you could have it easier . . . just testing.

> The DIVINE CHILD moves to cradle the GIRL on her lap.

GIRL: Girls who passed got white stars pasted on their foreheads and a certificate confirming their virginity.

All I wanted was a bath. I felt dirty. Not lily-white like the label on my forehead.

A label which encourages you to say look, I need to stay pure. I have not been deflowered, or something like that.

WISE WOMAN, GIRL, and DIVINE CHILD (*together*): Zizithethe zam ezi. Zizithethe zakho ezi. Izithethe zam zizithethe zakho.

This is my culture. This culture is your culture. My culture is your culture.

The GIRL gets up and approaches the WISE WOMAN.

GIRL (*echoed simultaneously by the DIVINE CHILD in the vernacular, whimpering*): What hurts me most, what I really want to do . . . the person I most want to talk to about this is you. And I can't.

The CHORUS appears suddenly, emerging only as heads through the two back doors.

CHORUS: Nesting. Digging into the unmade bed. Like a filthy little wave in and out of consciousness. Scoop and gone. Scoop and gone. Up and over the precipice and down . . . down . . . deep . . . and surface! Fright! Blink! The hand caught in the cookie jar. Not mine! How did it get in there? No. . . . not again . . . who me? Couldn't be! Then who? Number 2 stole the cookie from the cookie jar . . .

The CHORUS disappears suddenly, slamming the doors shut behind them.

GIRL: Because all good things come to an end . . . and I can still taste the chocolate chip on my palate . . .

DIVINE CHILD: Ten in the bed and the little one said roll over. Roll over. So they all rolled over and I fell out . . .

The WISE WOMAN sits again with her enamel bowl, cleaning herself and the flowers. The DIVINE CHILD stays curled up in a fetal position next to her flower pot. The WISE MAN enters with a doorframe on wheels.

WISE MAN: Which one are you now?
Rural or real?
Whose rules do you follow?

GIRL: Theirs.

WISE MAN: They both have rules.
Rural rules are real.
Urban rules are real.
Which traditions do you follow?
Which culture?
Are you real?

GIRL: That was me then.
Now . . . I am exposed. It is out in the open—wide shut. Naked . . .

When the itching comes, it always brings red swelling and a smelly discharge.

At least I can demand an extra cow for lobola.

Over the years it became easier—to switch off. The rashes remained—returned always to remind me.

Once when I went to the clinic they asked me if they could take pictures. They had never seen anything like it before. I said, "Sure, why not?" It didn't make any difference to me. They weren't going to photograph my face, after all.

The first time I found the courage to go to the clinic, it was painful. The nurses all looked so stricken and embarrassed; I could tell that they *all* wanted to see it, but they were afraid to ask because they were afraid that they would hurt my feelings.

But they wouldn't understand. Hurt. Me?

They look like me—on the outside, the surface. We are the same.

But I am not in their culture, in their reality, now.

So I cover it up. Again.

> The WISE MAN *places a door in the frame and moves it directly in front of the* GIRL.

WISE MAN: Hiding in whose culture?

Where do you fit in?

> *Echoed by* CHORUS.

GIRL (*whispers*): I don't know . . .

Door 8—Archetype of the Persona

A door slams. The GIRL *is confronted with her* PERSONA, *the mask she holds up to the world in order to protect herself from being vulnerable. One door becomes a symbol of a mirror. The* PERSONA *is revealed, represented by a white* GIRL *(Traditional/Western realities). The mirror-image game is played in silence.*

GIRL: Who . . . ?

PERSONA: I've been hibernating . . . waiting, for you.

> *A physical-movement piece is interspersed with the words.*

GIRL: What is it *you* want?

PERSONA: I want to be able to call you. I want to be able to knock on your door. I want to be able to keep your key and give you mine. I want to be seen with you in public. I want there to be no gossip. I want to know that nothing can come between us except each other.

WISE MAN: Follow it—your true self is really there. What exists and what might exist are pictured together at the core of reality. All the separations and divisions and blind alleys and impossibilities that seem so central to life are happening at its outer edges. If you could follow the map . . .

PERSONA: If I could follow the map further and if I could refuse the false endings (the false starts don't matter), I could find the place where time stops. Where death stops. Where love is. Beyond time, beyond death, love is. Time and death cannot wear it away.

    I accept you, for you.

    I love you.

GIRL: Loving you . . .

PERSONA: Loving you!

GIRL: Loving me?

PERSONA: Me, you!

GIRL: You, me?

PERSONA: Me.

GIRL: You?

WISE MAN: *Laughs.*

    The PERSONA *leaves, leaving behind the empty doorframe/"mirror."*

GIRL: Loving you . . . loving . . . *all* of me, is like lifting a heavy stone. It would be easier not to do it and I'm not quite sure why I am doing it. It takes all my strength and all my determination. Embracing all cultures in me, that make me, me. Is there any sense in loving someone you can only wake up to by chance?

    The DIVINE CHILD *runs and confronts the* GIRL *through the doorframe.*

GIRL: Will you always follow me?

DIVINE CHILD: Is life a straight line?

GIRL: Isn't there a straight answer?

DIVINE CHILD: Not in my universe.

GIRL: Which one is that?

DIVINE CHILD: The one curved by yours.

GIRL: I'm lost. I have to find me. Where am I?

    I am lost.

DIVINE CHILD (*chants, in various languages*): I am lost, I am lost. . . . Ek is verlore.

WISE MAN: She's right. I am the one who's muddling things up. How she lives is her dream.

    If I don't like it I should stay out of the way.

    If I don't like it I should say so and close the door.

Door 9—Archetypes Come Together

The GIRL *is faced with all the different parts of herself at once. Instead of facing them she runs into the "rain." The* WISE MAN *and the* DIVINE CHILD *guide her through this process and try to make her realize that she is the only one who can save herself. The* PERSONA *is also still on stage but isn't part of the rest; she becomes the authentic self, slowly taking off the white dress she is wearing and exiting, leaving the remnants of the "cocoon" behind.*

A door is brought on that is slowly dismantled (folded up) and ends up "consuming" the GIRL *She ends up standing on top of the folded door.*

GIRL: What's going on here?

All start repeating sentences from the play. They needn't repeat their own sentences, as all represent the GIRL. *Their dialogue has to build to a climax by the time she speaks again.*

TRICKSTER: Secret sits in the middle and knows.

DIVINE CHILD: The clock ticks, but only in time.

SHADOW: Poor little princess, stuck in a rut.

ANIMUS: Tonight we go deeper than most disguises.

ENTOURAGE: We're tailing one another.

WISE MAN: Moving forward, standing still.

DIVINE CHILD: Always you, always me, always this story.

PERSONA: You let me inside you.

ENTOURAGE: You're playing solitaire.

WISE MAN: You forget to be here!

ANIMUS: The beautiful half of golden hurt.

SHADOW: Condemned to be free.

ANIMA: I am the map that you redraw.

TRICKSTER: In silence and in tears.

The TRICKSTER*'s cloth body gets attached to the* GIRL, *so wherever she is, this shadow is following her.*

ENTOURAGE: None so blind as those who won't see.

DIVINE CHILD: Only you can save you!

The DIVINE CHILD *hands the* GIRL *an umbrella without any covering (just the silver spokes, the frame). The* WISE WOMAN *moves with her bowl to sit next to the* GIRL *on the shadow cloth, which has been dropped next to the folded door.*

The WISE MAN *uses the watering can and showers the* GIRL *with water, eventually drenching her in the cleansing rain.*

GIRL: Where do I take this pain of mine?

I run but it stays right on my inside.

So tear me open, pour me out!

There are things inside that scream and shout!

And the pain still hates me . . .

So hold me until it sleeps.

TRICKSTER: Just like the curse, just like the strain.

SHADOW: You feed it once and now it stays.

GIRL: So tear me open! But beware; there are things inside without a care!

And the dirt stains me! So wash me until I'm clean!

ALL: It grips you . . .
GIRL: So hold me!
ALL: It stains you . . .
GIRL: So hold me!
ALL: It holds you . . .
GIRL: So hold me . . . until it sleeps.

> *Long silence. Nothing happens, no one moves, all watch her intently.*
> *She screams again.*

So tell me why you've chosen me! I don't want your grip, don't want this need! Why?
WISE MAN: I want to be able to call you. I want to be able to knock on your door. I want to be able to keep your key and give you mine.
DIVINE CHILD: You don't have to be scared anymore.
WISE MAN: Your true self is really here. What exists and what might exist are pictured together at the core of reality. Follow the map.

> *The* WISE WOMAN *starts to wash the* GIRL'*s feet.*

WISE WOMAN: If you could follow the map further and if you could refuse the false endings (the false starts don't matter), you will find the place where time stops. Where love is.

I forgive you.
I forgive me.
I love you.
GIRL (*exhausted*): Loving you . . .
ALL: Loving *you!*

> ALL *echo as they disperse, leaving just her.*

GIRL: Loving me?
ALL: Me, you!
GIRL: You, me!
ALL: Me.
GIRL: You?

> *End.*

The Struggle to End
the Practice of
Female Genital Mutilation

Nawal El Saadawi

Changing a Social System into a Divine Law

Female and male genital mutilation (FGM and MGM) are not characteristic of any society or any religion, or any country, or race or color, or ethnic group. Like the oppression of women and poor classes, they constitute an integral part of the political, economic, social, cultural, and religious systems preponderant in most of the world—west and east, north and south, Jewish, Christian, Islamic, Hindu, and others. FGM and MGM were born of developments in history that led one class to rule over another and men to dominate women in the state and in the family unit, which together constitute the core of the patriarchal class relations.

But there are still many writers who close their eyes to these historical facts, for political, economic, and colonial reasons. They depict FGM and MGM as stemming from Islam, or they reduce these crimes against women and men to religious, cultural, and identity factors. For these thinkers, there is no link between sexual and class oppression; there is no link between global politics, national politics, and family politics; there is no link between the American military invasion of Iraq and oil domination and exploitation; there is no link between money and sex, no link between the material and spiritual, or between the body, the mind, and the spirit.

These dichotomies are still prevalent today and are inherited from the slave system that arose some thousands of years ago; they serve to veil the mind and to deceive women and men by hiding material-physical exploitation under a false spiritual-religious happiness or by changing the social system (made by ruling classes) into a divine law.

We need to study history and the three monotheistic divine books to understand why FGM and MGM arose in history. It is important to know that FGM is not mentioned in any of these books. MGM is mentioned in the Old Testament, but there is nothing about MGM in the Koran or New Testament.

In the Old Testament there is the following verse:

الإصحاح 17 (تكوين) يعقد الإله مع النبي ابراهيم عهدا يقول فيه ، أقيم عهدى بينى وبين نسلك من بعدك ... عهدا أبديا ... أعطى لك ولنسلك من بعدك أرض غربتك كل أرض كنعان ملكا أبديا ... هذا هو عهدى الذى تحفظوه بينى وبينكم ... يختن منكم كل ذكر ... فتختنون فى لحم غرلتكم ، فيكون علامة عهد بينى وبينكم ... فيكون عهدى فى لحمكم أبديا ... وأما الذكر الغلف الذى لا يختن فى لحم غرلته فتقطع تلك النفس من شعبها ، إنه نكث عهدى." (Genesis 17:8–14)

17:8: And I will give unto thee, and to thy seed after thee, the land wherein thou art a stranger, all the land of Canaan, for an everlasting possession, and I will be their God.

17:10: This is my covenant, which ye shall keep, between me and you and thy seed after thee, every man child among you shall be circumcised.

17:13: He that is born in thy house, and he that is bought with thy money, must needs be circumcised, and my covenant shall be in your flesh for an everlasting covenant.

17:14: And the uncircumcised man child whose flesh of his foreskin is not circumcised, that soul shall be cut off from his people, he hath broken my covenant.

As a medical doctor, I have known the physical, mental, and social problems of both MGM and FGM. It is common sense that a child (male or female) should not be cut into by knife under any religious or cultural or identity slogans. Never in my life did I perform such an operation on a female or male child. I feel it is a crime against a newborn child.

FGM: This crime was done to me when I was six years old. I wrote about it in my book *The Naked Face of Women* (1972), which was published in English in 1980 under the title *The Hidden Face of Eve*. The publisher changed the English title; I do not know why, maybe to link it somehow with veiling of women, or with Islam, though I never linked FGM to Islam or any religion or culture.

FGM is inherited from the slave system, or the class patriarchal system. It is part of the patriarchal package that includes: (1) cutting the sexual organs of female children, especially the clitoris, to guarantee their virginity before marriage and their fidelity after marriage; (2) veiling of women, isolating them at home under the authority of their men, and forcing them to work (at home or outside home) with no payment to guarantee their economic dependence on their men, and therefore their submission to any type of oppression; (3) severe punishment of women who do not obey their men; obedience to the father and husband is inseparable from obedience to God—a woman who betrays her husband is punished by death, but a man has the right to betray his wife, since God gave him the right to divorce and to practice polygamy; and (4) enforcement of virginity and monogamy by physical, mental, religious, moral, social, legal, political, and economic means, so that the paternity of their children is certain.

FGM is one of the means used to diminish women's sexual ability and social mobility, so that her husband will be sure of his fatherhood, sure that his children are his and sure that his children will inherit his land and money and carry his patriarchal name. Patriarchy is based on the name of the father.

From my experience as a medical doctor and a psychiatrist, I learned that FGM has nothing to do with the morality of women; it does not make them more monogamous or more faithful to their husbands. On the contrary, cutting the clitoris increases women's sexual desires, for two reasons: (1) because the brain is the main site of sexual desire and (2) because circumcised women have difficulty reaching sexual satisfaction with their husbands, they look for this satisfaction outside marriage.

It is my contention that freedom and responsibility toward the self and others should not be separable. Free uncircumcised women can be more responsible toward their families if they combine freedom with responsibility. Circumcised women can be less responsible if they are oppressed or veiled (physically or mentally). Veiling of the mind is inseparable from veiling of the body, since the body and the mind are inseparable.

In Egypt some religious Islamic scholars believe that FGM is a divine order, or at least a Sunni order according to Hadith by Prophet Mohammed, but other Islamic scholars believe that FGM and the veil have nothing to do with Islam. In much of the Muslim world, veiling of women has become a divine code. If you criticize the veil in Egypt today, you expose yourself to danger and censure.

Some people think that FGM is an ancient Arab, Egyptian, or African tradition, but FGM is a universal slave tradition and is not related to a particular race, color, country, or continent. FGM is unknown in most Islamic and Arab countries, such as Syria, Iraq, Lebanon, Tunisia, Algeria, Libya, Morocco, Saudi

Arabia, and others. Among the Arab-influenced African countries, only Egypt, Sudan, Somalia, Mali, Senegal, and Yemen practice FGM.

FGM Projects in Egypt

When I spoke and wrote against FGM in Egypt half a century ago, I was accused of ignorance by my colleagues in the medical profession. At that time, FGM and MGM were performed on all children in Egypt regardless of their religious background. In 1972 I lost my post in the Ministry of Health, the magazine *Health* was closed down, and my book *Women and Sex* was banned.

However, with the increasing awareness of the dangers of FGM, things have changed. Since 2001 the Egyptian government has been carrying out a national project to fight against FGM in sixty villages in Upper Egypt, with the aid of twelve local NGOs, the United Nations Development Program, and other international funds supported by Germany, Canada, Denmark, Finland, Italy, Holland, Switzerland, and the United States. The project consists of a series of training and follow-up workshops at the regional and local levels to coordinate and network FGM initiatives and create a wider platform for political support. There is a lot of government propaganda about the project, but as with all other government projects, it has a very limited impact on people, especially on the majority of men and women who live in poverty and ignorance and who are brainwashed almost every day by religious political groups.

The veiling of women and FGM are connected, and they have been on the rise in Egypt during the last three decades, with FGM performed on approximately 97 percent of the female population in Egypt. There is no law in Egypt that condemns FGM and considers it a crime. There is only a decree issued by the Ministry of Health, but it does not have the power of law.

FGM has been a deep-rooted custom ever since the slave-based patriarchal system. To eradicate it, there must be combined efforts to mobilize men, women, youth, and children so that they become organized and constitute a political and social power capable of changing the existing patriarchal values and laws. This mobilization needs real democracy. It needs freedom to organize and criticize. It needs a collective struggle against state dictatorship, against family dictatorship, and against false consciousness created by governmental media and the educational system. If the state itself is based on patriarchy, class, and religion, how can it fight against FGM (or MGM) which is a product of patriarchy, class and religion?

History of the Struggle to End FGM

Half a century ago, most religious men and medical doctors in Egypt condemned contraceptive pills and abortion. They defended FGM and MGM.

Today in Egypt, FGM is condemned by the government and by NGOs as well as by many doctors and religious men and women. But MGM is not condemned. When I wrote to the Minister of Health in 1999 about the dangers of MGM, I was attacked by government people and by most medical doctors and religious men and women (both Muslims and Christian Copts).

Inhumane religious and cultural practices such as FGM and MGM disappear with increasing awareness and health knowledge. But they are rekindled with the revival of reactionary religious-political movements.

Traditionally, the practice of veiling women was limited in Europe to conservative Jewish and Islamic groups. Today it is increasingly common among Islamic migrant communities in Holland, France, the UK, Belgium, and other countries in Europe. Sometimes it is accompanied by FGM. Both veiling and FGM are considered by the political and religious leaders of these communities as a necessary part of the Islamic identity, under the guise of so-called cultural relativism. It is part of the deception and brainwashing of women and poor men. It is happening in Egypt and many other countries.

The deception of cultural relativism has been going on for at least three decades. Deception is a form of violence against the mind; mutilation of the mind is no less a crime than FGM or MGM, and it is even more dangerous. It is used to mutilate the body and the soul, to justify violence against women and the poor. In some regressive opinions, women's rights are considered a direct attack against God's law, moral values, and sacred tradition.

Traditions (sacred or not) reflect systems of power in the state and in the family. They change with time and place. They are not fixed or immutable or eternal. They are selectively picked up by political groups to preserve the patriarchal capitalist structures globally and locally.

Global and Local Struggles against FGM Must Continue

When women fight for their human rights under any patriarchal system, they are labeled traitors to their religion, their country, their culture, their authentic identity, their morality, their chastity, etc. But we have to go on fighting: we cannot be intimidated; we must organize globally and locally.

There are about 150 million women worldwide who have undergone FGM. It is part of the violence against women by global, national, and family politics.

International and national politics should treat women's rights globally and locally in an equal manner, regardless of different cultural and religious beliefs.

We should reject the medicalization of FGM. It is a crime and should not be done either by safe or unsafe methods, in a mild form or in a semi-mild form. Cutting any part of the female or male child is a crime (unless there is a disease and the operation is a method of medical treatment).

Global struggle is the only path to a solution. Freedom has a high price, but the price of slavery is greater, so it is better to pay the price and be free than to pay anyway and be a slave.

Slow Poison

Makuchi

Manoji was lying on the bamboo bed his mother had placed in the parlor, positioned in a strategic corner where he could see the sunlight, if and when he was able to turn his head to face the *nsaa*. Yes, the nsaa, the sun; the two who now watched obsessively over him ever since the people stopped coming, ever since the relatives fled. Manoji painstakingly turned his head, each movement an effort that could kill him. His neck was rigid, the bones on his back creaked, his arms refused to follow directions meted out by an equally numb mind. The bones on his feet seemed to crackle, his knees knocked against each other, and he let out a quiet moan. He thought it might take him an entire day to turn his head; at least he hoped it was daylight. He had long ago lost the ability to stay in focus, to synchronize his being with trivial things like day or night. But he had to see the sun, that much he was certain of. He wanted to stare at the golden streaks slashing through the foliage of huge trees, burning through the eyelids of children who mocked its power, defied its scorching manhood, and played to the tunes of juvenile dreams. He wanted to feel those dreams again and again. . . . He wanted to see the sun, no, he wanted to feel the rays burn through his brown (or was it rosy-pink?) parched skin. He wanted to feel the sun on his estranged epidermis, toasting his emaciated, lifeless body and to taste the stench of burning fat in his mouth, in his nostrils, in his belly. He turned. One more inch, he told himself. He knew that inch would cost him. He shut his eyes, and just as he was about to make the move, called one memory to his rescue. Each memory lent him the support he needed to move his head an inch. Remembering took over, fighting the aches in his head, in his neck, in his body, with the fierceness of a hen protecting her young ones from the penetrating gaze of a very patient but hungry hawk. Remembering numbed the pain, and inch by inch, Manoji's face came into full view of the sun.

He gazes at the sun, his eyes wide open, blinking with the curiosity of a new-born discovering and pondering the world of humans. He suddenly feels an urge to stand, to lift his body, to stand up and walk; no, to float toward the sun. The hunger of a curious child who will not be daunted by vain threats is burning in him, through him. He has to stand up. He has to. He speaks to his legs. "Have I ever eaten and not shared with you?" he asks them. "Never," they reply. He doesn't know why but his legs actually move. He is pulling his knees up and they are saying, yes, go ahead, let's hit the floor, let's stand. He is dreaming, yes, but a good dream. He can feel his body swinging precariously upright. He is nauseated and has to place his bony hands on his knees to steel himself. Every effort, every single effort costs him. A lot. But he refuses to be paralyzed by the fear that threatens to glue his body to his bed. He has to fight the invisible paws that are forcing him to the ground. He lifts his hands from his knees and places them on the bamboo bed. He can feel the softness of the foam mattress his mother bought for him, the one she spent her savings on to give his bones some temporary relief. Most times, he doesn't notice the mattress is there. But sometimes he is grateful for her sacrifice. He moves his fingers and clutches its softness. His fingers say they are alive. He thinks he is alive. He awakens to being alive and smiles, in spite of himself. The mattress smells so much of death, how could he be alive?

He raises his head, holds firmly onto the exposed bamboo, and concentrates on the brightness advancing through the open door, almost sucking him into its vortex. He grinds his teeth, lifts his torso, and he is in the air. He can feel his feet on the floor. The house is quiet and he can hear the silence buzzing through his head. He begins to feel dizzy but knows he cannot afford to give in to the spasm moving like a wave through his bowels. And so he fixes his gaze on the receding shadow of the door and stares. He concentrates on the rays of the sun and stares. He moves toward them, gliding through space. He feels he is falling. He thinks he is falling and desperately grabs at anything he can touch. His hands can feel the firmness of wood. He clings to it, braces himself, and opens his eyes. He recognizes the door frame. He runs his fingers, a few inches, up and down the mahogany as if scratching a lover's back. He desires its firmness. He longs for its ageless demeanor of defiance. He is about to take a step forward when something catches his eyes. The image is bleary. He has to still himself and focus. An image is reflected back at him. It seems to be projected from within the far reaches of the closet, of the mirror hanging on the brick wall. He stills himself and waits. The image is moving closer, zooming in. He is struck dumb, startled by the old man staring back blankly at him. The face looks curiously familiar. It displays marks and features peculiar to his family. The prominent forehead, like his uncle's; the prominent, high cheek bones, like his mother's; the full head of kinky hair, the protruding, stubborn chin, like his father's. But the eyes, the haunting, scared eyes of a caged animal, whose eyes are these? Eyes like those of an owl. Eyes that look too big for his face; eyes that seem to be popping out of their sockets; eyes whose whiteness is frightening, a whiteness that seems to spread, overpowering the blackness of the face, highlighting two deep, dark pupils, spinning like a whirlpool at the bottom of a well. Manoji cannot place these eyes. He cannot place this bony face. He makes a supreme effort to lift his hands and feel the bones sticking through the cheeks. What is left of them. But the hands divert his attention from the face. The thin, long fingers with their overgrown nails look like claws. They are skeletal and remind him of the hands of the scarecrows he used to make with his father when he was a young boy and proudly display on his mother's farms. He tries to imitate the movement of the scarecrow's hands, agitating, stirring excitedly with the force of the wind, but the hands remain hanging in midair. They are refusing to follow his command. He cannot bear to look at those fingers. His hands slowly drop by his side. He can hear his clavicles creak. His gaze follows the clavicles down his bare torso. Manoji stares at his scrawny, wasted body. The brownness of his skin seems to have been bleached away, leaving behind an almost transparent pinkish surface. The dermis is disrobed, ugly in its nakedness. He traces the long lines carefully designed and left bare by exposed ribs. They are nothing like the tiger's, nothing like the zebra's. He can see the thin layer of flesh clinging desperately to the bones as he struggles to breathe in and out. Caught between the hollow lines are spots, huge dark spots. They are nothing like the leopard's. Some of the spots look like scars that leave an imprint on the skin after a bout of yaws. They are competing with shingles and scabies for space. He is thankful for the hard, dark crusts of the shingles that taunt him with a semblance of blackness. He knows these spots are bearing witness to the slow poison that has slowly but tenaciously been devouring his body, eating away his life. He has become a bag of bones. He has become a scarecrow. He fidgets with the wrappa wrapped around his waist. What is left of it. The wrappa falls to the ground. He doesn't hear a sound. He looks with bitterness at the two straight sticks that used to be thighs; he wants to knock on the protruding, round knees. He tries to make a fist but his fingers will not indulge him. He suddenly realizes he has missed something. He can't tell what it is. He has to think. What am I forgetting? he is desperately asking himself. He needs a memory, right now. He needs a memory to ignite his brain again. He is feeling dizzy. He wants to throw up, but there is nothing to throw up. He clutches the firmness of the mahogany, stills himself, and the old man in the mirror comes back in focus. The man is missing something, something between his bony thighs. Where is his manhood? What is this shriveled up, almost unnoticeable appendage, clinging ferociously to the pubis? Or what is left of it? It looks almost like a stamp affixed on an envelope. Manoji is feeling dizzy; he is choking; he is coughing; he cannot hold his sides, he cannot hold onto the mahogany. Its firmness is letting him go. He feels his hands gliding off the wood. He is falling. Falling. Floating backward to the ground. He feels as light as a wisp of smoke. He wants to see the sun. He wants to wrap his body in the folds of its golden warmth. He wants to remain suspended in its splendor. But he is falling. Falling. The last thing he glimpses in the mirror is the familiar face of his mother. She is standing, silently, right behind him. Their eyes meet. He can feel the heat. The sun is right there with him. He can feel its warmth enveloping his body, seeping through his bag of bones, melting the marrow, taking over his memories. He knows they will be kept in a safe place for him. He lets himself fall. Her arms are open. He is grateful he is falling into her waiting arms.

Manoji died the way he had lived: in the arms of a woman. At least that was the one thing, the one ounce of consolation he grasped firmly in the palms of his bony hands, in the wiry folds of his shriveled-up heart, when his spirit quietly and calmly abandoned his body, or what was left of it. My son passed away in my arms. I was sitting on the floor, holding him firmly to my chest, oblivious to the silence, the loneliness, the abandon that was threatening to sweep me away. I sat there, the hard floor beneath me, the only thing that reminded me I was still alive. Even as I held my son's lifeless body, I adamantly refused to accept his death. He is still alive, I kept saying to myself. It's not possible. He can't be gone, I kept consoling myself. But then, his usual paper-weight body began slowly and slowly to weigh down on me like a basin of water. I began to wonder how this had all happened. How had this little baby I carried just a few months ago on my back as I cleaned the house, as I cooked food, as I worked on the farm, as I went to the market, how had this baby come to this? When did this all begin? When? How had this happened to us? To our lives? I couldn't think straight. I knew I needed his memories. I needed to rememory his life in order to do the right thing for my son, in order to set him free. There was no time for tears. There was no place for tears. I held him firmly to my chest and his memories took over. I needed them to consume me the way they had consumed his body.

A few years ago, Manoji started going out with young women unusually bigger than the ones I had always seen him with. It isn't that he hadn't had big women friends before. This time was different. He stuck to big women only. I pointed this new preference out to him. "My son, why are you going out with all these fat women? What is wrong with you? Is this the new craze?" I asked him. "Hmmm," Manoji smiled and reminded me that the women were just "bigger." They are true African women, he enthused. True African women with flesh on their bones, he parroted. But I was not to be fooled and I kept on teasing him. One day, as he was about to walk away after one such conversation (I called them conversations; he called them unnecessary snooping on my part), he changed his mind and walked back into my house. He pulled up a chair, sat down by the fire, put those long hands calmly on his knees, and asked me an embarrassing question.

"Mother," he said.

"Yes, my son. What is it?"

"Have you heard about this thing they call AIDS?"

"What's that my son?"

"Come, mother, you know what it is. Stop pretending not to know."

"No, I don't know what it is. What is it?"

"Mother, you know it's an illness."

"An illness. What kind of illness?"

"Mother, you know what illness it is. You know it is that terrible disease people call 'slow poison.'"

"Slow poison? Are you talking to me about those lies your people from the Ministry of Health are spreading around the country?"

"Mother, they're not lies. You heard what that doctor said the other day at the community meeting."

"I know what he was saying. He was talking about a disease that eats people away, slowly, as if they had taken slow poison. But my son, only people struck with witchcraft can suffer such a disease. This is not something the white people and those strangers from the Ministry of Health should come here and talk to us about. What do they know about our witchcraft? What do they know about esotericism? Nothing. Absolutely nothing. I tell you they know nothing about our abilities to manipulate the natural and the supernatural, how can they know about slow poison? . . ."

"But mother, this is serious. . . ."

"Say what you want, my son, but let me tell you something. If those liars keep on coming here and talking about this so-called new disease that kills people slowly like the slow poison we cast on our enemies, then they will all suffer the same fate. . . ."

"But mother, they say this slow poison is different from our own. It is different because you get it by having sexual relations with a man or a woman who already has the poison in them."

"So, why sleep with a woman who has been poisoned, my son?"

"You don't know she is."

"Impossible. How can you not know when a woman has been poisoned. If you can't, then you are not my son. . . ."

"That's why my women are all plump. . . . They have good blood, unlike thin women. You can't be sure of their blood."

I knew what my son meant when he talked about bad blood. It had to do with our neighbor, a father who for three years had consistently given blood for his sickle-cell anemic child. But things never used to be like that. Over the years, his eight-year-old son had been given blood by almost every relative or friend living in this neighborhood. Previously, when the child got ill, three, four, or five of us would go to the blood bank with the father and they would systematically collect our blood, test it, and then give the right blood to the child. And then things changed. They claimed the government had run out of money. That testing blood from many people had become too expensive. They even started charging five thousand francs for each blood bag. If you have four people with you, that means twenty thousand. Imagine that. Who can afford that? People couldn't afford to give blood anymore. So now they pretest a sample and only collect the blood if the donor's blood is the right one. That's how our neighbor ended up as sole donor for his son. He gave his blood, gave his blood, gave his blood, and then one day the doctor said his blood was bad and could not be given to his son.

"How is that possible?" he asked the doctor.

"Your blood isn't good anymore," the doctor said.

"What do you mean, anymore? . . . I have been giving blood for three years and suddenly my blood isn't good? How? Has my blood group changed?"

"No, your blood group is still the same. But your blood now has a disease. Have you heard about AIDS? Your blood is HIV-positive. That means your blood has a disease and I cannot give your blood . . . I cannot give the disease in your blood to your child . . ."

"I do not understand. . . . I don't understand. . . ."

"I understand . . ."

"No, doctor, you don't understand. You know my son has sickle-cell anemia. . . . He needs my blood or he'll die. . . . Who's going to give my child blood? Who? . . . And now you're telling me I must stop. You're telling me I'm going to kill my child. You're telling me I am going to die. You're sitting here and issuing death warrants . . ."

"Well, it is not that simple. True-true, you are HIV-positive. But it might take a while before the real illness . . . AIDS—you get from this bad blood—manifests itself. Having HIV is not the end of your life . . ."

"How long?"

"It could be a few months, it could be years. . . . You see, this disease works like slow poison . . ."

"So it watches from the shadows of the bushes as its messengers eat you up, step by step, is that it?"

"Yes, something like that. When the time comes, you might begin to cough a lot. You might have big craw-craw all over your body. You will have diarrhea. You will pass a lot of water and fluids from your body. Then your body will begin to waste away because it is losing so much water, because of the slow poison in your body."

Our neighbor broke down in the doctor's office and cried and cried and cried. He came to the complete realization of the magnitude of this illness when the doctor referred him to the Presbyterian Mission Hospital. The doctor asked him to come and see Dr. Peter here at your mission hospital. Our neighbor was devastated. He came home a broken man. We couldn't believe it when we heard the news. How does a father deal with such news? It's always easier to deal with this illness when you don't know the person. You hear someone has this disease and you say, "oh!" or "sorry ooh" or "na which kana baluck dis now?" and that's it. There is a safe distance between you and that person. You express your sorrow because that's the right thing to do and life goes on. But when you know someone, like we knew our neighbor, someone for whose child we had all, at one time or another, given blood . . . when you know someone that intimately, and you hear they have AIDS, you are totally in shock. Shock. Pure and simple. You feel as if someone has divulged a terrible secret that should have remained sealed. You can't bear the weight of the bad news you are now carrying. You know they've been sentenced to death. You know they cannot reverse the verdict. You are conscious of their certain death. You withdraw your tears. Your tears desert you. Your tear glands dry up like the Sahara. You deny the illness, you banish it from your mind, but it won't leave. You begin to have nightmares about it. You get angry. You want to scream, you want to cry, but you can't. You think about the meaning of the illness, the ramifications: is his wife infected? What will happen to the children? You begin to think of them as orphans—and that, while their father is still alive. But then, that is nothing when you haven't come face to face with the person. It is worse when you come face-to-face with someone you know, someone you love who has AIDS. When I met my neighbor for the first time after that fateful trip to the hospital, I didn't even have the courage to extend my hand. . . . I . . . I . . . I couldn't extend my hand. What's a greeting? Something we offer freely, every day, to everybody—friends, family, and enemies alike. But there I was, standing in front of Pa

Ambrose, and I couldn't offer my hand. I found it difficult to extend my hand. It seemed to weigh ten tons. It couldn't move. Later, only later, did I realize that I had unconsciously moved my hands toward my back. I had pretended to scratch my back. I had fidgeted with the ends of my wrappa and had pretended to wrap it more firmly round my waist. I had done everything so as not to offer my hand. I had even looked at the floor, searching my toes for *jiggas* that were not there. I couldn't look him straight in the eyes. This man, with whom I had joked and laughed so often in the past . . . this man, whose children have sat down and eaten food with me in my house . . . who call me mother. Our conversation was monosyllabic, monotonous: Hello. Hello. Morning. Morning. Bright day. Yes. Are these your eyes? Yes. Yours? Yes. How are you? Fine. How have you been? Sick. Your son? Fine. You see what I mean? A stupid conversation like that. Taking us nowhere. Although I was on my way to the market, I turned around and went back home. I remember thinking to myself on the way home: at least the child is safe, for now. Ambrose should count himself lucky. He will not be branded a wizard for eating his own son. What about mothers who kill the babies in their wombs with this disease without knowing it? Tegheh kwu! Ambrose is lucky indeed. He will be fine, I kept saying to myself. I didn't eat all day. I was so disgusted with myself. I was overwhelmed with sadness. I had never known such sadness. I had never known the day would come when I couldn't bring myself to greet my own neighbor, my own friend, my own blood. How do things like these happen? How?

It was about then that my son became the "fat virgin" man. Virgins and fat women seem to be in demand these days! Apparently, fat women do not have AIDS, or so Manoji claimed. He said fat women were less likely to have slow poison. I know our culture has always placed value on the shine of a woman's skin, on the plumpness of her curves, and especially on what these curves say about her husband's ability to take care of her, but this new craze about fat women and no AIDS was simply beyond me. Who can blame him or all the men who began to think like him? When people have AIDS, they shrink away so fast you can't even recognize someone you knew. They might have to call out to you and say, it's me, so-and-so. Manoji was certain he had found the way to conquer this new ulcer that was quietly eating through the nervous system of our people. Then the time came and that fateful day came knocking on our door. My sister got ill and was wilting like a leaf in the sun, before our eyes. I didn't believe the diviner who said her ex-husband was bewitching her. So I took her to the hospital to get her checked for worms. I knew it had to be worms or something easy to treat. They tested for worms. They said she had worms. But they also said she was anemic. They said she needed a blood transfusion, and only after that could she go home and pursue her treatment by eating a lot of vegetables and liver. Manoji offered to give his aunt the blood she needed. But first they had to pretest his blood. And the nurse said she had to tell us first why they had to test it.

"So you were given some pretest counseling by the hospital staff? That's good."

"Yes, even though I didn't see any need for the lecture."

Anyway, that woman reminded me that we should be grateful someone was taking the time to talk to us before taking our blood. She made it clear that pretest counseling for HIV wasn't done systematically in most hospitals. She told us that doctors had difficulty explaining to people why the blood they were giving for relatives and friends had to be tested for AIDS. They had problems with donors who would refuse to give their blood for such a test or who would refuse to see or accept the results. She was relieved that wasn't the case with us. Manoji was prepared to do anything for his aunt, so he gave a blood sample and we waited. Waiting for the results was excruciating. Those six minutes we spent waiting for the rapid test are the longest six minutes I have ever spent in my entire life. Manoji, especially, made it feel like a lifetime. He paced up and down the hospital corridor. He bit on his nails. He stuck and removed his hands from his pockets more times than I could count. He was a nervous wreck. Anxiety was drumming tunes all over his face. The look in his eyes kept saying, What if? . . . What if I am? . . . What if I am HIV-positive?" My worried look reflected back the same at him. What if the result is positive? we kept asking ourselves. The question kept pounding through my head. The feeling was oppressive, overwhelming. The waiting was killing me. My palms were sweaty, my skin was aching. My blood pressure kept rising. My heart would not stop pounding. We were so nervous I wanted to open my mouth and scream, but my throat was completely dry. The wetness in my mouth seemed to have evaporated into thin air. Minutes felt like hours. You try to relax but you can't. You try to relax, you close your eyes but your eyelids are heavy and feel like rocks. Manoji paced up and down. Six minutes felt like six hours. Manoji paced up and down. Manoji bit on his nails. Six hours felt like six days. Manoji paced up and down. Manoji repeatedly stuck his hands in and out of his pockets. Six days felt like six years. . . .

"Please sit down," the nurse said softly, almost too kindly. "I am sorry I have bad news. . . ."

"   "
. . .

"I am sorry to tell you that we cannot take your blood. . . ."

"   "
. . .

"Mr. Manoji . . . you are HIV-positive, so we cannot collect your blood. . . . We cannot give your blood to your aunt. . . ."

"   "
. . .

"Please do not take this the wrong way. Being HIV-positive isn't the end of one's life as most people think. . . ."

"   "
. . .

"I understand how difficult this is, but . . . It's okay, Mami. Hold him. Let him cry. . . . It's all right."

"Sister, so what do we do now?" I heard a voice that sounded like mine ask the nurse.

Manoji's head was resting on my lap, his entire body convulsing as if fighting a bout of malaria fever, his hot tears leaving wet patches on my wrappa. I placed my hands on his shoulders, bent down, and rested my face on the back of his head. Our hearts were breaking like the sea waves that drenched our faces. After what seemed like an eternity, I felt the nurse's hand on my cheek, wiping away the tears.

"Mami Manoji, I am truly sorry . . . but I have to ask you . . . would you like me to test your blood . . . ?"

" . . . "

"Is it possible to ask someone else . . . another family member to give blood . . . ?"

I have to tell you that in all this tragedy, what hurts most is what happens to families when a family member is HIV-positive or has AIDS—the breakdown of the family as we know it. I didn't mind the furtive looks, the whispering, the gossip, when it came from strangers; after all they didn't know me. They didn't know my son personally. I came to a point where I cared even less when people withdrew their hands in midair of a greeting or stepped back when it dawned on them my son had AIDS. I was only his caretaker. . . . Why wouldn't they shake my hand? Why wouldn't they hug me? They withdrew their hands, their smiles, their words, as if I were the plague. I erected a wall in my heart and shut out their callousness as we navigated from one clinic to the next and between hospitals. I forgave them their ignorance. But how could I forgive my own family for slandering and deserting me and my son? They called my son a womanizer who had inherited his philandering ways from his mother. My son, a philanderer and I a prostitute! Imagine that. They all fled. The cowards. They deserted me. They were scared of me, as if I were a witch . . . as if I would curse them with slow poison and watch them die faster than my son. The cowards! They watched me from the bushes, as I shouldered his illness and his ailments; they watched as I cooked his food, cleaned his wounds, cleaned his body, removed the feces from incessant diarrheal bouts that threatened every day to kill him. I watched my son hurt as he coughed. I watched my son hurt as he drank water. I watched my son hurt as fluids drained out of his body like water disappearing in the sand. I watched my son waste away on the bed as friends and relatives stood safely in my nsaa and talked to me through the open door.

"Take him to the native doctor," they'd say. "I know so-and-so. I hear he cures people who have slow poison in their blood. Take your son to him. He has a good reputation. He is the best in the land. Take your son to him. He will cure your son. . . ."

The hospitals had said over and over that there was no cure for AIDS and I had believed them but when you have gone through what I have gone through, you begin to believe that they must be lying. You begin to say to yourself that there must be a treatment for the white man's slow poison just as there is a treatment for our slow poison. At least with our slow poison, all you need is to know who cursed you in the first place, and that person can be persuaded to lift the curse and let you live. In the case of the white man's slow poison, you don't know who poisoned your blood, so how can your blood be treated? Some people even warned me that my son did not have the white man's slow poison but had been bewitched by one of my own relatives—my paternal granduncle, to be exact. Traditional medicine was the only cure my son needed, they insisted. Why was I wasting my time with white man medicine, they queried. I wanted the death of my son, they accused. Those frightened dogs, with their tails tucked between their legs, accused me of eating my own son! And without realizing it, I was moving my son from one medicine man's compound to another.

"Did the native doctors help?"

"No."

"So you decided to come back home?"

"Yes. I came back because I couldn't afford it anymore. They had taken all I have: the liters of palm oil, the bundles of salt, the goats, the fowls, the money—those vultures! And they were killing my son with all sorts of concoctions that made him weaker day by day instead of purging and cleansing him of the poison, as they claimed. I had to come back. I came back because I wanted my son to die at home. To die at home with dignity. To die at home among his people, his ancestors. His people might have forsaken him but his ancestors would not. Never."

"I hear you."

"But I also came back home because I heard of your services. I heard about the charity work that the Presbyterian Mission was doing around the village for people who are dying from slow poison like my son. Sister, it is a great thing that your mission, your people, are doing for us. It is a shame that your mission charity has taken on the responsibility of our government and our own families. Help, concern, kindness are things we do and offer each other because we're family. Now, other people . . . total strangers, have replaced our family. . . . It is a terrible thing that is happening to us. This monster is threatening the very foundation on which our family institution is built. What are we going to do? What are we going to do . . . ?"

"Oh, Mami Manoji, I didn't know you still had tears in your eyes. . . . Here, let me dry your face. . . . You look like a little girl who is getting married when you cry like that. . . ."

"Sister, you know I lost the desire to laugh. Why are you making me laugh? . . . I tell you, family is dead. Family isn't what it used to be. Not when it comes to AIDS. No, not when it comes to AIDS."

" . . ."

"Can I ask you something, Sister?"

"Weh, Mami Manoji, you know you can ask me anything."

"Why does your hospital not keep people there, I mean, in the hospital itself?"

"It wasn't always like this. We used to hospitalize our AIDS patients. But as you know, ours is a small hospital and we do not have as many beds as we would like to. Our AIDS patients used to take up beds . . ."

"So? I thought those beds are meant for patients."

"Yes, but they were taking up beds for months. Some, for long, long periods of time—years. And besides, they were . . ."

"Certain to die anyway . . ."

"Yes. We had to face the fact that they were all going to die, and so instead of keeping the patients in the hospital, we decided to send them home. We created the association of nurses who would run an outreach program so that we could visit them weekly and provide them with care at home. Even though the hospital funds the outreach program, the program actually cuts costs. . . ."

"Sister, I have to thank all of you. Every day, I invoke the gods to come to our aid. I pray to the ancestors each night before I go to bed, that they bless us with more programs like yours. Your outreach program has done more for me than my own government, than my own family. Manoji and I both looked forward to the weekly visits your AIDS teams paid us. Your visits put a rare ray of hope and anticipation into our lives. We couldn't have survived without the drugs you provided weekly for his diarrhea, the vitamins, the pain killers . . . We couldn't have survived it without the weekly counseling, the attention, the encouragement, the strength you gave us to move forward. Your visits were a morale booster that helped my son more than anything else. Those visits helped a mother deal with her grief. They helped my son and I watch him pass away in dignity. Sister, you should have seen him. When the time came, he wasn't afraid to go. He made peace with himself. He said good-bye in my arms. . . . My son died. My son is dead, and still, I have to carry the stigma of what killed him like a badge. AIDS has claimed my son. AIDS has branded and banished me from my people. Do you know some fled before his body was even in the ground? They were disrespectful of their own blood. Fewer people attended and participated in the death celebrations. Death—life—we all celebrate; an event we all flock to, to cry, laugh, sing, dance, eat, and drink until we get drunk, whether we're connected by blood or not. They shunned him, even in death. Death! Life! . . . What kind of a disease is this that, like leprosy, is amputating our families, extremity by extremity, limb by limb? What kind of a disease is this that is taking away our words, cloaking us with silence, numbing us with fear? Eeh, Sister, you tell me."

Just Keep Talking

Two Poems

Cheshe Dow

8.8 Months Ago

It is cold outside
She is in a small room
Nothing but a thin sheet of
Something that looks like asbestos
Radiating a little heat
To keep them warm

The women huddle around it

Most of them
Are sick
Some are dying
Of a disease their combined cultures
Know nothing about

They know only
That the symptoms hurt

An older woman stands up
She needs the toilet
The woman doesn't make it to the door
She is leaking

Nthusa, tlhemma nthusa   Help me, please help me
Ijoo tlhe bathong   People of my home
Cancer *ke a e tshaba*   I am afraid of cancer
Ke a e tshaba   I am afraid

She is trapped in the small room with
The leaking woman

The odor is pungent
Not one woman covers her face
Silently they bow their heads

The old woman wipes the floor
Plugs the leaks that are now hers
And asks their forgiveness

She does not see the old woman again
She doesn't have to
She will never forget her.

AIDS

She stands over a grave
She will be standing over another one next week
She has learned not to stand too close
She has learned to find someone to whisper to
It doesn't much matter about what
Just keep talking.

Tell Me a Lie

Ann Kithaka

Tell me a lie.
Tell me that this redness
That turns my lips to pepper hue
Is a result of overzealous use
Of some abrasive chemicals in my lipstick
And not the precursor of
The dreaded AIDS virus.

Tell me a lie.
Tell me that this itch
That persistently invades my skin
Is a result of an allergy
Triggered by an eating orgy
And not the herald of
The dreaded AIDS virus.

Tell me a lie.
Tell me that these night sweats
That drench my shirt and shin
Snatching my sleep and dreams
Are a sign of early menopause
And not the precursor of
The dreaded AIDS virus.

Tell me a lie.

Tell me that when,
Bedridden and forlorn,
I shall lie, eyes fixed heavenward,
Regrets of conquests past and present
Will not haunt me,
Hurrying my tired soul to

A quickened and shameful end.
Yes, lie to me and then lay me out
To die.

Prayers and Meditation
Heal Despair

Pauline Dongala

When talking about healing, it is impossible to separate these four words: suffering, pain, prayers, and strength. We human beings are not meant to suffer; our lives should be enjoyed and fully lived. But there are times in every life when suffering and pain are unavoidable. For me it was when my family and my extended family were swept up in the civil war in my country, the Republic of Congo (not to be confused with the former Zaire).

When political ethnic tensions erupted into civil war in 1998, my country entered a period of unimaginable terror. In the capital, Brazzaville, fighting turned a peaceful place into a hell on earth. Houses were looted and bombarded and civilians were randomly killed. Checkpoints were built, at which many people lost their lives. Both sides used barbaric tactics to assault each other. Women and girls were raped. On the streets rival groups paraded with the heads of dead people stuck on poles.

One night, when about forty friends and relatives were seeking shelter in my house, our compound was attacked by fighters looking for people they deemed their enemies. They launched rockets and shot at the compound all night. We were terrified, all lying on the floor, some vomiting and having diarrhea, not knowing what the next minute would bring. We were just praying all the time. When things quieted down late in the night, we left the house and fled.

Leaving the house was frightening and very dangerous. We could see rockets in the sky, looking like fireworks. On both sides the fighters were kidnapping girls and boys and torturing people—the barbarism was unspeakable. Dead bodies were found floating in the Congo River. People were killed for not having money to bribe the gunmen or because they had some precious things on them, like a nice pair of shoes, a watch, or jewelry. You could be killed just for being on the wrong side of whatever bloodthirsty fighter you might chance to meet.

We managed to leave the capital, leaving behind us all our belongings and wandering in the bush and neighboring villages. At that time my husband was away, lecturing in the United States, so I was running on my own with three young children, all girls. I was constantly praying, seeking God's protection, trying to keep positive thoughts around us. It seemed to be working. At one checkpoint a militiaman who knew me shouted to his friend, "This woman is from our opponents' group!" I thought to myself, "If my time has arrived, please, God, take care of my children." But a second voice came out of the crowd, calling, "Leave her alone and let her go!" At another checkpoint a soldier pointed a gun at me because I did not have my identity card with me, but once again Providence was with my family and me and we were allowed to proceed.

For a while, we were hiding in the forest and the jungle, and we endured a terrible period of starvation. When we knew that we would soon run out of food, we started taking turns eating. The men and children would have a meal one day, the women the next day. Sometimes we only were able to eat three meals a week.

Later the civil war reached the regions where my extended family lived. During the bombing and shootings I lost two brothers, my aunt, two cousins, and one niece all in one day, all civilians. The rest of my family also left their houses and sought refuge in the jungle.

At that time my husband's friends in the United States, including Philip Roth and PEN-International, were able to secure a teaching job for him at Bard College. Although most of the embassies were evacuating their people and refusing to grant visas to the seekers of asylum or to those who wanted to leave the country, my husband was finally granted a visa for him, me, and our three girls to come to the United States. Our arrival there was somewhat of a media event: the *New York Times*, the *Boston Globe*, and several other magazines covered it.

Behind us in the Congo, the tragedy continued. The population fleeing the war was still in the jungle, without any assistance. I had no news of my extended family. My mother, who is diabetic, managed to survive six months without medicine. Dozens of people died during that period due to lack of medicine, snakebites, malaria, starvation, etc. I lost a third brother and so many members of my extended family—cousins, nephews, and nieces; my brother-in-law and friends; the list is very long. Although I was safe in the United States, the lack of communication with my country was hard to take. I had to live without knowing what was going on with my family.

I was emotionally and spiritually devastated each time I heard about another death back home. I lived with deep pain and I had no peace and happiness. I was always swinging between disbelief and rage. I wanted to sit with my family to mourn those who died, to have a sense of closure for their deaths. I was sick and crying every day, going to the hospital almost every week with pains in my stomach and terrible headaches, but clinically nothing helped me.

Gradually, deep in myself I was reminded that I should turn to prayer for my inner peace. I kept hearing a voice repeatedly saying to me, "Violence is not the answer when it comes to violence." To ease myself I sang songs of sorrow and comfort.

Since I had been exposed to prayers at a very young age, I turned to meditation and I began to pray every day. My parents were Christians and my grandparents, who were traditional healers, taught us the importance of prayers in healing. I knew that although there is no magical answer to suffering, I had to focus on dealing with the pain, day by day, using prayers and meditation to heal myself.

In time, I began to feel revived and energized. When I first arrived in the United States, I was not ready to take on any kind of work, other than learning English. To keep myself busy, I started making stuffed African dolls at home. When I was growing up, my mother taught us how to make dolls. We were six sisters, and she could not afford to buy six imported dolls to satisfy her girls. My sisters and I made dolls by recycling our old fabrics, and I returned to this practice during my first months in the United States.

At first the goal was to distract myself while I stayed alone in the house during the day, during the time when my husband and children were out. Later, the work became more intentional. I started naming the dolls after friends and relatives whom I was missing, such as my late brothers. Others I gave names like Auntie Mountounou or cousin Yala, or I gave them affirmative names like Peace, Love, Strength, Comfort, and Courage. I displayed them everywhere in my house, and they helped me to keep in my mind the presence of all those people and qualities that I loved.

The dollmaking became very soothing for me. In each doll I intentionally tried to create and focus on something that I wanted to see accomplished. I connected this work to my grandparents' practice of traditional healing. After every healing session, they would give the patient something to mark the end of the work and strengthen the healing. For example, when a child who had had a seizure was treated traditionally, he would be given a copper bracelet to crown the end of the treatment. Sometimes it was a belt made of a specific grass to wear, or in some regions, a gourd or a tiny basket filled with herbs. For me, the dolls were similar to these traditional healing objects—and the patient who was being healed was myself.

In time I became stronger and stronger. I put my anxiety and sadness on God's altar. I prayed and asked for peace and calm. I asked for guidance, clarity, and help. I started to do, not to dwell, and not to be blocked in by my losses. I asked in my prayers to meet wise and kind people who could help me along my path. I asked in my prayers to find faith and love.

I began a prayer circle, praying for others, especially for those who were going through difficult times. I always pray for women who are still living in war zones, because I have experienced that horror. I know what they feel when a bomb falls, or when the sound of a bullet or a rocket hits close by. I know the anxiety they feel when they run out of food and wonder what to give their children. I know how humiliation resonates in the mind of those who are powerless in front of diabolical torturers and rapists.

I pray also for warlords to have their consciousness raised so that they understand that those they are killing are also human beings and have the right to live their lives, instead of having their dreams stopped by violence. I pray constantly for peace and love in the world.

Prayers and meditation have been the most powerful cure I have found in my times of despair. I find strength, hope, and healing whenever I connect myself to the pure spiritual Source and let myself be the receptacle of divine healing.

Part Five

Taking a Stand

*Women as Activists against War,
Environmental Degradation, and
Social Conflict*

The contributors to this section use writing as a tool of activism, seeking to open a window for readers into the issues of violence, social conflict, and environmental deterioration that plague many African countries. In "A Poem Written in the Ink of the Blood Shed in Rwanda," Nathalie Etoké of Cameroon offers a fierce eulogy for the million dead in the Rwandan civil war of the 1990s, writing about the horrors of the Rwandan genocide in order to move beyond it toward peace and reconciliation.

In the excerpt from her novel *Biography of Ash*, written in Arabic and not yet available in its entirety in English, Moroccan human rights activist Khadija Marouazi sheds somber, resistant humor on the plight of a political prisoner enduring harsh interrogation by security agents, evoking the stubborn humanity of Africans even under the most desperate circumstances.

In her essay "Women's Responses to State Violence in the Niger Delta," Nigerian journalist Sokari Ekine documents the devastating social and environmental consequences of the oil boom in the Niger Delta, particularly for women. The discovery of vast oil reserves in the Delta should have been a boon for the people of the region, but instead the government has allowed foreign oil companies to seize control of the resources and has played one local tribe against another, keeping them occupied with fighting each other while the region as a whole sinks into poverty and environmental decay. Women have been used as foils in this internecine struggle, subjected to rape and violent displacement from their communities at the hands of government forces as well as various militia groups. Ekine seeks to inform readers about the seriousness of the problems confronting the Delta region and to amplify the voices of the women who are stubbornly resisting the government's efforts to silence and subdue them.

Ugandan China Keitetsi was the first African girl soldier to tell in writing the story of her experience. As a child of eight, Keitetsi was lured into one of the militias fighting a protracted civil war in Uganda, and she spent the next ten years living the brutal life of a child soldier, "fighting for her life," as she says in the subtitle of her autobiography. For girl soldiers, duties include not only handling an AK-47 but also sexually servicing the older men, including her officers. The sections of her autobiography included here show her remarkable strength and courage under the constant stresses of her circumstances. Keitetsi is one of the lucky ones who survived her years of military servitude, and today she lives in exile in Denmark, working to end the damaging practice of kidnapping children and forcing them to become soldiers.

Finally, this section includes transcripts of an interview with Wangari Maathai of Kenya, the founder of the Green Belt Movement and winner of the 2004 Nobel Peace Prize for her work with Kenyan women in a widespread movement to reforest a countryside devastated by unregulated logging, development, and burning. Maathai, now a member of the Kenyan Parliament, was for years harassed by the government and was jailed several times for her outspoken protests against the development practices of state agencies and companies. She never gave up, and her success continues to inspire environmental activists all over the world, who look to the example of the Green Belt Movement as a model for collaborative popular resistance to unsustainable and damaging business and governmental policies.

As the African continent grapples with ongoing issues of social conflict and political corruption and tries to balance the need for economic development with environmental conservation, women in every region of Africa are increasingly coming to the forefront to demand that their needs and rights be taken into account. Likewise, women have emerged at the vanguard of negotiations in post-conflict regions, "waging peace" on behalf of their families and communities. The placement of women at the heart of the Millennium Development Goals promulgated by the United Nations and the passage of Security Council Resolution 1325 in 2000, as well as the election of Ellen Johnson-Sirleaf as President of Liberia in 2005, were clear markers that women from Africa and other emerging world regions are beginning to make their voices heard in the halls of power.

A Poem Written in the Ink of the Blood Shed in Rwanda

Nathalie Etoké

A man chops another man's legs with a machete
He has to exterminate the Inyenzi,
the cockroaches . . .
A Hutu is killed because he was hiding his Tutsi friends

A Hutu woman buries the fruit of a forbidden love
The child is still alive
Fighting for his life
He doesn't understand
He keeps saying:
Mummy stop playing!
I don't want to play anymore
Stop playing!
He must die . . .
His father was Tutsi . . .

Tutsi women are raped
Murdered afterward
Few have managed to survive
Some of them are pregnant
Some of them are HIV-positive
Some of them are pregnant and HIV-positive

How to raise a genocide baby?
How to raise a genocide HIV-positive baby?

What nursery rhymes will be sung?
Nursery rhymes of horror
What bedtime stories will be told?
Stories of terror . . .

People are killed
The United Nations is not concerned
The United States is not concerned
The Organization of African Unity is not concerned
You are not concerned
I am not concerned
Nobody is concerned
How could we stand aside and look?

Some Africans killing each other
It happens all the time
Who the hell cares?

Symphony of screams
Accompanied by
Silent tears
Nobody hears them

Cacophony of machetes chopping up
Legs
Arms
Skulls
In the house of God.
Where was God?
Is there any God?

Imana

Imana
Imana

Talk to me

Imana
Imana
Imana
Show me your face

Harmony of pain . . .
The Tutsis are dying
Their bodies are flowing in the bloody river of genocide.

2004
Ten years later
The international community is trying to make sense
    of the unthinkable
People are talking about remembrance
They are making apologies
They are voicing their regrets
They are shedding tears of shame
The horror must be told to prevent another horror.

Frankly I don't give a damn about what they say . . .
I keep on asking myself, how did it happen?
Why did it happen?
Is it going to happen again?
How could human beings be so inhuman?
How can one comprehend the incomprehensible?

How does it feel today in Kigali to be Hutu or Tutsi?
Is the ANGER gone?
Is the RANCOR gone?
Is there room for genuine LOVE?
Genuine PEACE?
Is there room for RECONCILIATION
After such a display of HATRED?

When I think about Rwanda I sometimes cry.
Are the people of Rwanda still crying?
Are they still mourning?

Sometimes I feel
So useless
So hopeless
In front of the world's miseries
I have nothing left except
                          Sympathy Empathy Compassion

The aching in my chest reminds me that I/We have
A heart to feel the pain of the others
A spirit in touch with the spirit of others
Praying for Love
Asking for Forgiveness
Looking for Happiness.

The beautiful smile of this newborn reminds me
That there was a time
Not so long ago
When Hutu
Tutsi
Twa
Used to live together and love each other.

The beautiful smile of this newborn gives me Hope
The beautiful smile of this newborn
is the beginning of a New Era.

Poet's Note: On Writing Poetry:
Resistance, Transcendence, and Survival

In a collection of essays entitled *Sister Outsider*, Audre Lorde wrote: "For women, poetry is not a luxury. It is a vital necessity of our existence. It forms light within which we predicate our hopes and dreams toward survival and change. . . . Poetry is the way we give help, give name to the nameless so it can be thought. The farthest horizons of our hopes and fears are cobbled by our poems." Following Lorde's footsteps, I believe poetry allows one to express hope, fear, change, and a will to survive. I do not write poetry when I am happy. My desire to write poetry emerges from a feeling of sweet sadness, which is born from hopelessness, anger, disillusionment, and a strong will to go beyond the nightmarish depiction of Africa. Although disenchantment and melancholy are at the roots of my poetic adventures, they paradoxically help me to conceive of a promising future through an ambivalent gaze. As I write about the catastrophes and tragedies that plague the continent, I insist upon the courage and tenacity of African men and women and their ability to confront adversity.

In "A Poem Written in the Ink of the Blood Shed in Rwanda," I try to say the unspeakable. Through poetry, I want to see how one can confront the dichotomies of life, how one can transcend without undermining or negating the horror of the Rwandan genocide. Poetry gives me a psychological space where hope and reconciliation can be expressed. The act of writing thus becomes an act of sublimation, a way of coping. In this poem, the horror of the Rwandan genocide is addressed, then reoriented toward an ethic of peace and reconciliation. The creative impetus seeks to go beyond the tragic.

"A Poem Written in the Ink of the Blood Shed in Rwanda" is an act of faith. I write about chaos in order to escape chaos. I write about a nightmarish past because I dream of a better future. I write about death in order to celebrate life. I describe hopeless situations because I do not want to lose hope. I write because I want to bear witness to what happened, to recreate what happened, what should have happened, what will happen.

In the words of June Jordan, "Some of us did not die, we're still here. I guess it was our destiny to live, so let's get on with it." Despite their trials and tribulations, African people are still standing. They bury their dead. They cry. They sing. They dance. Sudanese in Darfur are fighting for their lives as I write. Survivors of the Rwandan genocide are trying like all of us to find happiness, love, and peace. Raped women in the Democratic Republic of Congo are getting together, sharing their stories, singing therapeutic songs, crying tears of sadness and tears of joy, trying to forgive and forget the rebels who destroyed their bodies but not their souls.

In an increasingly globalized world, Africa is too often portrayed as a museum of horrors in which desolation and pessimism are the major artistic patterns. As the French philosopher Albert Camus put it in *Le mythe de Sisyphe*, "Il n'y a pas de soleil sans ombre, il faut connaître la nuit" [There is no sun without shadow, so it is essential to know the night]. Although Africa tends to be viewed only as a place of darkness, decadence, and despair, we must remember that the sun shines in Africa too. Poetic writing is an act of resistance, an act of freedom, an attempt to understand the complexities of the African experience through a literary form that conveys our sorrow, our joy, and our dreams in the midst of chaos and uncertainty.

Excerpt from
Biography of Ash

Khadija Marouazi

There, where my body seemed to lie a great distance from me, I put my hand on my leg, on my fingers, and I couldn't tell they were mine. My thighs. My legs. My waist. Everything was dry and withered. It was the dryness that scared me. Every time I placed my hand on a part of my body, it was as if I had placed it on a piece of damp wood. By the third day after I had been blindfolded, it seemed to me that I was one of the walking dead. I began to notice that my body was becoming frighteningly emaciated. I continued to deteriorate as a result of the torture and was constantly dizzy. As soon as I woke up and touched my body, I felt like collapsing again.

I disappeared into slumber and woke to the sound of scratching underneath my bed of cardboard. The scratching continued, and that's what annoyed me. The sound began to move from under this bed, directly to my ear. I jumped up violently and with considerable effort. I pulled the cardboard up from where it lay and shook it a little, hoping that the source of the scratching sound would fall from one of its folds. I got down on the floor to look at some of the holes in the walls. In the right-hand corner, I discovered a burrow. I threw myself violently to the opposite corner. There was a tail curling up into it as fast as a flash of lightning. I held my breath. The tail turned over and the head appeared. It was a mouse! With what remained of my strength, I rushed to the door and proceeded to bang on it. I was screaming at the top of my lungs when the Hadj entered my cell with keys in hand. I didn't know what he was expecting of me. Nor did I know what I was expecting of myself after all of this screaming. Finally, I surprised him with a request to use the toilet.

Until the moment he inserted the key into the lock of my cell, I wasn't sure that I was going to ask him for anything except to get rid of the mouse and to fill the hole with cement. I don't know what compelled me to ask to go to the toilet.

"You people only take pleasure in going to the toilet. If you were to exchange your shit for words, it would be better for you and us both, for God's sake!"

This is what the Hadj said as he flung open the door of my cell in front of me. Had I revealed the truth, I would have handed them a point of weakness on a golden platter. The distance between my cell and the toilet was quite long, and it was necessary to walk between two facing rows of cells. The Hadj's cane urged me along quickly. I pushed the door open and went in. I opened my fly and urinated with some difficulty, as there was nothing there, but I wanted only to prolong my time there so that I wouldn't have to return to the cell. Perhaps if I took my time, the mouse would leave and go someplace else. The problem with the hole was that there was the possibility that another could appear at any time. Dear Lord! I've got to get a hold of myself. I'll try. I'll try. The Hadj knocked twice and yelled: "Hurry up. Are you constipated?!"

I came out clearing my throat, my hand on my fly. My steps were heavy when the Hadj pushed me forcefully back into my cell. He locked the door and left, while I remained standing on my tiptoes, my back pressed up against the door. I fixed my gaze on the opposite corner, on the mouse hole where that little silvery-gray creature had forced me to play blind man's bluff again after all these years.

The other kids used to insist that I join them, and when my turn came and I closed my eyes, they would take the opportunity to grab hold of any small soft piece of cloth, a piece of wool, or some other piece of material, tie it up in a knot and throw it at my face.

"Moulin, look out, a mouse, a mouse!" They would jump around and run away while I remained, dancing in fear. I would scream with all my strength. I would cry, and when I got wise to the fake "mouse" that they threw at me, I would tell them to get lost, filling my hands with rocks, and the alley with screams. It wouldn't stop until Youssef convinced me to fall into the trap yet again, whenever my turn came up in the game of blind man's bluff.

My God, the mouse is here after all this time. I'll play the game again here and now, even though this is no place for games. I got tired of standing; there was no point. I moved the cardboard a little in the direction of the door in order to sleep as far as possible from the mouse hole. However, I feared that this would raise the Hadj's suspicions so I pushed it into the middle of the cell and lay down. I stretched out a little, but I couldn't force myself to forget about the little silvery-gray mouse. I began to convince myself that he could do me no harm, comparing his size to mine. What could he do to me compared to what the agents do? Could I handle all of that, yet kneel down before this silvery-gray mouse? No, no way. I tried to cover my eyes, but it was in vain that I tried to distance myself from him.

Three days of rolling right and left in a fitful sleep out of which the slightest scratching would wake me—the jangling of keys; one of the comrades heading to the toilet; another one crying out because of his wounds. I was like a clock, wound up by the slightest noise. The room became even gloomier. I kept my eyes open until they bulged. Perhaps I would catch a glimpse of him. He was dark gray when I saw him in the daytime. Perhaps he left and another, or others, came in his place. Who knows? I never knew that there was something called "morning" in here. However, the presence of this silvery-gray mouse forced me to make it out, or at least to imagine I had. It was only then, in the morning, that it was possible to see the hole, and to distinguish between the one that went in, and the one who came out.

I don't know how sleep overtook me, but one morning I woke up with something running over my outstretched hand, causing me to renew my screams as he entered his hole. The Hadj opened the door accompanied by two nervous-looking agents who dragged me to the "hospitality" session. I didn't ask for the toilet this time.

I didn't think about the torture rituals, for our detainment had lasted more than two years moving between secret prison and *garde à vue* detention. The judicial police accompanied us, even to the district attorney and the investigating judge. They would use our bodies as ashtrays, and as practice dummies for their *cravaches*. I learned from the prison doctor afterward that with us, he could not figure out why our wounds kept appearing anew despite our transfer to this location more than three months ago, whereas the wounds and scars on the rest of the comrades had stopped bleeding and appeared, relatively speaking, to be healing.

While the question of my position on the inclusion of the Kida region in our nation was drawing its bloody lines on my body, and placing electrical charges and cigarette burns all over me and on my genitals, I remained obsessed with that mouse. Did he enter his hole? Did he leave it? For the first time, I was distracted from the torture with other things. My responses to their questions remained limited.

"Is your secret organization in favor of the annexation of Kida or not?"

"We're still organizing ourselves internally. Discussions among us only concern general principles and planning. This issue has not been put forth yet."

"Son of a bitch! And eradicating illiteracy and meeting with workers and posters and announcements. . . . You call these things 'organizing principles' and 'structural planning?!' Tell it to someone who cares and shut up!"

They cut me off with a strong slap to the face. I felt heat where a rivulet of blood flowed from my nose (I often had nosebleeds during torture sessions). I heard the cravache smack the ground all of a sudden.

"Take this dog out of here at once!"

A unit of agents came out and the Hadj rushed me to my cell, holding onto my arms and dragging my legs along the ground. I was prepared to prolong my time anywhere—in the toilet with its awful smell, in the torture room with its gloomy colors and whips, in this cement hallway. The important thing was to not go back to the cell, where waiting for me were that hole, fear . . . and the mouse.

The fear that lurked, waiting for me when I entered the cell, was not the same as when I entered the torture room. A shivering overtook my entire body as I threw myself inside. Lmima, come. Come look at your son now.

The Hadj locked the door behind me and I stood there whimpering in a strangled voice. All this torture and it's only this mouse that appears to me strong as an elephant. I imagined that if they knew of my fear of the mouse, and my complete collapse in front of it, they would organize a celebration for intelligence units worldwide. The upper echelons of these organizations would review their programs, and they would give supplementary lessons to their units aimed at seeking the weak spots of a detainee—just as we were able to drive Haydaoui the carpenter out of his mind when we were little, with the single word "honey," which we would lob at him while running away; or as we used to be able to do to Abdelghani ibn Elhai who would be reduced to hysterical laughter when we tickled him on his sides, or under the armpits. As for me, it was enough for them to throw me a mouse.

I mulled over these fears and noticed that I was still standing. I stretched out on the floor a little, and sat with my legs out in front of me. I put my hand on the ground and leaned my head back, placing it on the wall. No sooner had I placed myself in such a position than I felt a movement. I jumped up immediately and fixed my gaze upon the hole with my eyes shooting out like darts. I crouched down and remained like a shepherd fearful of a wolf getting into his sheep's enclosure. Then he appeared, but I had neither the power nor the strength to face him. Even if I did possess such courage, I was barefoot. I didn't have a shoe to stomp on him. I remained thus, in a crouching position. He came out and began to poke around his hole. He wasn't silver-gray as I had seen him the first time, and as I had remembered him. I held my breath lest the slightest movement turn him back to his silver-gray color, which would definitely bring him toward me. He continued to walk to the center of the cell, which I had always considered so small. But now he made me look at it in terms of corners, a middle, and sides. He got to the center and stopped, pausing, while I remained holding my breath. He made himself into a ball in his place, tracing a circle on the floor and sitting in the middle of it as if performing some sort of yoga movements. I swallowed my breath once again, nearly bursting with laughter. Would Youssef ever believe that I had sat face to face with a mouse? He moved a little, then returned to where he had been without disturbing me at all. Oh God, what is it he has discovered? "Come here, come here. Is it possible for you to leave me alone? Or is it possible that we become friends?"

I spoke to him in a voice that was barely audible. I told him the reason for my discomfort: that my fear of him came from the time when he bit the hand of my father, the neighborhood holy man, the fqih. My father had put his hand inside the hole next to the bench where he hid his Quran (I was studying with him—he had sat me in the first row), and when he took his hand out of the hole, blood flowed from his finger and he threw the Quran away. The other kids screamed out of pain for their fqih, my father. The grocer, Bajloul, came and killed the mouse. When he saw the frightening pallor that my father had taken on, he informed us that it was not a normal mouse, that it was poisoned. This was confirmed with a visit to the neighborhood doctor. "You see, I had to hate you. It was the first time my father's horse had ever stumbled. A horse armored in gold. Despite lessons in natural sciences that followed confirming that poison is not found in all mice, time did what it did. This contract with all mice, or should I say against them, was enough to confuse me. Now you appear nice enough, as if you are cast from another mold entirely. Perhaps the mice of the fifties are different from those of the seventies. Twenty years or more is surely enough to change a person, to make him obedient, even to melt and re-form him entirely. Why not the same with a mouse?"

I glanced at him again. He couldn't have weighed more than the smallest starling. He was a faded gray, like dirt. His eyes were like grains of salt, their color impossible to determine. His mouth and his nose were two dots at the end of a line.

Only now will we reconcile. Perhaps we'll even become friends. He moved in place, without leaving his spot. No! It's not just a matter of getting to know one another and reconciling. I'm going to name you. I'll find a name for you. True, we have reconciled, but I don't think the matter of getting to know one another will be completed in a day, at least not on my end. I know your kind. If it weren't for the other animals, you wouldn't be here living and breathing. It was only when the boat filled with dung that everyone was disgusted and complained about it to Noah. So he squeezed the elephant's tail and a male and female pig fell from it, and they proceeded to eat all of the manure that had gathered in the ark. When the pig sneezed, you two—the male and the female mouse—came out. It follows, then, that were it not for the pig's sneeze, you wouldn't exist. I'll find a name for you so that any time I say it, you'll know I mean you. But what shall I name you? What shall I name you after all this hubbub, and after we have given in to one another, or at least after I have given in to you?

I've got it! I'll name you Salman Hissa, and why not?!

Thus began my relationship with Salman, and thus did it develop in unexpected ways.

After the beginning of the trial, they put us in an old wing that had been designated by the colonial administrators for prisoners associated with the nationalist movement. That day, I waited for Salman to emerge, after things had returned to normal. No one expected that Salman Hissa would jump to the top of the list of detainees and that he would be the cause of the reinterrogation of all the comrades in order to find out who he was. It was his name I yelled out when the interrogators colored my flesh with their handiwork. My torture continued for many more days. Perhaps Salman felt the duration of my absence and left, never to return. I yelled his name with no rhyme or reason. I didn't think about the lines of blood on my body when the interrogators stopped their whipping and one of them yelled in my face:

"That's what you said yesterday! Who is this Salman? Is he the head of the organization? Is he the one who formulated the special document saying that Kida shouldn't be annexed by us? Tell us, who is Salman?!"

They started to hit my ribs again. I felt a fire consuming my joints, followed by an icy coldness. I repeated the full name:

"Salman Hissa."

They took me back to my cell where Salman was sitting in the middle of the floor as if nothing had happened. I saw him and I smiled. All units would begin looking for Salman, and there he was, sitting with me in my cell. It took no more than a day and a half for their special intelligence apparatuses to verify that this name could not be located on any map in the country, among the living or the dead. It had never occurred to me before that mice were responsible for meticulously dividing up the map, unless it was of a species specific to colonization. They took me and read more than twenty names that resembled the name of Salman Hissa: Ahmad Salman. Ashour Salman. Salman Aicha . . . And I assured them that I knew him by one name only: Salman Hissa.

"Have you met him?"

"Yes! But no more than four times."

They wanted a description of him so I gave them Salman's precise features: small, slight, thin. Coloring like dirt. Narrow eyes. With a mouth and nose smaller than a grain of wheat.

"Did he wear glasses?"

"I don't know. Whenever I met him, he wasn't wearing them. Maybe he wore them at other times."

"Did he visit you alone or was someone with him?"

"The four times we met, there was a woman with him."

"Same woman?"

"No."

Salman seemed vague and general. That's all they extracted. They closed the file on me in order to open an investigation on the comrade who went by the activist name of Salman Hissa.

When they began to group us together and put us in one wing, we were heartened by the beginning of the trial, but it was a sad day due to my separation from Salman. He went into his hole, but did not emerge again. I dragged my legs slowly toward the open door of the cell after exposing them to the wind and screaming out. I looked back at it like a lover who sets a meeting with his beloved in a specific place, only to find the morality police have come to make sure that he knows that standing in this place is forbidden. I kept turning back in the direction of the hole with the distant hope that perhaps he would appear again.

Women's Responses
to State Violence
in the Niger Delta

Sokari Ekine

Introduction: Violence in the Niger Delta

For nearly fifty years, Nigeria has been a militarized state, even when so-called civilian governments, including the present one, have been in power.* Militarization in this sense consists of the use of the threat of violence to settle political conflicts; the legitimization of state violence; the curtailment of freedom of opinion; the domination of military values over civilian life; the violation of human rights, extrajudicial killings, and the gross repression of the people.

A militarized state is one in which violence becomes a crisis of everyday life, is disenfranchising politically, and is physically and economically debilitating.

*Author's note: The testimonies used in this paper were taken during fieldwork undertaken by me and other members of the Niger Delta Women for Justice (NDWJ) and the Ijaw Council for Human Rights (ICHR) between 2000 and 2003.

The Niger Delta is a region of Nigeria that has been subjected to excessive militarization, with violence being used as an instrument of governance to force people into total submission. It is a region where the majority of the people live in abject poverty and where women are the poorest of the poor. The Niger Delta has no infrastructure, no services, no electricity, no water, no communications, no health facilities, and poor, inadequate schools. At the same time, the Niger Delta is the source of billions in profits produced from oil pumped out of the region by multinational oil companies.

The multinational oil companies (mainly Shell, Chevron/Texaco, and Elf) have treated both the people and the environment of the Niger Delta with total disdain and hostility. They have worked hand-in-hand with a succession of brutal and corrupt regimes to protect their exploitation of the land and people by providing the Nigerian military and police with weapons, transport, logistical support, and financial payments. In return, the Nigerian government has allowed the oil companies a free hand to do as they wish, and they have established one of the worst environmental records in the world.

The Niger Delta region covers some twenty thousand square kilometers and has a highly complex ecosystem and a high level of biodiversity. It is a largely rural, densely populated rainforest area that includes many rivers, creeks, ponds, and mangrove swamps, with more than six million inhabitants. Due to gas and oil extraction, the Delta has become an ecological disaster zone. It is a place where rusty oil pipelines run through farms and in front of houses, where huge gas fires rage day and night in massive pits and towers, spewing out noxious gases and filth amongst people's homes and farms. Oil spills and fires are a regular occurrence, often causing the death of local people and the destruction of wildlife and property.

On many occasions, the spillages lead to raging fires, as in the case of the Jesse fire (October 17, 1998) when more than a thousand people were killed and thousands more were left homeless, many with horrendous burns. In a region where medical care is scarce and only available for the rich, it is easy to imagine what happened to these people. Ponds, creeks, rivers, and land are soaked with thick layers of oil.

The usual response of the oil companies to such spills is to accuse the villagers of sabotage. It is hard to understand why the villagers would commit an act of sabotage that would increase the environmental damage and pollution of their land and prevent them from engaging in their livelihoods of farming, fishing, and trading. In this case, the pipeline in question was buried six feet deep (many pipelines in the region are built above ground, running through farmland and through villages), and the oil spilt from underneath. Villagers are rarely compensated for land or damage to property from oil spillage or fires.

After nearly fifty years of oil exploration and exploitation, the people of the Niger Delta have begun to organize across ethnic nationalities. Beginning with the Ogoni Bill of Rights in 1990, each nationality has issued its own declarations (the Ogoni Bill of Rights, the Kaiama Declaration, the Aklaka Declaration of the Egi people, the Resolutions of the First Urhobo Economic Summit, the Oron Bill of Rights, the Warri Accord, and the Ikerrwe Charter) stating their intention and determination to reclaim control over their land and resources, as well as their commitment to a pan-Delta alliance.

Whenever the dispossessed communities demand environmental, economic, and social justice, their protests are met with violence. When they demand proper compensation and an end to environmental terrorism, the response is more violence. Whenever the people have demanded corporate responsibility and respect for human rights, the Nigerian state has unleashed a mass of violence against the people, including judicial and mass murder, torture, rape, the burning of homes and property, and complete militarization of the Niger Delta by an unrestrained, irresponsible military force.

The Niger Delta is a wilderness of violence unchecked. It is a region where life is surrounded by constant fear of state-sponsored violence: fear of walking, fear of travelling, fear of crossing the path of the armed forces and paramilitary police, and fear of rape, beating, and death. As in other parts of Nigeria, corpses are left on the road until they are ground into the tarmac, suspected thieves are either burnt or stoned to death, and the bodies of the disappeared are never found or even looked for. In the Niger Delta, acts of violence are committed by agents of the state who have total license to abuse without fear of retribution. Acts of violence are most often conducted in a public space, in order to increase the humiliation of the victims and their community and also to reassert the perpetrators' power. For example, women are often raped in public, in order to shame them and their communities.

Gendered Violence and Strategies of Resistance

Violence is not just a physical act; it exists at many levels and can take multiple forms. Violence is always an abuse of power. It is about humiliation and disrespect for persons, their property, and their environment, whether direct or indirect. In the Niger Delta, women are subjected to sexual violence including rape, forced prostitution, and sexual harassment (hissing at young girls and women when they are passing, touching them, mocking their bodies, and so on); physical violence (beatings and murder); violence against property (breaking up and burning of homes and shops); and environmental violence (burning of gas flares, leaking and old pipelines, oil spills, pollution of rivers and ponds). All of these forms of violence explicitly and implicitly impact women's lives precisely because it is women who are the homemakers and the farmers, women who fish the waters, trade their produce in the market, and care for their children, husbands, fathers, and brothers. Violence against women does not happen in a sociopolitical vacuum; it is a reflection of the unequal relationship between women and other groups within the society. Within a militarized society such as Nigeria, violence is condoned and permitted when perpetrated against the poor, against those who are seen as worthless, voiceless, and invisible.

In the Niger Delta, women are both victims of violence and agents of resistance. Women in the Niger Delta channel their resistance into a variety of forms, including dancing and singing; collective action such as demonstrations and strikes; testimonies and silence; culturally significant responses, such as stripping naked; refusing to change work routines and habits, such as opening up market stalls or collecting water; participating in women's meetings; and struggling to maintain their daily routines amid the chaos and violence that surrounds them. Of all the forms of resistance to violence, escape is considered the most extreme, as it is usually only ventured in dire circumstances (Green 1999). During the invasion of Odi Town in 1999 many townsfolk took flight, leaving their lifelong, meager possessions, often losing family members during the escape and eventually returning to find other family members killed, their homes burned to the ground, and property looted. For women this crisis was particularly difficult, as the following interviewees explain.

MOPO burned houses and looted property. I ran to Irri with my three children because it was close. When we returned, the whole village was hungry with nothing to eat. . . . We women struggle to feed and educate our children. No one could go to the farm. (Comfort Ogoro, Oleh Town)

I left everything to run for my dear life and pleaded with people to let me in their canoe with my children. . . . I pleaded with people to take my children. I didn't even know the destination they were running to. . . . Later I started to trace my children. . . . As God would have it, none of them died and at the end all of us came here. When I saw my house I cried. . . . People were hugging me. We will survive this thing with God. (Odi woman)

When the soldiers came we were in our various houses, we only heard that soldiers had come and surrounded everywhere. Since the soldiers were coming we were all afraid. Everyone started packing and running away, we were not able to withstand soldiers. We carried a few things and we left. When we came back, we saw all our houses and food had been burned down, along with the money that we had left in our houses. Since then we have been trying to manage with nothing. We are lying on the ground with nothing to sleep on. (Amasin, a primary school teacher in Odi)

We ran to a nearby village called Odoni. We were crying, "Our houses are finished." We also heard the gunshots and knew people were being killed. Others ran to the bush. Those who could not get boats ran to the bush. You know, that time was a flood period and water was everywhere, the whole bush was covered with water and some of the people were standing on trees, hanging like that for days. There was no food for them as they stayed in the bush for a long period, up to one week. Women, not men, only women; the men were dead. One woman was captured; she came out with her children because they couldn't stand it (the bush) so the army was feeding her with *gari* [cassava]. The soldiers did that — gave people burnt gari to drink and burnt yams to eat. (Imgble, school teacher Odi Town)

Elderly women are especially vulnerable. During the invasion of Odi Town, for example, many of the elderly women refused to run with their families and stayed to witness the horror of shooting, burning, and looting by soldiers. One elderly woman explained how soldiers broke the doors of her house and started stealing personal property. They came with a big truck to pack all the things they looted, she said, and some of them even slept in her house. Elderly women were usually protected from physical violence by their age and status as mothers and grandmothers and in some instances the soldiers ended up giving them food, albeit very meager amounts.

The act of testifying can help to heal the physical and psychological trauma experienced as a result of violence. For women, testimonies reinforce the reality of what has happened and provide an effective way for women to manage their suffering. It is a way of telling outsiders: this is our life, this is how we live, and this is the justice we demand. The testimonies and interviews collected by activists and researchers in the region are all examples of women speaking out about their personal and community experiences of violence. Women told their stories of rape, beatings, sexual harassment, the burning of their property, the arrest and murder of their husbands, sons, fathers and brothers. They spoke of the loss of their fishing ponds and farm lands to pollution and of the poverty of their lives. They spoke about the lack of employment opportunities for the male family members and the harassment of their young sons by police and army personnel. They spoke both of the support and, in most cases, the lack of support they received from their spouses and traditional elders in their activism. They spoke about their decisions to take action and the consequences of those actions.

Other Strategies of Resistance: The Power of Silence

A less obvious kind of women's resistance is the act of silent resistance, by which I mean silence of words and of actions, or of choosing to do nothing. Before undertaking fieldwork for *Blood and Oil*, I had never considered silence as an act of resistance. However, when interviewing groups of women, I observed that there would often be some who did not speak or who spoke very little. Although as a researcher and observer "listening to their silence" was difficult, I was very conscious of the need to respect it. I began to be aware of how powerful these silent voices were. I saw their silence as an act of defiance and strength and another way to manage the pain of their lives.

Traci West observes that resistance includes any coping mechanism used for survival, including silence when it is used as an aid to the survival and healing of the individual (West 1999). In other words, what may appear as doing nothing is, in effect, *making a choice not to do something.*

For example, the military often targeted male youths in particular and a number of women I spoke to had sons, brothers, or fathers who had "disappeared" during a crisis. Mrs. Imiko described how "when I heard they had killed my brother, arrested my father (aged ninety-one) and my family was missing, I didn't know how I can find myself again. . . . They came here to leave their trademark, sorrow, tears, and blood." Another woman from Odi Town recounted how she lost her son in the violence: "We were all in this house but when we heard gunshots, everyone took to his heels. My son ran in a different direction from myself and others. . . . I have not seen my son since then, not even his corpse. I have six children and my son is the last and I am feeling I will not see him again. I am not happy about what they have done."

These women could have done a number of things to help get their sons back or at least learn more about their whereabouts, such as collaborate with the army or police or even prostitute themselves, but they chose not to. They remained silent to the oppressor both in words and in their actions.

Another example of silence that remains at the forefront of my mind took place in the small town of Kaiama in Western Ijaw. On December 11, 1998, representatives of over forty Ijaw clans issued a communiqué known as the Kaiama Declaration and created the Ijaw Youth Council (IYC) to administer the affairs of the Ijaw youth. The communiqué called for an end to forty years of environmental damage and underdevelopment in the region and asserted the right to ownership of resources and land by the indigenous people. In response, the Nigerian government created a Naval Special Task Force and on December 29 sent fifteen hundred federal troops to the nearby state capital at Yenagoa and occupied the surrounding area. Following a massacre, rape, and the burning of properties in Yenagoa on January 1, 1999, the army invaded the town of Kaiama on January 2. On January 4, using Chevron helicopters and boats, the army invaded seven other Ijaw towns.

Twenty-five women were interviewed in the town of Kaiama about the events of that period. One particular woman stood out because, unlike others, she was not interested in speaking. We learned that her son had been killed on the day of the invasion. The story was simple. The family had all fled when they heard that the soldiers were coming. Her son ran back to the house to get something he had forgotten and was shot dead in the stomach. Standing face-to-face with her silence was overpowering, as was her grief and loss. She chose a strategy of insulation by disengaging herself from her surroundings and continuing to live with dignity, refusing her violators any sense of victory. In this instance, she had to face her son's murderers every day, possibly even selling them foodstuffs from the stall she runs to support her surviving children. Her silence, her stance, and her body language did not allow them to take away what was left of her.

Sexual Violence and Community Responses

Rape, sexual slavery, and forced prostitution are all acts of violence and demonstrations of power used in times of war and conflict. Rape, often under orders and sanctioned by military and paramilitary police forces, serves to gratify the soldiers, feeding their hatred of the enemy while also being used as an effective weapon to spread terror amongst the people. In the Niger Delta, rape and other forms of sexual violence have taken place repeatedly in communities that have been invaded by the Nigerian army or where paramilitary police forces have been used to quell demonstrations or to set an example of what will happen if the people assert their human rights.

Forced prostitution and harassment, particularly of young women and girls, are regular occurrences. One of the interviewees, Blessing, explained that the soldiers and police often force girls to "befriend" them. If they refuse, they are threatened with rape and beatings. Blessing had managed to avoid being "befriended" by her lack of fear and sheer stubbornness. She said that at first she tried to make friends for protection and had been bought drinks, after which attempts to force her were made. She said the pressure was terrible and most girls just gave in. Another woman reported seeing a soldier walking into the bush with a girl of about twelve years. After the interaction (the woman did not know what took place), they came out and the child was given money by the soldier.

Community responses to rape have varied widely depending on tribal customs, as can be seen in the following two case studies of rape in two different ethnic nationalities.

The town of Choba, an Ikwerre community in Rivers State, is the headquarters of a pipeline construction company called Wilbros Nigeria Ltd. (a subsidiary of Wilbros Group, an American company). Community relations between Wilbros and the people of Choba have been poor, mainly as a result of the company's lack of respect for Choba and its people, as well as its failure to employ local people, which prompted a number of demonstrations against Wilbros. In June 1999 the youth of Choba began a series of demonstrations and sit-ins outside the gates of Wilbros. On September 17, 1999, a memorandum of understanding was signed between the Choba community and Wilbros, with the latter agreeing to a number of demands.

However, the youths of Choba were dissatisfied with the company's slowness in implementing the agreement. They demanded that six hundred Wilbros employees be replaced immediately by Choba residents, and they again organized a sit-in and demonstrations. On October 28, 1999, the mobile police (a paramilitary force) invaded Choba and unleashed murder, the destruction of property, and rape on the people of the town. In this instance, the rapes of women by soldiers were captured on film by a journalist and published in the Nigerian daily press. In response, Nigerian President Obasanjo declared that the photographs were fake, since *his* soldiers would never do such a thing. The response of the women of Choba was one of insulation, a turning inward toward their community, and initially the whole community of Choba closed in on itself, refusing to speak to outsiders. However, some months later and after much perseverance, a reporter for the *Nigerian Vanguard* was able to elicit a few interviews with sons of rape victims. Their mothers had had to cope not only with the trauma of being publicly raped but also with the shame they and their community felt when their photographs were published in the newspaper.

In Ikwerre culture, married women who have been raped must be separated from their husbands. This is explained in an interview with one of the women leaders of Choba, Mrs. Alice Okocha, who had been giving support to the women and trying to seek help from the Rivers State government.

> It is a taboo to rape a married woman. . . . Until the gods are appeased, these women cannot sleep with their husbands and cannot cook for them. It is our tradition and we have to respect it, not just for the sake of respecting our custom but because there are grave implications for disobedience. . . . These women come here every morning to cry that I should help them out of this dilemma. They beg me to go and meet the government [officials] to provide what it takes to appease the gods so that they can live their normal lives.
>
> After a time, we rallied our women to protest to the wife of the governor so that she could help us to push the case, but we were arrested and detained for four days. It took the intervention of well-meaning elders before we were released. . . . We, the women of Choba, appeal to those behind the ugly events to come and do the necessary things to appease the gods. . . . This is important to us because without these rituals, these women are as good as divorced. (Okpowo 1999)

Though the women had become separated from their husbands because of the rapes, this should not be seen as a totally negative response by the community. It can also be seen as an acknowledgement of their pain and suffering. The women supported each other and organized themselves to demand help from their village elders and the governor's wife. Their response was steered by their need to "appease the gods," an essential part of their healing process, so that they could move on and return their lives to some kind of normality.

In Ogoniland, the responses of rape victims and their families were very different. The troubles in Ogoniland came to a head in November 1993, when the Nigerian military government began a three-year campaign of violence, murder, rape, burning, looting, beatings, and torture against the Ogoni people.* For the Ogoni women, resistance was a daily norm as every day they faced both the impact of Shell's destruction of their environment and the presence of the Nigerian army and mobile police. Women were harassed on the way to their farms, on the way to their markets, in their villages minding their homes, and at night when they were asleep. In interviews with members of the Federation of Ogoni Women's Organizations (FOWA), woman after woman stood up, named herself, and described in graphic detail the rapes and other types of sexual violence she had been subjected to.

They started beating the women, dragging them into the bush. And they started loosening their cloths and raping them. . . . My friend was pregnant. One army man just used his leg and hit her stomach and she miscarried. That was the beginning of suffering in Nyo-Khana.** (Comfort Aluzim)

They started beating us, and they took away all that we were carrying to the market to sell. They took our things, our bags. They asked us to raise our hands and jump like frogs. There was an old woman with us who could not jump. What the army man did was to use his double-barrel gun to beat the old woman's back and she fell down. (Mercy Nkwagha)

One day we were demonstrating. We sang as we moved from our town to Ken-Khana. Singing near the main road, we met face to face with the army. . . . They asked us to lie down on the road. After using the *koboko* [whip] on us, they

---

*The brutal military dictator General Sani Abacha came to power in November 1993 and one of the first things he did was create the now-notorious Rivers State Internal Security Task Force (RSISTF) under Lieutenant Colonel Paul Okuntimo and appoint a new military governor of Rivers State, Lieutenant Colonel Dauda Komo. These two, together with Shell Oil, spent the next three years terrorizing the Ogoni people, a campaign that culminated in the judicial murder of Ken Saro Wiwa and eight other activists on November 10, 1995. Following the execution of Ken Saro Wiwa, the women of the Federation of Ogoni Women's Organizations (FOWA) became prime targets of the RSISTF who, in the words of a FOWA member, "were looking for us the way children look for rats in the bush."

**Ogoniland is divided into six kingdoms (or clans): Babbe, Eleme, Gokana, Nyo-Khana, Ken-Khana, and Tai.

started kicking us with their feet. They dragged some of the women into the bush. We were naked, our dresses were torn, our wrappers were being loosened by a man who was not our husband. They tore our pants and began raping us in the bush. The raping wasn't secret because two people were raping you there. They were raping you in front of your sister. They were raping your sister in front of your mother. It was like a market. (Mrs. Kawayorko)

Unlike in Choba, the Ogoni women were able to stand up and publicly rally to protest the violence they had suffered. Through organizations like FOWA and the Movement for the Survival of the Ogoni Peoples (MOSOP), the women of Ogoniland were highly politicized and engaged actively with elders and youth in the struggle against Shell's activities and for the political auton-omy of Ogoniland. They also used their position and status as mothers to work with the youths, who were in effect their sons or the age of their sons, as this Ogoni woman attests:

During the period, the women of Tai Kingdom suffered a lot. The army came to Tai Kingdom because we have some oil fields. Many of the women were beaten; many of the houses destroyed. At that time the women decided that, dead or alive, they would still hold their meetings. FOWA women had their meetings in the bush. We worked with the youth wing of the movement; the youth of Tai dug a very big pit in the ground and we the women entered the pit and the youth used bushes to cover us. (Ogoni woman farmer)

In Ogoniland, women were not ostracized or excluded because they had been raped. "Our men just take it as what happens, because they know their wives did not just go out like that but were forced. The other women took it the same way," a FOWA member said.

Going Naked: Women Occupy
the Oil Companies' Headquarters

FOWA's response to violence was a combination of collective action, individual courage, and sheer defiance in the face of military and environmental aggres-sion. More recently, women of the Niger Delta have used both collective action and traditional techniques in response to the complete neglect of their envi-ronment, health, education, infrastructure, employment, and general under-development by the government and multinationals.

Between June and August 2002, thousands of women occupied no less than eight oil facilities belonging to Chevron Texaco and Shell Petroleum, including Chevron's main oil terminal at Escravos in Delta State. This series of direct ac-tions by women in the Niger Delta was unprecedented for a number of reasons.

First, never before had so many women taken a series of actions against an oil company within such a short period of time. Second, the actions, in particular the initial occupation of Escravos oil terminal, were highly organized. The women divided themselves into seven groups, each occupying a different strategic area of the complex, including the main office building. Third, because the actions taken by the women (mothers and grandmothers whose ages ranged between thirty and ninety) were organized and collective, as well as in the interest of the community at large, they had the complete support of their communities, including their husbands, the youths, elders, and chiefs. Finally, and most importantly, although in the first instance the actions were taken separately by the women from three different ethnic nationalities, in the final occupation, for the first time women from three different ethnic nationalities (Ijaw, Itsekiri, and Ilaje) came together in a united action against corporate irresponsibility, putting aside previous interethnic hostilities and grievances.*

The women occupied the operational headquarters of Chevron-Texaco and Shell Petroleum singing songs of solidarity to protest years of plunder of their rural environment by the oil companies. During this siege some eight hundred women were injured during a particularly brutal encounter with security forces belonging to the oil companies. Here the voices of the women speak of their coming together and their grievances:

> The rivers they are polluting are our life and death. We depend on the rivers for everything. . . . When this situation became unbearable, we decided to come together to protest. Ijaw, Itsekiri, and Ilaje, we are one, we are brothers and sisters, it is only people who do not understand who think we are fighting ourselves. Our common enemies are the oil companies and their backers. (Mrs. Bmipe Ebi [Ilaje])

---

*The youth and elders in particular of these three ethnic groups have been engaged in violent clashes at various times over issues relating to oil. One of the strategies used by both the multinational oil companies and successive Nigerian governments has been to deliberately exploit existing tensions between the various ethnic nationalities in the region as well as to encourage antagonisms between youth and women, elders and youth, and elders and women in towns and villages. Violence is instigated by bribing chiefs and elders, paying compensation to one ethnic group and not the other, changing local government boundaries that conflict with traditional ethnic boundaries, and bribing youths and elders, especially where women have been at the forefront of local activism and protest. Since the 2002 series of protests ended, there have been further demonstrations and direct actions by the women, and the struggle for justice continues. It is therefore particularly important to stress the solidarity between women from different ethnicities in this instance, which is due to the women's understanding that in such a desperate situation, cooperation is essential to success. Their political awareness of the divide-and-conquer tactics encouraged them to put aside previous hostilities to come together to fight their common enemy.

> We don't want Shell, Chevron, Texaco, or any other oil companies again. They should leave us alone. We don't have guns, and we don't have any weapons to fight them. Since they have treated us like this, we are prepared to die. (Mrs. Rose Miebi [Ijaw])

The reasons behind the occupations and demonstrations were not new. Again the words of the women explain it best:

> Chevron sends effluent into the creeks. The fish from this river when eaten smell and taste of crude oil. (Mrs. Funke Tunjor)

> Last week [July 15, 2002] there was a fire outbreak at Escravos; the air was polluted such that the rain was black. . . . Fowls that drank the water died. (Chief Ogoba)

> If Chevron no keep the promises, next time I ready to go naked. (Mrs. Funke Tunjor)

The women were relentless in their protest and demands, and in a final act of defiance confronted the oil companies with an ingenious indigenous weapon: they threatened to remove all their clothes in what is known as the Curse of Nakedness. The stripping off of clothes, particularly by married and elderly women, is a way of shaming men, some of whom believe that if they see the naked bodies, they will go mad or suffer some great harm. The curse extends not just to local men but also to any foreigner; it is a powerful weapon, not used lightly and one that has many precedents.

Women in the Niger Delta used their weapon of the Curse of Nakedness as a last resort because they had failed by other means to have their demands met. Though greatly feared and rarely used, nakedness as a form of protest is legitimate within the cultural context of the Niger Delta and one of the few occasions when women are able to maneuver themselves into a position of power. Because it is rarely used and used only under extreme provocation, it remains a powerful weapon of collective resistance.

Conclusion

It is important to acknowledge the wide variety of strategies of resistance employed by the women of the Niger Delta. If one only considers direct actions such as demonstrations, rallies, and nakedness as valid responses and acts of resistance, then we negate the suffering of all the other women who do not respond in the same fashion. Women's responses that at first glance appear to be passive may actually be seen as a show of strength, if one's expectations and preconceptions are set aside. For example, "sitting on oneself"—that is, to stand with dignity as a mature woman—is a silent response that can become a very powerful act. Individual acts such as these are ways of managing suffering on a personal level by turning inward to the self, family, and community, and must be acknowledged as effective individual forms of resistance to violence.

References

Alidou, Ousseina, and Meredeth Turshen. 2000. "Africa: Women in the Aftermath of Civil War." *Race and Class* 41 (4): 81.

Davies, Miranda, ed. 1994. *Women and Violence: Realities and Responses Worldwide.* London: Zed Books.

Drew, Allison. 1995. "Female Consciousness and Feminism in Africa." *Theory and Society* 24: 1–33.

Ekine, Sokari. 2000. *Blood and Oil: Testimonies of Violence from Women of the Niger Delta.* London: Center for Democracy and Development.

Green, December. 1999. *Gender Violence in Africa: African Women's Responses.* New York: St. Martin's Press.

Nordstrom, Carolyn. 1997. *A Different Kind of War Story.* Philadelphia: University of Pennsylvania Press.

Okon, Emem. 2002. *Report of the Niger Delta Women for Justice (NDWJ) on the Delta Women's Siege on the American Oil Company, Chevron-Texaco in Delta State, Nigeria.*

Okpowo, Blessyn. 1999. "Interviews with Ikwerre Women." *Vanguard Newspaper.* December 4. Lagos, Nigeria.

Turner, Terisa, and M. Oshare. 1992. "Women's Uprisings against the Nigerian Oil Industry in the 1980s." Paper presented at Canadian African Studies Association Annual Meeting, Montreal.

Turshen, Meredeth, and Clotilde Twagiramariya, eds. 1998. *What Women Do in Wartime.* London: Zed Books.

West, Tracie. 1999. *Wounds of Spirit: Black Women, Violence, and Resistance Ethics.* New York: New York University Press.

Excerpt from *Child Soldier: Fighting for My Life*

China Keitetsi

Editor's note: We enter China's story when she is eight years old, on her own, and is picked up by soldiers from the National Resistance Army (NRA), an opposition militia headed by Yoweri Museveni. China began her testimony with the following dedication: "I would like to dedicate this book to all child soldiers who are alive, and to those who didn't make it. May your souls rest in peace."

A Mark for Life

I stood on the main road, deciding whether to go back to the old man. I would tell him what had happened. Maybe he would let me stay and work for him.

I felt scared standing out there with the moon and stars with their bright light shining brighter than any streetlight. I walked and walked, and after some time I noticed something was wrong. I hadn't seen the old man's house and wondered whether it was the same way I had come the day before.

I couldn't feel my body. I stood there trying to think, and when I couldn't find a solution, I got on a train. I woke up when the train stopped and it was still night outside.

I got off the train and walked until I saw the end of the road. All my fear had gone and I felt stronger than ever. Then I saw a flash of light and thought of turning back. I was exhausted. I decided to walk toward the light but was stopped by a man's voice. "Stop! Who are you? Come closer," he ordered. He was surprised when he looked down at me.

"What are you doing out here in the middle of the night?" he asked. "I'm looking for my mother," I replied. He pointed his torch at me and asked about my father. "He's dead," I lied. I was still answering questions when a group of men appeared from the bush with guns on their shoulders. Everybody stood there looking at me and I was very afraid.

I relaxed when some of the men began to speak my language. All of them were very dirty, and they were dressed in torn clothes. The man seemed content with my answers and told me to go to sleep. I was puzzled and kept on looking at him, wondering where the house and bed were. Suddenly he smiled and laid two torn blankets on the ground. He told me to go to sleep. Although the blanket smelled bad, mosquitoes forced me to cover my head with it. I woke up to the voice of a man commanding, "Left-right, left-right," and when I looked around, I saw children of different ages marching next to a man in military uniform. I could feel an excitement growing in my stomach. It was like a brand new game and I wished that I was there marching along with him.

The man from yesterday approached me with friendly but strange eyes. Before he could speak, I asked to join the others, but he refused because of my swollen feet. Soon after getting up, we all had to leave. I couldn't understand why. Some of the children knew why. They said that the NRA had just attacked Kabamba military barracks, and we had to move to a new place.

The NRA had many groups and each one had its own operational areas. We never stayed in one place. We were always on the run from the government army. We moved our camp to another place, and on the third day I was allowed to join. I felt excited as I marched alongside with them.

After what might have been two hours of marching, we had a break of fifteen minutes. The grown-ups sat alone and the children sat in groups. I sat alone looking at their faces. Many of the children seemed to have been there for some time. It was hard for me to join in with them because I didn't speak their language. After the break, some were lined up behind gun lines at a practice site. There were twelve children, each with an AK-47. They had a few seconds to dismantle their guns and to put them back together again.

The following day we trained in taking cover and charging with bayonets, but the AK47s were bigger than most of us so we charged with wooden sticks. On the third day of my training, an instructor came straight toward me in the line at the morning parade. The hard-looking tall man stood in front of me, looking straight down into my eyes, and asked my name. Scared and frightened, I looked down. "Look at me, China eyes!" He roared and my head shot up to meet his eyes. Then he pulled me out of the line and commanded me to march in front of the others: "China! Left-right, China, left-right!" From that day on I was known as "China."

My foreign name made me famous, and most of the children became my friends, although our different languages were a problem. I spoke Kinyankole and there were only a few who spoke it. I had to learn Kiganda and Swahili as fast as I could. Most of the kids were of the Baganda tribe who speak Kiganda, but Yoweri Museveni considered Swahili to be the language we ought to speak, as it belonged to no one. He thought using an "international" language would end tribalism. He taught us that the differences between us shouldn't matter any more because we were all fighting for freedom.

My training didn't take very long—not because I was a fine child soldier who would be fearless on the battlefield, and not because I was a fast learner. The simple reason was the NRA was short of men, and they could not afford to spend time training new soldiers.

After being taught a little about warfare, we were divided into different fighting groups. I was one of those who couldn't carry an AK-47, so we helped carry the leaders' things—cups, pans, ammunition.

A month after I left the training grounds, I was picked for a special assignment along with a few other children. I was excited because I would be seeing the action I had heard so much about from the older children. We walked through the bush, getting our instructions along the way. Soon we hid on the perimeter of the bush that surrounded the dirt road. The commander told us to go to the middle of the road, sit down and pretend to have a good time playing with the sand. After a while, government troops approached in a huge convoy, but we continued playing as though we were alone. The convoy stopped—the first cargo truck was right in front of us. When most of the soldiers jumped out, we did as we had been instructed, running back into the bush to our fighting group, who then opened fire on the enemy. But it didn't happen quite as I had been told. The sound was terrifyingly loud and everything on the road seemed to splinter into pieces as rocket-propelled grenades (RPGs) hit the trucks.

I was more frightened than ever and about to run for my life when one of my comrades held me down behind a tree.

Our side won, and after the battle everybody ran to the road and began undressing the dead soldiers. Every one of us, except the senior officers, needed something to wear. It didn't matter that it was the enemy's military uniform—anything was okay with us. I stood and watched from a distance as the enemy's boots and underwear were shared out. I was confused, having been told that I was fighting for freedom. I never imagined that it would include stealing from the dead.

My excitement turned to sadness when I saw the wounded enemy scattered around crying for help, and suddenly it became hard for me to think of them as my enemy. Those who had surrendered had their arms tied behind their backs in the most painful way. When I looked around at my comrades, they seemed to be enjoying themselves. It convinced me there was nothing on earth that human beings liked more than to torture and laugh at their prey. The captured troops were escorted to our camp. Our comrades kicked them and spat at them, and when we arrived, the officers were shot dead. Yoweri Museveni welcomed us with convincing words. For playing with the sand we became the heroes of the day. . . .

The Battle

My group and I were at a place near Rwenzori, resting away from the sun. It was around three o'clock in the afternoon when Salem Saleh, a senior officer and Museveni's younger brother, arrived. In his briefing he told us it was time for the NRA to overthrow Dr. Milton Obote. I saw him smile as he said it. He and the mobile brigade had captured something called a Katusha, a special weapon, the day before. This had struck a blow to Obote's soldiers.

Before leaving us, he assured us the NRA would be in power within weeks. Our morale was strengthened by his assurance and he left us singing. Soon after Saleh left, our battalion commander took over the briefing. He told us to prepare ourselves because we were to attack a government camp about four kilometers away. After the briefing, my friends and I just looked at each other, saying nothing. I prepared my Uzi and then stripped off the side pockets and shortened my huge uniform. When I put it on again, I felt lighter and safer because I knew that the amount of ammunition I carried would decide whether I survived or not. I was afraid but couldn't show it, as I was scared I would be called a coward—we were always checking one another to see who was afraid. If you were afraid, many of the children would laugh at you and we all hated that. Many of us would do anything to be seen as heroes, and it didn't matter that we were scared—we still pretended to be cool.

A woman soldier told us to sleep and slowly we made our beds on the grass. It was a struggle because the mosquitoes and my anxiety would not let me sleep. All night I wondered what I ought to feel. Staring at the starlit sky, I tried to feel the right way until the time came to shed blood.

Guided by the moon and the stars, we walked through the bush until we found our fellow soldiers already in position. Our platoon commander told us to kneel down and wait for our orders. Still safely hidden in the shadow of the last trees, we looked at the sleeping enemy camp. We waited for half an hour with the painful stings of busy mosquitoes draining our blood. We couldn't defend ourselves because we'd been told not to make a sound. All I did was bite my lips. Then we heard the first rapid fire of AK-47s, which meant that now we had to kill every living thing in the camp. . . .

The massive fire of our guns made the wild screaming of goats, hens and people get fainter and fainter over the next three or four hours. When we entered the camp, goats and hens were lying in a heap with soldiers and their women who had been visiting. They were all dead, baking there in the hot morning sun. . . .

When it was over, we had to move on because the enemy, who was better equipped than we were, didn't leave us alone for long. Sometimes we had to walk for a whole day without camping anywhere because military helicopters would pass over our heads, telling us to give up or face what they called "wipe-out." But we couldn't give up because we had already promised, we had crossed our hearts saying we would finish what we'd started. We walked with our belongings on our heads, trying to keep up with the grown-ups in a place burning like fire, with our small dry lips crying for water.

Just as I lost all hope, they decided to end our pain and one of the commanders suggested we go to a nearby village to ask for water. . . . As we approached the village, we were alarmed by the smell of rotten meat, but we ignored it and carried on. In the village we saw our fellow comrades lying on the ground with liquid leaking out of every opening they had in their bodies. I shook my head and closed my eyes. I realized there was much destruction still to come. I knew I couldn't change my situation. I tried as hard as I could to look after myself because I knew that hardly anybody managed to escape and no one could see their families. The ones who tried to get away were captured and suffered terrible deaths—we had seen it happen right in front of us. And even those who stole food from civilians were tied to trees and shot. . . .

After going through the village, a government helicopter suddenly appeared. We had to quickly throw ourselves down and hide. We waited for the heavens to fall on us.

After the terror had ended and we felt safe enough, we stood up in panic, feeling our bodies to see if we were hit. After checking myself, I looked around to see if any of my friends were hit, and to my despair one of them was lying on the ground. When I walked toward him, he was quiet, as though in a heavy sleep. I tried to wake him up, but he didn't respond. It was hard for me to believe that he was going away from us. He was a small wise child who always comforted us, telling us to be strong and not to worry.

A minute or two passed and our platoon sergeant took us away from him, telling us he was dead. We had no time to cry. We joined the group and continued walking. My thirst and hunger were replaced with silent tears and I saw flashes of our comrades dead on the ground in the village. I was confused and afraid because I finally realized the terror I had seen could also happen to me.

Finally we arrived at a place with water. Beside it was a bush where we were told to rest.

I was awakened by Museveni who arrived with a group of soldiers. He stood there in front of us, as always with a stick in his hands. . . . In his speech, he told us that we were fighting for freedom and against *ukabira* or tribalism. . . . As most children didn't know what had happened to their parents, he told us that they were killed by government troops and those who were still alive were in jails, and that their hope was for us to liberate them. Everybody stood and shouted: "Yes, Mzee, yes Afande!" with our guns in the air. Museveni smiled and held his stick in the air as well. But I was different. I knew where my parents were. I just hoped to stay alive so that one day I could go home and kill them. I decided they had to pay the price for the pain I was in. . . .

A few days later my five friends and I were transferred to the fifth battalion, and when our new commanding officer, Stephen Kashaka, saw us he ordered two of my friends to join his platoon bodyguard. Many of the officers liked to have children as their bodyguards because they acted without asking questions. And they were loyal to their Afandes. We were involved in everything—killing and torture was the most exciting job for many of us. We thought it was the way to please our commanding officers.

We would increase our brutality toward our prisoners just to get rank, which meant more recognition and authority. But we were too young to realize that what we did to the enemy would haunt our dreams and thoughts forever, no matter where we were. We committed terrible acts to please our leaders, and in return they betrayed us. I guess they never thought of us as getting older, or of what would become of us. I suppose they knew we were unlikely to survive the frontline. We had to endure much more than most adults ever see in a lifetime.

The Fate of Two Friends

One afternoon I was sitting in the shadow under a tree with my friends. We were talking about our experiences when a parade was called. A commander from another unit stood in front and two platoons were told to march and I happened to be in one of them. We were told that we would be taken to join a new unit, which would attack Simba battalion in western Uganda. When we arrived, I felt my misery disappear because I saw the smiles of my old friends Narongo and Mukombozi. I regained my confidence and strength as I greeted them with their arms around me. I wondered what I would have done without these two women because at that moment everything else seemed cruel and ugly.

Our senior officers were Fred Rwigyema and Julius Chihanda. Rwigyeme was loved by many. He was tall, handsome, and a great commander who didn't only persuade us to die for the glory, but also reminded us of the importance of staying alive. On the way we disarmed a police post and the men gave up without firing a single shot.

We continued our journey for most of the day but after Kamwenge we found a place to camp until dawn. Many people came to our camp to greet us and spoke sweet words to us. We watched them sing "We love you liberators." Even the children were excited to see us and many people brought gifts and food for us—but sadly we weren't allowed to accept anything.

I felt proud and so did my comrades, and I began to realize that we meant more to these civilians than to most of our commanders and leaders. It was time to leave again, and our plans had for some reason changed. The original plan had been to leave a couple of hours earlier to attack a sleeping enemy camp, but it was now morning with a rising sun in the sky.

Simba barracks was situated on a hill, close to the main road. We arrived, cut the fence, and seconds later, both sides started shooting. We killed most of our enemy who had been inside the barracks. Others were busy charging the dead while we checked on our casualties. As some of us cried over our lost friends, a new surprise attacker started shooting at us from the other side of the hill.

Everyone ran for cover. Many of our comrades were shot in the back in this first confusion of running for our lives. Still, we kept on fighting with one spirit. Mukombozi wasn't able to take cover because she would shoot the RPG from her hip, and this day it proved to be fatal. Mukombozi was killed by a gun on an anti-personnel vehicle.

When Narongo saw what had happened, she climbed into a tree and began shooting. Rwigyema ordered her down, but she refused. No one saw her body falling, but when we withdrew, we discovered Narongo was missing. When I realized these two women had died, I felt like running away to my father's home, miles away from where we were. Then I thought of what his reaction might be when he saw me in uniform with a gun on my shoulder. Would he scream or kneel down and beg for forgiveness?

Many of us were terrified as we walked down the hillside toward the main road and saw blood running like little rivers and being sucked into the thirsty ground. But, as always, all we could do was blink and swallow the pain. . . .

The next mission was to attack Masaka barracks. When we arrived, the enemy was on high alert to defend their barracks. The shooting erupted and soon both sides were losing men. . . . I was getting "drunk" on gun smoke, making it impossible to see whether my bullets were killing the enemy or not. All I could see were the dead bodies from both sides. One thing I promised myself was never to get up and pretend that I was bullet-proof. I took cover, always shooting when I was hidden on the ground, and when an enemy fell I would convince myself it was my gun that had killed them. The battle went on for much longer than I'd expected, even with the much-feared fifth battalion on our side.

The enemy's bullets fell on us like hail and we had to retreat. As I ran away, everything I owned felt as heavy as boulders, and I thought of throwing my Uzi gun away, only that was a serious offense, so I began with my cap. But it did nothing, I still felt heavy. . . .

The fifth battalion now had a new commander, Ahmad Kashilingi, who had been appointed by Museveni after Kashaka left. Kashilingi was a Munyankole and a former Idi Amin soldier. He was well trained in combat and in administration and tall enough to look a giraffe in the eyes. He had a beard that gave him the nickname Kalevu, meaning "goat's beard." . . . The fifth battalion was ordered to be on the ready because we would soon advance and cross a small, heavily guarded bridge, Katonga Bridge, a few kilometers from Kampala, the capital.

At the parade, we were told that the Mobile Brigade was doing such a good job that soon they would take over the capital. Now that I had survived two major battles, I knew I had a big chance of seeing this city which most of us kids could only dream of. Before we left for Katonga, we obtained a lot of brand new cars. I saw officers knocking over expensive cars, men who didn't even know how to start them.

Was this really what we had been fighting for, I asked myself, watching the senior officers doing the same, running up and down with women who were wild about these new freedom fighters. The soldiers had not washed for days. I suppose these women were perfectly unaware of it, or perhaps they just enjoyed the smell. All of this happened in a small town named Lukaya.

I watched all of this madness while my comrades and I relaxed under a tree. Three fat women approached us. They invited us to a nearby bar and took me for being a boy too. I enjoyed being seen as a boy, so I told my comrades not to say anything about my true identity.

We drank what they offered us and it was the first time any of us had tasted alcohol. All the people in the bar were crazy with excitement about our presence. We laughed and laughed, looking at their gestures as they eagerly offered us drinks. We didn't care whether we got drunk or not because we knew our leaders had no time left to see what we were up to. We were getting drunk and the women began to touch us. Whenever my woman got too close to the truth, I removed her hand. She laughed at me and assured everybody that I was afraid of women.

My comrades burst into laughter although I noticed they too were afraid. I wanted to see the minds of these strange beings, so I was patient. The women were wild and tried with more strength to touch us between our legs. When this happened, all of us got angry. We stood up, pointed our guns at the shocked women, and forced them to raise their arms above their heads. At that moment, a soldier walked into the bar. I noticed his mouth open and close in surprise before he spun around and disappeared.

A minute later he returned with a drunk commander. We began to laugh when we saw him swaying from side to side, telling us to leave the stupid civilians alone. On our way out, he asked why we were in such a situation and we explained that these women wanted to rape us. He was satisfied with that because he knew our only strength was our guns. Suddenly he sat down in the middle of the street laughing, pointing at me. "Did they even want to rape China?" When he had finished rolling around with laughter, we moved on to another bar, where a lot of women went wild there too. The commander enjoyed telling everyone how terrified we were of the women.

I was thinking about my mother—whether she did the same things as these women. Anger grew inside my stomach, and suddenly I felt like shutting everybody up with my gun. I left the bar and sat myself against a tree watching the nightlife. Everyone except me seemed to have found a partner, and the loneliness seemed to have been made only for me.

We stayed in Lukaya for a short time, enjoying our time away from the war. At the parade we were told to bear in mind that we might be needed at any time, and afterwards my comrades and I discussed our previous battle. We assured each other no battle could be as big as the last one. We would survive many more.

We agreed that no other frontline could ever frighten us again—we were real fighters now. Then a message came from Museveni or Saleh. Senior officer and commander of the fifth battalion, Ahmad Kashilingi, was ordered to take us across Katonga and capture Entebbe International Airport. We were briefed and told to prepare ourselves for a morning attack.

I was one of the first who was ready with my Uzi on my shoulder. Worried and excited, I watched the sun rise while the drivers ran around looking for which trucks to drive. Most of them had glowing red eyes, and I knew they had been drinking all night. Nearly everyone was ready to go. Then I saw a terrible sight. The commanders, including our battalion commander, were all drunk—Muslims and non-Muslims alike. We went to Katonga but couldn't go ahead with the attack. Big guns were lined up behind the bridge, ready to tear us to pieces. We were ordered to dig in so we began digging holes in which to take cover. As I dug, I remembered I had promised myself never to judge a situation before it happened. The only thing separating us from the enemy that day was the river that only a fool would think of crossing under fire.

Later that day both sides started firing, though neither side took the initiative to cross the narrow bridge, which I am sure every soldier considered suicide.

We were stuck at Katonga for about four months, until Kashilingi was ordered to cross the waters—within hours. I looked at our side and saw nothing as large as their weapons on the other side. At first I couldn't believe the order was real, but I couldn't have heard incorrectly. Museveni and his brother were the only ones who could give orders like that one. He knew very well how devastating this could be and I began to think he was being careless with our lives.

I wondered whether he would keep any of the promises he had made when he was a hopeful rebel. We moved over the bridge, and we were falling like flies, but the commander shouted at us to move. We continued through bullets and hand grenades. Suddenly one of my friends nicknamed "Strike Commando" went down. He shouted, begging for help, but not one of us could stop to help him. We managed to push the enemy back but we lost many soldiers. I walked among the casualties, looking for my friend. When I went to see the dead, I was interrupted by angry comrades who raged at the bodies of the enemy with fists and boots.

I could not cry even though I knew my friend was dead. I couldn't cry for fear of breaking down. I had come this far, though I never seemed to harden. It was strange to see children with a lust for killing and torturing. They could even smile after a "rare killing," competing to earn nicknames like Commando, Rambo and Suicide. I hated feeling sorry for others, even the enemy. I had crossed the line. I had used up both hands to count my fallen friends.

Now it was time to decide. I was broken, but I was still kind and unselfish. Now I thought I needed to be a strong, full-blooded killer—if I only could.

Soon every child carried more than three magazines tied to their AK-47; many of us had up to six magazines each. I guess we all felt that being seen with so many magazines would impress our leaders. We forgot about our shoulders and soon many of us started walking like old men.

All of us need someone to love us and if your parents haven't given you love, who will? Some children's parents were dead, and those who were alive had let us down. Now we had to search for love from strangers and they too looked the other way. We were on our own, and we were forced to find love and compassion in the wrong places. We were forced to get love from a gun.

We were told our guns were our mothers, our friends, our whole world, and we must rather lose ourselves than our guns. At night our leaders would come and steal the guns from us, and the next day they would ask us where our guns were. You would look everywhere and they would beat you and roll you in the mud, accusing you of giving your gun to rebels, or they would say you had sold it. After the beatings, they would give you your gun and say to you: "That's what happens when you lose your mother." Whenever I went to sleep, I wound my gun belt around my neck. Still, I was afraid to fall asleep. . . .

Once again we had to leave. We were driven along the blood-stained main road. Bodies were scattered everywhere; dogs were eating some of them, but I watched without any feelings, remembering how they had just killed my friend.

On our shortcut to Entebbe, a helicopter attacked us. We were better equipped now, shooting at them with a .37-caliber artillery gun, and soon they retreated to the Victoria Nile. We carried on fighting and when we were told that Kampala was only a few miles away, we were filled with hope and saw the future promised to us.

After a few days, we faced a strong and well-equipped enemy. They seemed as if they were all prepared to die. Kashilingi begged for reinforcements, though no one came to our rescue. "Let not one of you die here—fight and defend yourselves!" he commanded. Weeks later, the enemy had retreated and I could see hope in all our faces. . . .

In Kampala, raging civilians were chasing government soldiers, and everybody ran around in chaos. The street was on fire with our enemy's screams. They were burned in car tires, but there was nothing we could do about it. We just walked through the streets pretending everything was in order.

When we arrived in the inner city, I couldn't see anything like the impressive descriptions I had heard. But before I could feel too disappointed, we were overrun by thousands of happy citizens. Some were crying, others knelt down to thank us.

For the first time on Ugandan soil women were armed and walked as proudly as any man. Many looked as if they had forgotten the war, which was replaced by bright eyes of hope, but I couldn't feel that way. I couldn't loosen up because I knew there was more to come. I had learned never to feel secure until I could see the next valley or look around the next corner.

Don't Get Mad, Get Elected!

A Conversation with Activist Wangari Maathai

Danielle Nierenberg and **Mia MacDonald**

Jailed, harassed, and vilified by the autocratic regime of former President Daniel arap Moi, Wangari Maathai is the founder of the Green Belt Movement (GBM) of Kenya, which has supported the planting by women of over twenty million trees in that country since 1977, while also advocating for better governance and human rights. In December 2002 Maathai was elected to Kenya's Parliament as a member of the Green Party in the country's first free election in decades. In January 2003 she was appointed Assistant Minister for Environment, Natural Resources, and Wildlife. She was interviewed in Nairobi in November 2003, a little less than a year before she became the first African woman to win the Nobel Peace Prize.

What's it like, going from being a prominent government critic to being part of the government itself?

People were very happy that I was elected. What they don't quite appreciate is that if you're not the minister, there are many things you can't do because you are now working under another person. I try to be persuasive, but [things are] not moving as fast as I would have liked. One of the major challenges is that we inherited a system that had been riddled with corruption and looting of public resources.

What does your being in government mean for environmental activists around the world?

Many of the environmentalists with whom we started in the 1960s and 1970s did end up in government, and a number of them became ministers. Sometimes when I'm frustrated I remember José Lutzemberger in Brazil. He was minister for the environment [1990 to 1992] and we were all very excited about that. Then he felt so tied up that he resigned. Because many of us are driven by idealism rather than politics, we have to train ourselves to be patient. I'm very excited, actually. Sometimes when I go into Parliament I reflect that to be in this house is a very big privilege. There are 222 of us [members of Parliament] in a country of 30 million people, and there are 16 or 17 women. I try to remind myself of the responsibility.

What are the most important lessons from your work with the Green Belt Movement that you can apply to your work in government?

One of the most wonderful things we did was to [help] ordinary people become seedling producers—what we call "foresters without diplomas." Our main thing was to try to make people understand the linkage between good governance and conservation—how an environment that is well managed helps to sustain a good quality of life. That is what produced the tree-planting campaign. We created a movement that was not only taking action to save the environment but also was about the responsibility we have as citizens to change the government.

I'm working with the Green Belt Movement to continue producing seedlings in the thousands. I'm waiting for the ministry to be able to say we can buy these seedlings. If we said we could buy these seedlings, we would get them in the *millions*. You'd put a lot of people to work in the rural areas. You'd be putting money into the hands of very poor people and they'd be working for it.

What initiatives are you working on now?

I wanted to start a national tree-planting day, and I thought that Easter would be a wonderful time. It's a long weekend. Kenya is almost 85 percent Christian. People here are crazy about religion and Jesus and the crucifixion, and to get a cross somebody has to go into the forest, cut a tree, and chop it up. I thought there would be nothing better for the Christians to do than to plant a tree and bring back a life, the way Christ came back to life.

What are the main challenges Kenya's environment faces?

How to recover forest cover, save our wildlife, give ourselves adequate water, and curb pollution. Forest cover has been reduced very quickly, to about 1.7 percent [of the country's area]. The level recommended by the UN Environment Program is about 10 percent, at the very minimum. Two-thirds of our country is arid, semiarid, and desert. We are an agricultural country and we are very vulnerable, with the Sahara Desert right here. We need to increase forest cover, and the only way you can do it is by involving the people.

Is reforestation really possible, despite population and development pressures?

It is doable. We have a high population pressure, but we tend to congregate in the one-third of our country where we have water and good soil and forested mountains. But two-thirds is out there and should be utilized more. I've been advocating reforestation in those areas with exotic species of trees that grow fast, are commercially exploitable, and [until now] have been planted on the mountains. We should plant fewer exotic trees in the mountains and more indigenous trees there, because we also want to protect the catchment areas and the diversity of plants and animals.

Exotic species can do very well in dry areas. But this is also something that will require some convincing, because for the last eighty years or so we have been planting exotic species for the timber industry, cutting indigenous forests to replace them with exotics. Slowly, they will see sense in taking plantations of exotic species to other areas.

What about corruption and land grabbing, which was a focus of your work with the Green Belt Movement?

We have sent all the foresters home, because so many were corrupt and were destroying the forest. They are being reinterviewed to see whom we shall keep and whom we shall let go. Involving the public [in managing the forests] is very important because the public has been persuaded to perceive the forest as being the property of the government—none of their business. These foresters were able to destroy forests while the public watched. The public didn't raise the alarm and it was left to a few organizations like ours. But the more people get involved, the more we can fight corruption at the local level.

The other area where we are fighting corruption is in the wildlife sector. Our biggest problem there is poaching, and we also have conflicts with wildlife.

Wildlife needs vegetation, and animals are coming onto farms looking for food, and then people complain. We are trying to go back to Parliament and have a law giving us the mandate to compensate [people who lose livestock or property, or are injured by wildlife]. On one side we compensate [and] on the other side we are saying, "You must rehabilitate the forest with indigenous vegetation so that we can give the animals their habitat and reduce that conflict."

Are you thinking that being in government may not be for you?

No, no, no, no, no. For me it is the next step and a very, very important step. I sit in Parliament sometimes and remind myself, "You're really making laws here." If a law is made, then you actually have an opportunity to influence future generations.

What's been the impact of your gender on your work?

If a man had been endowed as I have been, he would probably have been able to accomplish much more because the opportunities would not be so controlled. But I also know that I've been lucky because I have gone through many stages in my life—some successful and some not. I think that many women, especially in Kenya, relate to my story because they can read something in it that reminds them of their own story.

Do you see yourself as a role model for women in Kenya or even globally?

A lot of women were very encouraged by the fact that I won an election. Maybe it would have been different if I had been [appointed]. They would probably have said, "Oh, some man somewhere decided to give her a position." I represent an ordinary woman—it's very different from coming into a position because of your inheritance.

Sometimes I've had difficult times, and I think having those and overcoming them for women is very important—[showing] that you don't have to be down and out. You can get back up. That's what a lot of women relate to. I also think that's what men relate to now, because they figure, well, the story stopped being the story of a woman who is belligerent or a woman who is resisting being put in a certain place.

Do you see yourself running for president one day?

Well, that is far-fetched right now. What I'm interested in is to see that I can make an impact in the government. What the future will bring, I really don't know. There are a lot of very vibrant young men and women coming up; by the end of the second term I'll probably be feeling I'm too tired.

Do you think former Moi government officials are saying, "I can't believe that troublesome woman got in there"?

People who were in the Moi government are probably confused. They probably don't believe I can sit still and not be shouting at them. At the same time, I marvel at the fact that they are not in the government and we are.

Part Six

Writing from
a Different Place
Perspectives on Exile and Diaspora

This section opens up the complex terrain of African women in the diaspora, as women from four different African countries reflect on their experiences living abroad, which force them to confront racial discrimination, cultural miscommunication, and the gradual shaping of a new definition of what it means to be an African woman living outside of Africa.

Ghanaian Kuukua Dzigbordi Yomekpe uses her name as a starting point for exploring the ongoing interactions between her cultural origins and her current location in the West. It's important to recognize, Yomekpe says, how "those of us of African descent who carry the baggage of colonialism, imperialism, and racism . . . are forever working through our baggage." This can be a productive process, however, especially when it takes the form of powerful writing to be shared with a wider audience in the hope of creating a strong transnational community for African women sojourning abroad.

Moroccan Touria Khannous asks how, at a time when modern Western liberalism clashes with Islamic culture, can Muslim Moroccan women in the diaspora negotiate Islam? How can they maintain their identity in a global world? Khannous delves into Moroccan history as well as her own upbringing to explore contemporary Moroccan women's multifaceted resistance against religious fundamentalism, nationalist fanaticism, Westernized liberalism, and patriarchal oppression. Writing her own story of resistance, Khannous takes her place among generations of Moroccan women who have been agents of change throughout history, speaking and writing publicly against forces of oppression.

In "Knowing Your Place," Nigerian Diana Adesola Mafe takes the fighting words of Chicana Gloria Anzaldúa as her starting point; Anzaldúa advises young Third World women writers to "throw away abstraction and the academic learning" and write from personal experience, "not through rhetoric but through blood and pus and sweat." Mafe, the biracial daughter of a Dutch mother and an African father, responds to this call with a deeply personal narrative of her experiences with racism in her adopted home of Ontario, describing the cultural disjunction she often feels among her Yoruba extended family. Mafe ends by asserting her right to claim the liminal space of the borderland between cultures as her proper home.

In "Letter to Clara," Cameroonian Susan Akono writes to a young woman she met in a classroom in Spain, who made an indelible impression on Akono when she unthinkingly reduced her to a stereotype of the poor, hungry, uncultured black African. Her offensive comment made Akono so insecure about her own identity and her place in Europe that it launched her on a lengthy process of self-definition, which ultimately left her stronger and wiser. Though she herself comes from a privileged African background, she will choose to "identify with all the people at war, all the people battling against prejudice, injustice and sheer misfortune," and she knows she will never be made to feel so insecure about her identity again.

African women in the diaspora are constantly renegotiating their liminal place—between generations, between cultures, between geographic locations— a process that can be fraught with discomfort and marginality but which can also create a position of strength from which to comment on both worlds, as the contributors to this section demonstrate.

Musings
of an African Woman

Excerpts from a Memoir in Progress

Kuukua Dzigbordi Yomekpe

All Because of a Name (2001)

Claiming your name with all its baggage of ancestral memory brings a certain comfort that is very cathartic.

It is 12:16 a.m. on Wednesday morning—the *day* on which I was born. To us Ghanaians this is very important since most of us are named according to this day. I have just finished reading the preface and some of the introduction to a book written by one of my professors from college. I finally sign my name in a book that I have owned for almost four years. Without thinking I sign "Kuukua Dzigbordi Yomekpe" with oomph; I realize that I like the sound of my own name, my African name.

Why I had never given any earlier thought to protesting my European name is beyond me. Of course, most people I knew in Ghana strove to be regarded as "white" or Europeanized. From my maternal grandmother, who tried to make proper ladies out of my sister and me by teaching us the proper use of cutlery at teatime or the mannerisms of a lady, to the nuns in habits, who charged us 10 *cedis* for speaking our native tongues during recess, everyone made it their business to ensure that this new generation of children was brought up right, trained to fit into the mold that the colonizer was creating for the so-called educated African. Then there was the Anglican, and later, the Catholic Church, to which my ancestors had been forced to convert, that demanded that all baptized children of God be named after saints—of course it came in handy that most of these saints had English names! So with all these forces working against me, it was no surprise that my name was, and had been for twenty-four years, Melody-Ann D. Yomekpe and not Kuukua Dzigbordi Yomekpe.

I can recall feelings of shame when called upon in class to enunciate my "full name" or to tell my teachers what my middle initial, *D*, stood for. The teachers, also victims of the colonizer's brainwashing, didn't make these feelings any easier to deal with, ridiculing the sound of my names. These names, inherited from my father, originated from the Ewe tribe, who occupied the eastern part of Ghana and were not thought to be among the most assimilated and Europeanized of the Ghanaian tribes. I grew up hoping and praying that someday I would be married off to a man from a place outside of Africa and then my last name would change and I would never have to blush when asked to pronounce my last name again! Yes, it was a traumatic experience for a child who strove against all odds to be Europeanized. There were even occasions when I denied the existence of that side of my heritage. Denying my association with my father's tribe always cost me dearly because quite a few of the students in my class were also members of this tribe and this denial was always seen as a betrayal. I would think to myself that they would do the same if they had names like mine, which meant "gravestone."

I'm sure you are trying to figure out how merely scribbling my name in a book could rouse such deep feelings within me. I guess this goes to show how deeply rooted in culture we all are, especially those of us of African descent who carry the baggage of colonialism, imperialism, and racism; we are forever working through our baggage.

This brings me to the real reason for writing. . . . I have been suddenly seized by an overwhelming desire to reaffirm myself with a sort of "return-to-the-roots" ritual, and at this point in my life reclaiming my true name—my Ghanaian name—seems to be the most appropriate ritual. Although in my case I wouldn't be actually changing my name, I would only be reclaiming what has been mine all along, the name that shame and brainwashing has prevented me from affirming.

Although some of my Ghanaian friends have kept their original names and used both—the Ghanaian and the baptism-inspired, church-assigned one—I had never even thought about doing this till now. Was it because I was so steeped in the culture of becoming "white" and fitting into the mold of the colonized

African that I just couldn't be bothered with the local homegrown name? Or was it because I was bombarded with enough messages while I was busy forming my fragile identity that I actually bought into the whole idea that the less I identified with my people and culture, the easier it would be to transition? Well, whatever the reason, I never before felt this strongly about returning to the use of my native name: Kuukua Dzigbordi Yomekpe—Kuukua for female born on Wednesday in the Akan tribe, Dzigbordi for child of patience, and Yomekpe for gravestone, both from the Ewe tribe.

It is 12:45 a.m. and I am seriously thinking about what it would take to make the official change. Would I do this at any cost? Would I be willing to teach people how to pronounce my "new" name? Would I still answer to "Melody-Ann"? Oh the joys of being a product of colonization!

I Am Beautiful the Way God Made Me! (2002)

It is such an awesome feeling when you finally come to the realization that you love yourself, and I mean the whole person—the hair that is not quite straight but not entirely nappy either; the thick or thin lips; the hips that may be too much, or not quite nearly enough; or the fingers that are short and stubby, or long and skinny—the whole package!

As I stand in the shower washing the hair that, thanks to all the latest developments in beauty products, is now straight and sleek, I run my palms over it and smile to myself. I could tell the story of my life with the stages through which my hair has gone . . . from the nappy short Afro days, to the days when I was trying to grow my hair and attempted several of the painful procedures to which most women of African descent resort, right down to the first time I got "approved" to get a perm for the Christmas play.

During the nappy days, if I sported an Afro it was not for any institution-defying purpose but rather that I had not made it to the barber shop or that I was desperately trying to escape my grandmother's not-so-skillful use of the scissors and miserly attempts to save money by doing it herself. A perm was "bad for you," she said, not because it meant we were buying into the whole idea that straight was the "good" way and nappy was the less beautiful "other," but because "the chemicals were bad for your brain." Maybe it is the one redeeming moment when my grandmother was not preaching her lesson of "on becoming white . . . ," but this did not make me feel any better: I wanted a perm because that was what every cool girl in my class had and darn it, I wanted to be cool too!

As I rinse my hair and put in the conditioner that detangles the nappies, I proceed to scrub the chocolate-brown skin of mine and yet another thought comes to mind. My . . . yes, you guessed it! My British grandmother to the rescue again! This time with lessons on how to become hygienically "white."

"Scrub that body!" she would scream, "maybe eventually some of that black will come off and you can start to look and act more like your mom and me." This would normally be followed by lectures of why my mother should never have married my father, whose tribe was not Europeanized enough, topped off with how none of us, my mother's children, took any of that silky *bronyi* (white) hair that was in our genes (my grandmother is mulatto). Abuse? No way! Proper upbringing served with extra doses of love? Yes! That's how she saw it and I'm sure she would still defend her methods of proper child rearing to this day.

After such lectures, I would dutifully scrub away or be scrubbed on those days when my childish hands and love for water made it impossible for me to complete the task. Little did I know then that I would grow to hate the very vein that carries that hint of British in me.

So today, recalling this history that lies behind taking showers, I slow down the habitual and automatic scrubbing that has become an unconscious routine; I refuse to scrub away any of that beautiful chocolate-brown skin! It has taken me all my life to become comfortable in the body God gave me. I am five feet seven, with chocolate-brown skin, brown eyes, and black hair, which now has traces of faded Cherry Coke color in it, and I am thankful every day for this black woman that God created. After three years of growing my natural nappy hair, sporting braids, and having texturizers, I have finally settled, for now, on the bone-straight, sleek, relaxed hair that I'm sure would allow me to pass for a member of my grandmother's British family if I were to ever wish to be inducted into that secret society.

Life in the Land of Opportunity (2004)

The leaves on the tree right outside my window gently stir with a wind that only blows about every ten minutes. The air is hot and sticky and humid. The leaves rustle and move, yet no breeze enters my room to ease the stifling heat. The neighbors' air-conditioning units kick on and drown out the sing-song voice of the man who is having a highly animated conversation next door.

As I gaze out and try to take in my surroundings, I realize how this crowded apartment complex reminds me of the Korle Bu flats back in Ghana, which house civil servants who work for the government hospital. I think to myself, life in America is just a coated version of life in a so-called Third World country. True, the thickness of the coating makes it easy to dismiss this theory. People work so hard all day only to retire to this in the evening: a conglomerated, cacophonous display of miniscule living quarters. For the amount of money people pay for a place here, they could be living in a five-bedroom ranch in some developing country free from all the stresses of life. Sure, some of the finer amenities of life might be missing, but these would be minor, considering the amount of space and peace of mind one would enjoy.

So what makes my life different from that of an average Jane living in a developing country? Maybe the constant running water here; Jane would certainly have to be rationing or walking a few miles to a well or a community pipe. Then there is the electricity that seems to burn all day long, by which these people in the other apartments are cooling their living spaces. Or could it be the microwave, coffeemaker, or George Foreman grill? All seemingly necessary appliances for existence in America, yet I beg to differ! These are all mere trappings of the life we choose to lead in this here "free country," to which members of developing countries, en masse, escape with hopes of amassing wealth and returning to establish a mini-America in their homelands.

Noble goals! No doubt! But realistically, how many of these people ever end up leaving America to return to their homelands? How many actually achieve that goal of returning home to recreate better versions of the lives they had here in America? Very few! The average immigrant Jane ends up getting caught in the lifestyle of consumerism, and with the onslaught of bills, even a trip home to visit aging relatives or bury a dead family member becomes unaffordable, a debt to be added to the credit consolidator's list. Some remain trapped in America because of the real danger of not being able to return, once having left, because of immigration regulations.

As I write I wonder, Who am I really writing for? Who is my audience? My people, my fellow developing-country citizens who, like me, have left oftentimes better living conditions to come to America with the hopes of "finding greener pastures" and "making their fortunes" in this land of opportunity? If this is my audience, do they even care?

Immigrants make up the bulk of the population in America; everyone left some place to come and "make it" here. Different reasons propelled each ethnic group that migrated here but the one underlying reason, regardless of which group, seems to be the promise of finding something better than what they had. In the process of "making it" we all lose important parts of ourselves: an accent, a difficult-to-pronounce name, the foods from which our clothing used to reek, the culture that used to emanate from our very beings. We lose these parts of ourselves in an attempt to blend in, to become one of the majority. Sadly though (or is fortunate?), most immigrants can never quite complete that process of blending in.

Just when you think you've perfected the pronunciation of a word or gotten the meaning of some idiomatic expression right, some person somewhere comes up to you on the pretense of making conversation and asks: "So, where are you from?" or, my all-time favorite, "What are you?" I love to give people like these hernias because I calmly proceed to say casually, "The Midwest,

Ohio!" Of course they don't get the hint and so they continue to probe: "No, I mean where are you really from?" They know they are right—you look different, you sound different, you must be different!

That's when I kick myself for ever leaving my country, where I was not "different," to "seek greener pastures." What most people do not realize or refuse to acknowledge is the fact that this country, America, truly only belonged to one group of people, the Native Americans. These original owners were sacked and mistreated, much like what happened in my country, colonized by the British. America today is made up of centuries of people from other places; people who looked and sounded different back then, some brought in by force, others driven by the search for a better life—the same reasons that still bring immigrants in today.

So if we're going to be so picky about who is "different," then shouldn't we all return to our original homelands? But of course there are quite a few Americans today who cannot trace their ancestry back to their original locations, so where does that leave them? I suggest a new identity: ambassadors for peace, embracing and extending warm welcomes to all new immigrants.

A Moroccan Woman in the Glocal Village

Reflections on Islam, Identity, and Cultural Legacies

Touria Khannous

I grew up in Morocco, in the city of Fes. Located at the crossroads of Africa, Europe, and the Middle East, Morocco is widely known to Americans through the media, which often features exotic scenes of its old medina and its folkloric spectacles. Paul Bowles's novel about Morocco, *The Sheltering Sky*, was adapted for the screen; Moroccan filmmaker M. A. Tazi's films are available on DVD. Articles in the travel section of the *New York Times* have featured Casablanca, Marrakesh, and Essaouira, to name a few. Morocco is often evoked as a beautiful place with a rich history, culture, and landscape.

But little is known about the large university at the outskirts of Fes, which houses a student body that is estimated to be about fifteen thousand. The university has an intelligentsia, and it attracts a diverse body of students who come from the city as well as the neighboring regions. Faculty and student strikes are a common occurrence at the university. Police cars and army vehicles are often parked near campus in response to unrest among students, sometimes caused by conflicts between Marxists and Islamists, or unrest stirred by students from

the former Spanish Sahara, some of whom are not in favor of Morocco's annexation of the Western Sahara to its territories. During my student years at the
university in the 1990s and my time as a faculty member in the early 2000s, I
was often caught up in an eruption of this violence. Afraid of being beaten by
the police, who do not distinguish between culprits and innocents, I had to run
for my safety. Not belonging to any of the political camps, I often felt voiceless
and invisible. This atmosphere of unrest inheres in the university setting to this
day, and student activists are frequently arrested and put on trial.

The unrest dates back to my childhood. Morocco is an open society
compared to other Muslim countries, but there are taboo topics. Growing up
in Morocco was culturally enriching but politically repressive. The monarchy
was oppressive: coups were attempted, dissenters were jailed, and newspapers
were banned. Throughout the 1970s, censorship was widespread, following two
coups d'état against Hassan II, in 1971 and 1972, from which he miraculously
escaped unscathed. With rumors of secret detention camps and prisons, I was
too fearful to speak out or voice opinions. Any reference to the political arena
would elicit stares from my parents, who did not want trouble. My childhood
years coincided with the Green March of 1975. At my elementary school,
my schoolmates and I were instructed to memorize nationalist songs in celebration of Morocco's claim to the Western Sahara. Thousands of Moroccans
participated in the so-called Green March. Moroccan public space was filled
with nationalist songs and symbols which distracted from the increasing tension. I knew all the nationalist songs, and I waved Moroccan flags in public
celebrations.

While patriotism helped ease the political tension enveloping Morocco
at the time, the Green March marked the beginning of the conflict with the Po-
lisario Front's guerillas. The secret Tazmamart prison, which was opened in 1971
in a remote rural southern region of Morocco, became a symbol of the king's
oppressive reign. French journalist Gilles Perrault's book *Notre ami le roi* (1990)
finally disclosed this secret prison to Moroccans, which ultimately prompted
the authorities to close it. Survivors of torture in Tazmamart have since written
memoirs about their years of incarceration.

In Fes, my family life was also overshadowed by oppressive family laws,
which circumscribed my legal status, along with that of other women. I soon
started to question the discrepancy between Islam as a faith that has the most
liberating potential for women, and the legal codes that restrict the rights of my
female relatives. My sister could conclude a contract for her carpet business,
but she was not trusted to be the sole witness of such a contract. The testimony
of a woman is worth only half of a man's in Morocco.

In the postcolonial period, promises of women's liberation were not fulfilled, despite King Mohammed V's attempt to emancipate women from traditional constraints. In an oft-cited symbolic gesture, King Mohammed V, upon

his return from exile in 1956, publicly took the head scarf off his daughter Lala Aicha, encouraging Moroccan women to likewise relinquish the veil and be involved in public activities. In the early post-independence period, the nationalists encouraged women's liberation, firmly believing that women's equality and advancement in the public domain would strengthen socioeconomic development. The nationalists' efforts to educate women bore fruit, as, for the first time in Moroccan history, women professionals emerged in all fields. Despite women's accomplishments during this period, the family law drafted by the *Ulema* (jurists) under the leadership of Mohammed V's son Hassan II set women back fifty years.

The juxtaposition of these incompatible gestures raises questions about women's status in Moroccan society. Family laws purportedly based on Islamic law, regulating such issues as marriage, divorce, and inheritance, were for the first time codified in imitation of French law. Traditionally, Islamic law welcomes multiple interpretations and the diversity of opinions, but in this case the set of family laws based on Islamic Sharia became stultified and closed to debate or reinterpretation. These crippling laws did not reflect the spirit of Islam; they were the product of the new secular, modern but still patriarchal state, which continued to constrain the legal status of Moroccan women.

Male and female activists protested the Moudawana (the Family Code), which reflected a dogmatic interpretation of religious precepts. Worse, it legalized gender discrimination, stifled dissent, and prescribed a hierarchical and traditional mode of life in the domestic sphere. These discriminatory laws, upholding the view that women are minors in need of male guardianship, prevented women from achieving their full potential in the socioeconomic and political sphere. The constant calls by activists for reform expressed real determination to change Morocco into a modern society where women could be integrated into the public sphere.

In Fes, I also grew up with the legacy of European (especially French) colonialism, and my languages before English were both Arabic and French. Unlike many of my generation who went to private schools that introduced them to French at an early age, I attended a traditional Koranic preschool, in which I memorized verses from the Koran and learned how to inscribe the Arabic script on clay trays. I was later exposed to French, but my traditional family, who spoke only Arabic at home, had kept me far removed from this second language. I could not explain my distance from French and later embrace of English, but eventually I realized that there is no anomaly in my attitude toward these foreign languages. I turned away from French because in Morocco, French was the language of domination. It was synonymous with colonialism and it is in French that the Moroccan colonial experience remains embedded. English too is a language of empire, but not of the empire that imposed itself on the culture where I was born and raised.

As a young woman, I revered my gentle and supportive father too much to rebel against the Arabic tradition. As a figure who inspired me to work hard and succeed academically, he was also a guide for my developing identity as a liberated woman. I would later use that very education and liberation, which I achieved with his encouragement, to change my mother. I knew that my mother was, of the two, the more keenly intelligent, but deprived of an education, she felt disadvantaged. My mother nurtured dreams and yearnings beyond what she was able to fulfill in her life, and she hoped that I would fulfill those longings. A strong woman with great interpersonal and management skills, she could have envisioned herself as a leader and a force in her community, if it were not for her illiteracy.

Her strength came from her own mother, who, like hundreds of other Moroccans in the aftermath of World War II, migrated from southern Morocco to escape starvation. At eighteen, and in the absence of her husband, who was a migrant worker in Algeria at the time, she traveled north together with her children. For the first ten years in the north, my grandmother worked on various farms while she peddled fruit and bread with her two young daughters. My grandmother's strength rested in her ability to resist poverty and dependence on the money her husband occasionally sent her from Algeria.

Although my mother was raised during a time when Morocco tried to improve the lives of women, men's sexist attitudes regarding women often prevented wives and daughters from benefiting from education, particularly within rural communities. My mother attended Koranic school through age ten, at which point she left school to help her mother. Frustrated by her own domestic experience, my mother desired a better life for me. She wavers at times between expressing regret at the opportunities she missed and satisfaction at my own achievements. As a student and young academic, I was aware of my own potential to help her achieve some degree of liberation. I showed her the possibilities available for women in the public sphere, beyond her traditional domestic environment. I once invited her to come to work with me, and I often brought her to public conferences in Morocco, which helped introduce my mother to a space into which she did not normally venture. She later recognized that even if I took after my father, I was very much her daughter. Gender works in peculiar ways. People expect "like mother, like daughter," but inherited traits do not always correlate with gender.

Valuing tradition but unable to take part in the mosque (in my tradition the mosque was for males), I learnt more about Islam from my teachers than from preachers. In the postcolonial period, Moroccan educators were adamant about preserving the Koranic tradition and its literature of laws and commentaries, and the Arabic language with its great literature and lore. But my task was also to reconcile those traditions with the reality of my global existence. I realized early on from reading French and English literature that, unlike the traditional religious culture of Morocco, which emphasizes obligation, the Western way emphasizes rights. Slowly I learned to assert myself, and I was seriously studious. Thus I discovered that there *are* other ways than rebellion, one of which is to supplement the inherited rules while still remaining loyal to one's community of origin. I tried to make sense of my life and relationships and to retain some autonomy under pressures both institutional and domestic. Abetted by a Fulbright scholarship to an M.A. program in English at Brown University, I went to the United States and to English, the language which I love.

I was not impelled by the desire for liberty or safety when I decided to leave Morocco in 1993 to pursue my graduate studies in the United States; I felt free and safe enough in Morocco as long as I did not need recourse to the law. In moving to the United States, I crossed significant cultural borders between my traditional Muslim society and the more diverse American society. Moving between two different cultures, and having to negotiate the shifting cultural codes and traditions, was not easy. The strain of going back and forth and struggling with self-identity made my first years in the United States extremely challenging.

On American campuses, I was continually asked about Islam and growing up Muslim. As I tried to create a space of critical, open dialogue, I fell in love with the work of postcolonial scholars who were involved in imagining a form of globally responsible education that could address the cultural identities of others. In America, bold headlines connected the image of terrorists and suicide bombers to the greater concepts of Islam and veiled women. I became an intercultural communicator, trying to dispel negative stereotypes about Muslim women and show their complex agency and their often ambivalent relationship to Euro-American ideals of liberty. When invited into open debate about the Muslim Woman, I wondered aloud how the history of biased representations is affecting current discourse and how biased images of Islam feed into this fear of difference. I saw this fear magnify to huge proportions in the aftermath of the September 11 attacks, when all things Muslim could evoke panic.

In April 2003 I went back to Morocco intending to embark on a new career as a university professor. It was my first time in Morocco since King Mohammed VI had succeeded his father to the throne. I could sense a breeze of change and freedom this time. The new king is known as a modernizer who has reformed family law and improved human rights; he has expanded democracy in Morocco. Changes in Moroccan law under the present king proved the compatibility of Islam and modernity with regard to emancipation of women; Morocco seems to be exemplary on this point and other Islamic nations may have to rise to the challenge.

I was disappointed to learn, though, that the Moroccan university is still not free of the tension, censorship, and fear that had prevailed in the early 1990s. In my classes I incorporated intercultural communication to reduce ignorance-based fear and increase international understanding. My attempts were constantly challenged. In 2004 a student threatened to boycott my exam for having shown the photograph of a Western woman during my Introduction to Media Studies course. Moroccan students are torn between modernity and tradition; they are also deeply troubled by the discrepancies and contradictions of today's Morocco.

Now, I teach in the expansive, "multicultural" United States of America, whose people mostly do not know the Maghreb, not even the word. The word *Maghreb* is not likely to be in their dictionaries, and it does not appear in my old French dictionaries either. Arabic words, however, are entering colloquial French, and they will soon appear in English. American dictionaries now already have words such as *djellabah* and *kasbah* (sometimes spelled with a *c*), terms that are specific to the Maghreb and to Islam, not just words related to strife and holy war like *jihad*. These are familiar terms of a religion and culture that is too little understood in this country where I reside. I see myself in an ambassadorial role, in effect; but an ambassador, more than other persons, needs self-understanding and clarity about representation. I myself represent a few reconciliations.

Therefore I speak to my English-speaking students from a global perspective. In my classes, I bring French and Arabic along with English to often-monolingual Americans, and I am continually exploring the ways in which we are all part of a global culture. This is not new for black or Jewish people who have been in the diaspora for thousands of years. But now so many of us are in the diaspora: Chaldeans in Detroit, Georgians in Queens, Poles in London, Ukrainians in Bologna, Colombians in Central Falls. A new generation of Moroccans is also migrating all over the world. Some of them are born "abroad." Many study, work, and live in the United States. They are engaged in art, literature, science, commerce, and politics. They are young and cosmopolitan citizens of a global world; they are also part of the Internet generation. Skype and Facebook are their means of communication. While in some deep, still unexplored sense, they feel Moroccan, they are now transforming Morocco into a glocal country.

I try to establish a shared orientation with my American students, often through the common denominator of popular culture: living in the glocal village, we all recognize the same headlines, listen to the same songs, and watch the same sitcoms and movies. We also all have unrecognized background assumptions, which go unrecognized precisely because they are accepted and taken for granted. Mine turn out to be Moroccan generally, with Berber origin behind that and black African way back; African generally. My family history started in the south of Morocco, in a small region bordering Algeria, where people are to this day stratified according to race and ethnic heritage. Haratins (former slaves) are segregated from Shurfa (Arabs), and Berbers are separated by language difference. The Haratins, who had been traditionally enslaved, are at the lowest rank of this southern community. My grandparents, themselves Haratins, had decided to leave that past behind when they left the south and its racial tensions for more opportunity in the north in the late 1940s. But even now that racial past still haunts my family.

We can investigate all the complexities about our past and yet come to some simple formulations. Each of us can say "I," the singular; and yet each of us is a world. I started early to ponder the complexities of my family's origin. When I am older, I would like to have as uncomplicated a view about my life experiences as my father, even though he had had a strenuous childhood in the south. He once said to me toward the end of his life: "I have nothing against anybody, and I think nobody has anything against me." I would like, after all the complications, to be able to embrace simplicity in this way.

My marriage to a foreigner, a Muslim who is often mistaken for a non-Muslim, has made me learn, and now assume, that life is not always simple. A Moroccan woman cannot be involved in a romance or a marriage with a foreigner. Once a Moroccan woman marries a foreign man, whether a Muslim or a non-Muslim, it becomes everyone's business to have—and to voice—unfavorable opinions about her marriage. There are of course interfaith marriages and interfaith families in Morocco. I often wondered how they deal with major life events (birth, adoption, coming-of-age, marriage, divorce, death). In Morocco, marrying a foreigner is neither simple nor easy. It took a court battle and a lawyer to obtain my marriage papers and to later acquire citizenship for my daughters.

People who ignore the subtleties of mixed marriages and focus exclusively on "the controversial relationship" mainly react to categories of identity, and they do so from an orientation of exclusivity. In their reactions, they are mainly upholding doctrine and dogma, and when they cling to tradition, exclusivity, and certainty, they risk seeing people as Us and Them. People can be right for themselves, but they need to see the differences between themselves and others and to accept that not all people are alike. The truth is that we are not free to choose whom we would love, but we should be disciplined enough to have jurisdiction over what we do about it.

So will we consent to be simply stereotyped, or will we demand to be recognized for who we are? What I see is that with enough motivation it is possible to quarrel bitterly and long over religious differences, squandering resources and blighting the world. Yet the three major monotheisms have enough in common that with sufficient motivation it should be possible to find reconciliations where they are necessary—while still allowing for, rather than trying to erase, differences. Some interpretations may be considered more authoritative than others, and we all submit to some authority, but we have some choice about when to submit and when to pay the price of rejecting authority that seems abusive, illegitimate, or counter to our own spirituality.

A young friend of mine startled me once with the question "Touria, how do you feel about being a woman?" I didn't "feel" about it; I was busy *being*. I had to realize, though, that I knew how I "felt" about being female, and also about being black, Moroccan, Muslim, an American resident, a scholar, a teacher, a daughter, a mother, and a wife—but I had lost sight of the question, What about being a *woman*? My parents, though they dealt with other thorny issues, never had to deal with a situation in which color and religion were so complicated by questions of gender. My response followed their examples, rather than an ideology. A lifetime of study and experience is brought to bear when I am confronted with difficult questions, and my answers express who I am and who my parents and teachers have been.

I am not called upon to defend Islam. I am not called upon to fight against colonialism and racism or to defend Moroccan independence. I am not called upon to make a feminist critique of sexism. I am not called upon to unravel Mediterranean complexities or to make peace in the Middle East. What then do I have to offer that has not been offered? As a woman, I am a mother's daughter and a mother of daughters. I am a transmitter of culture. The culture I transmit has been fought over and is itself evolving. Instead of being dogmatic, I am goal-oriented. In other words, I approach the world not in terms of battles, but from the perspective of the legacy I inherited and want to pass along.

Knowing Your Place

Diana Adesola Mafe

In the spring of 1980, a few months before my birth, Gloria Anzaldúa wrote a letter addressed to "Third World Women Writers." This letter, published as "Speaking in Tongues," has only just reached me. Perhaps I was not ready for it until now. Gloria writes: "Throw away abstraction and the academic learning, the rules, the map and compass. Feel your way without blinders. To touch more people, the personal realities and the social must be evoked—not through rhetoric but through blood and pus and sweat."

More to the point, she writes: "*Put your shit on the paper.*"

This is a hard lesson learned. I have not yet thrown away the map and compass. But I have tucked them away, out of sight. And I will try *not* to reach for them until this piece is done.

The man's features have since become fuzzy in my memory. But I recall thinking that he looked sinister, despite the bright sunshine and the warm brick thoroughfare. We had already sized each other up by the time we brushed shoulders, walking in opposite directions along a university walkway in southern Ontario. A number of stereotypes had crossed my mind. Words like *hick* and *redneck*. I too was guilty of prejudice that day. I had taken in his overalls and his swagger, met his white gaze, and immediately become guarded. My expression blank, my heartbeat inexplicably fast and my gaze unwavering, I remember marching on. As we approached each other, he slowly removed the lollipop he was sucking, revealing a tongue stained bright red. Then, so softly that I almost did not catch it, he whispered a solitary word in passing: "Nigger."

To this day, I am hesitant to admit what was murmured to me as I strolled across a pleasant campus on a late summer afternoon. He spoke so quietly, almost gently, that I thought, indeed hoped, that I was mistaken. I replayed the moment in my mind and tried desperately to convince myself that I was hearing things. The wrong things. After all, people misconstrue meaning all the time. But *that* word is decidedly hard to *mis*construe. And I was sufficiently rattled.

My identity, my right to belong, had once again been called into question. Ironically, or perhaps appropriately, I was in the midst of preparing for my doctoral comprehensive exams when this incident happened. And the postcolonial literature I was doggedly wading through came surprisingly alive after that day.

Academic objectivity melted. Terms like *subaltern* and *other* jumped off the page. In true epiphany fashion, I *became* the subaltern and the other. On a more mundane level, I became pissed off. A complete stranger had seen me, labeled me, and dismissed me in one fell swoop. I felt like I had been stamped on the forehead (Nigger) and mailed off somewhere (Return to Sender). Although cultivated on the plantations of the southern United States, the notorious *N* word is clearly international in its currency. And this particular individual was not averse to adopting the word when "necessity" dictated.

My intrinsic reaction, naive as it may sound, was utter bewilderment. Because only one thing mattered to that man on the walkway: he was white and I was not. And that simple equation, responsible for innumerable tragedies in human history, had triggered this unpleasant experience. That stranger clearly believed that I was out of place. I needed to go somewhere that would suit him and (he probably thought) suit me much better. *Back to Africa?* Yet there was a real possibility that I did not belong there either.

After all, a few years ago I was affronted on another walkway, an *African* walkway—and not by a white man but by a black woman. The occasion was my cousin's wedding in Nigeria, the woman was my aunt, and the walkway was smack down the middle of a massive Anglican church. In standard Yoruba style, the wedding was ostentatious. My entire family was dressed in traditional clothing. Since I had reached that "end of adolescence" stage where rediscovering my cultural roots was "cool," I donned a bright yellow *buba* and *iro*, draped the stiff *aso-oke iborun* over my shoulder and allowed a relative to tie the matching *gele* on my head, all with little complaint. The church was full of people milling around and searching for seats, including the aforementioned aunt, whom I had not seen since I was a child.

She sailed toward me, her elaborate starched head-tie not unlike the prow of a ship, and waited for recognition. I smiled politely, which produced a stark crease in her brow.

"Do you know who I am?" She demanded in very precise English.

"Um . . ." I faltered.

Scornful of my ignorance, she proceeded to outline my genealogy and her own formidable place in it. Visibly pleased with herself, she then instructed me to kneel down and show the proper respect. My response, in hindsight, was probably not the wisest course of action. Much like the biblical Sarah in the face of the Almighty, I laughed, unconvinced that my aunt was being serious. Serious she was. Incensed by my chuckle, she placed surprisingly firm hands on my shoulders.

"Come on! Don't you know your place!?! Just who do you think you are? You'd better kneel down in a hurry!" In full view of everybody who had packed the cathedral that day, she forced me into a kneeling position, gloated for a brief moment, and then sailed off, leaving me like flotsam in her wake.

Like the incident with the man on campus, this episode with my aunt evoked confusion, humiliation, and anger. I am willing to admit, however, that on this occasion the fault was partially mine. Since I had dressed the part, it was inevitable that I would have to *play* the part. Did I think I would shake her hand? Or kiss her on both cheeks, in the tradition of my European mother? It was a Yoruba wedding and kneeling is what Yoruba girls do when they see their Yoruba aunts come bustling toward them. But, my inner voice protests, I am only part Yoruba! I don't even speak the language! These are not really my traditions!

The upshot on this occasion, indeed many occasions, was that I had been reduced to something one-dimensional and inadequate. Like the man on the university walkway, my aunt had completely ignored all of the cultural experiences that shaped my awareness. So while my respective anecdotes are not immediately analogous, they do share a common resonance. A white man called me "nigger;" a black woman made me kneel. But both read me according to their own rigid ideas about race, gender, and culture before quickly trying to put me in my "appropriate" place.

Admittedly, as a mixed-race woman, knowing my place, appropriate or not, has always been a difficult thing. I was born to a Dutch mother and a Nigerian father—the only brown baby in the Dutch maternity ward. My cosmopolitan parents brought me "home" to Nigeria when I was two weeks old. I grew up knowing a smattering of Yoruba, rudimentary Dutch, and fluent English. Along with my two siblings, I attended first British, then American schools in Nigeria, where the student populations were always a diverse mix of nationalities and cultures. Summer vacations in Europe and North America expanded what I thought were already pretty broad horizons. By the time I arrived in Ontario, a curious, cagey, and slightly arrogant seventeen-year-old, ready to pursue an undergraduate degree in fine art and English, my sense of identity, cultural or otherwise, was decidedly fraught.

Now, almost a decade later, I am a permanent resident in Canada. I still have both a European and an African passport. I speak Canadian-accented English, a language that neither of my parents own as their first. My field is postcolonial literature. And my place remains unfixed; my sense of belonging inevitably poked and prodded by those who allege a stronger claim. People from both sides of the Atlantic nervously eye the stakes I have driven into their soil. And sometimes I am the one who denies the right to belong, pulling up the stakes with both hands, unwilling to accommodate the traditions that literally come with the territory.

Should I have reacted differently on those two occasions? Some people certainly think so, advocating that I should have "given the white guy the finger" and "told my aunt to shove it." While these responses may have felt good, they would hardly have been productive. Perhaps I should have delivered an impassioned speech, resisting my oppression with the power of my voice. Or would that have reduced me to yet another stereotype, pegged before I opened my mouth as the angry black bitch with the "bring it on" attitude? Or perhaps the insolent girl who shamefully ignores ancient traditions and talks back to her elders?

My place, regardless of citizenships, languages, or accents, may forever be in flux. And that is not necessarily a bad thing. *Home* has always been a relative term. So who do I write as today? What passport will it be? Do I write as a young African woman questioning the "old ways"? Or am I the African woman facing the challenges of emigration to a predominantly white society? And what about the world of truly "ivory" towers that I have chosen to enter, where any "ebony" at all becomes representative? Such questions could be posed ad infinitum so I will settle on three things that I know to be firm amid the flux and that represent my own personal resistance, whether to a white man or a black woman, for oppression crosses all boundaries. I write *as a woman*; I write *as a woman of color*; and, simply, *I write*.

Letter to Clara

Susan Akono

Contemplating *Lectura* is like contemplating you, Clara. The woman portrayed by Romero de Torres has the same full face, the same lavish eyebrows, and the same jet-black hair.

I thought I had already forgotten you. However, as I look at this painting, I realize that it was no more than self-delusion. A year later, your barb is still stuck in my skin, my flesh, and my blood. A sentence. A mere sentence. I thought I had it all, but it took only a single sentence of yours to annihilate my happiness. Maybe they were right, those ancients who claimed that the gods were jealous of the bliss of mortals. But what if your venom was rather a trick used by destiny to help me become aware of my condition as a woman at war?

While my eyes remain riveted on *Lectura*, the painting gradually gives way to a class of about thirty students. I remember that it was an unusually sunny autumn afternoon. With time, I began to think that it was the Madrid sun's way of waving goodbye to my naiveté. Until that day, I had assumed that I was beyond the reach of human stupidity and cruelty in the presence of fellow university students. I suppose I had to be disabused sooner or later. But was so much callousness really necessary to propel me on the road to maturity?

I found reading Tomás Rivera after Thomas Pynchon refreshing. I was captivated by the former's direct and poignant prose. And so I said enthusiastically when Martha asked for our views on *Y no se lo tragó la tierra* (*And the Earth Did Not Devour Him*). Everybody seemed to share my opinion. Martha was about to conclude the lesson when your high-pitched voice was suddenly heard: "I can understand why a poor black African who has known hunger would be more than interested in the tribulations of wretched Mexican immigrants in the United States, but we are dealing here with art and it is necessary to transcend one's personal experience." Spared as I am by nature from blushing or displaying any other epidermal sign of shame, embarrassment, or bewilderment, only my wide-open eyes betrayed how much I was overwhelmed by these feelings. As with the rebellious young hero of Tomás Rivera, earth did not devour me either. I had to endure the sepulchral silence that followed your comment.

I wanted to retort, of course. No. Not retort. I wanted to bellow, "You stupid bitch! Are you really suggesting that only war survivors can grasp and appreciate the moving depiction of the misery inflicted upon humans by war in, say, Hemingway's *For Whom the Bell Tolls*?" But the lump in my throat was too big. Gigantic. There was no way I could utter a single word.

Some of our classmates then burst into laughter. Others booed. Some others expressed their surprise at your insensitivity.

"Let's call it a day, Martha," came a man's voice.

I went into the underground and boarded the train like an automaton. Only after two stations did it dawn on me that I had taken the wrong direction. I opted to stay on the train—because line 6 is circular, I knew that I would reach my house eventually. It took me fifty minutes, instead of the usual ten, and so I had plenty of time to chew over your venomous words.

For these Westerners, it appears, I am just a poor black African, a wretched famine survivor. Sure, not all of them think that. But how many do? How many share Clara Mencía's view but, unlike her, dare not say so? Or rather, do not feel the need to say so? Take the case of our classmates. Granted, some did indeed censure Clara's insensitivity. But none told her that being African was not synonymous with being starving. In other words, they all think I am a famine survivor. What else can one expect from people coming from a society in which the only news reports about Africa are restricted to the three or four countries ravaged by war or famine? Even among the educated, how many Westerners know that there are more than fifty countries in Africa? What images does Africa evoke here? Big-bellied and skinny-legged black children; warring black clans and waves of illegal black immigrants rescued in extremis from the sea, exhausted by hunger and cold.

I remembered how I burst out laughing when, five years earlier, I went to say goodbye to one of my neighbors in Yaoundé. When he heard that I was going to Europe, he rebuked me for leaving our peaceful fatherland for a war-torn territory. Still laughing, I drew on my hazy geographical knowledge to explain to him that Bosnia was just a tiny, very tiny, part of the European continent. Little did I know that my fit of laughter was bound to turn into a long wince of pain, as similar misinformation, which I did not expect to find in a developed country, would wreak havoc with my life.

I cannot recall exactly when your venom began to poison and shatter my existence, Clara. All I know for sure is that it was at my workplace that its disastrous impact first became apparent.

I had been awarded a grant to work as a part-time translator at a Madrid publishing house. Before, the other grant holders and I used to work in a friendly atmosphere. We were bound by a sort of tacit agreement that consisted in working while always trying to have a good time. Our laughs were, almost daily, the subject of light-hearted remarks in the publishing house. "Let it go, it's just the Lewinskys," people used to say to deter anybody who would attempt to stop us.

I told my fellow grant holders nothing about your wounding remark, but nevertheless its poison leached out. It has taken me some time to realize it, but now I know that I started to mistrust and even resent them for being white Westerners and therefore, I presumed, as misinformed about Africa and prejudiced against black Africans as you.

Mistrust and resentment took over my heart, my whole being. First I began to skip the coffee break instead of joining the other grant holders as I used to. Then I took on the habit of working more than my required daily four hours. I suppose I wanted to win over our boss. I craved praise and admiration.

Your venom had dented my self-confidence to such an extent that I became boastful to conceal my insecurity. I so much wanted to show that I was much more than a poor black African or a wretched famine survivor. I took any opportunity to brag about my strikingly handsome American boyfriend, my excellent marks, or my mastering of several African and Western languages. My fellow grant holders soon found me unbearable and cold-shouldered me.

Although I was still studious and eager to attend classes, I became extremely reluctant to express my opinion. I bet you noticed that with glee, Clara. Like a knocked-out boxer forced to endure the victorious roars of the opponent, I restricted myself to listening silently to our classmates and, sometimes, to you.

I could not help mistrusting all Spanish people in the street. If, for instance, one of them looked at me, I assumed that they harbored such nasty thoughts as: "Look at that black African woman. She is really lucky to have escaped starvation. Doesn't she look good? Nothing like her fellow black Africans we see on TV. No wonder they would do anything to get here." If, in a train, any of the seats next to me remained empty, my conclusion was: "Of course, they do not want to sit beside the black woman."

Your venom also hijacked my love for Norman. It slipped into our relationship and steadily erected an insurmountable barrier between us. My identity crisis and subsequent insecurity made both my life and his a misery.

Though Norman's skin was even darker than mine, I began to mistrust and resent him too. Not for being a poor African, this time, but for being a privileged wealthy Westerner.

If he gave me a book by Javier Marías, José Saramago, or Philip Roth, I would mock and ask him whether he was unaware that as a poor African woman, I could not enjoy the literature of the rich. More than once, when he bought me flowers, I told him that instead of wasting money on such a frivolous present, he should have given it to a charity and saved the lives of several starving children. If he did not hold my hand when we walked on the street, I accused him of being ashamed of me. And if he held it, I would provoke a row by inquiring if he guided me because he thought there were no roads in my native Third World country.

Norman decided to break up with me after a particularly blazing argument. He reminded me how he had made it clear when we met that he wanted a harmonious relationship. While he admitted that I had made him very happy for two years, he complained that things had changed in the last six months. I had become so stupid, sarcastic, unkind, and spiteful that he could no longer stand me.

I tried to plead with him. But Norman strode away before I could say anything. Though I acknowledged that our relationship had been going downhill for some time, I was shocked at the drastic step taken by the man I knew I still loved. I had not yet realized how much your venom had affected me, Clara. I was still unaware that I was no longer the woman with whom Norman had once fallen in love.

The yellow dress. No, the red. I think the yellow suits me better. It highlights my thin waist and my pear-shaped bottom. I feel irresistible when I am wearing it. But this is not about me. It is about *him*. In which dress will *he* find me irresistible? I remember reading in that Senegalese women's magazine, *Amina*, that men find suggestive clothing sexier than revealing clothing. The red dress is certainly less revealing than the yellow. Besides, I know that he likes it because he told me so one day. He has never seen the yellow and he might not like it. What a disaster that would be! So let's play safe. I will wear the red.

But what about my hair? Should I have it loose or tied? And what about the make-up? Should I give it the full works or something a bit more subtle? And the bag? Should I choose a big or a small one? And the shoes? Should I wear a high-heeled or a low-heeled pair?

I had sworn to myself that I would win back Norman. I did not want any bitch to snatch him from me. I had insisted so much that barely three days after our break-up and, despite his avowed intention never to see me again, he had agreed to do so. I started to get ready four hours before our rendezvous. I was about to leave my house when I decided to take a last look at the mirror. At first, I smiled with satisfaction. But then, something within me suddenly broke. Although the red dress, the sophisticated make-up, and the stylishly tied hair made me appear stunning, I was devastated. I looked at least six years older than my twenty-four. I was pathetic. While there was still a frozen smile on my lips, my eyes were far from smiling. They were unrecognizable, harsh, terrifying, full of rage and resentment.

I called Norman to excuse myself. I crumpled into the sofa as soon as I hung up. I had, at long last, understood what was wrong. No dress, no make-up, no amount of sophistication could help me win back my ex-boyfriend. As things stood, I could no longer tug his heartstrings, for I had lost my former self, the self that had captivated him almost three years earlier.

I needed to start fighting to become my own person again, or an even better individual. I had no idea how long it would take me to do so. But I knew I had no right to make Norman unhappy or prevent him from seeing somebody else in the meantime.

Granted, I have not yet forgotten you, Clara Mencía. But I don't think I would ever let either your barb or that of any other prejudiced individual lacerate my life again. Supposing I were to see you one of these days, what would I do? I am sure I would be totally honest. I would invite you for a coffee and, while you would be sipping it, I would tell you everything that has happened to me since that fateful autumn afternoon.

No, I would not speak about that. I would do my best to obtain your address and, afterwards, send you as many letters as necessary to make you perceive the full impact of your venom on my life. I would keep copies of these letters as a tangible reminder of what can happen when one allows a bump in the road to become a Kilimanjaro.

I made a terrible mistake, Clara. You set me a trap and I fell headlong into it. I now know what I did wrong, though. You alluded to my origin to defeat me, and you won because I attempted to fight with the same weapons without noticing that they were rotten.

You boasted about what fortune has given you. And I did the same, instead of realizing that to boast about fortuitous circumstances is to transform oneself into a slave of fortune. Has little Leo, the few-week-old son of the British prime minister, gained an *A* with honors in an exam failed by Rosita, the little Mozambican girl born at the top of a tree?

Listen, Rosita, do not follow my example, do not feel ashamed of your condition. For whoever mocks you is a hundred times more miserable than you. I was not born at the top of a tree, but my duty as a human being is to identify with you. The shame is not even remotely yours, but humanity's, for letting that happen. For a long time, I have tried to dissociate myself from the squalor with which you associated me. But it's over now, Clara. I did not pass any exam to be born to Cameroonian diplomats, any more than you did when you landed your wealthy Spanish parents. None of us did anything to avoid being born in war-torn Sudan or Kosovo. But unlike you, I shall identify with the less fortunate. From now on, I shall wallow in muck and mud.

That I did not know hunger is completely irrelevant. Let me paraphrase Aimé Césaire and tell you that from now on, my mouth will be the mouth of the hungry who are too hungry to speak.

So you think one is only moved by experiences similar to one's own? Think again, Clara. One is not always one. In my case, one is, at least, five. For while I am a pure black woman, I can silence neither the white part within me nor the yellow nor the brown nor the red. In other words, I cannot silence my humanity. No I cannot. I shall identify with all the people at war, all the people battling against prejudice, injustice, and sheer misfortune.

My mouth will be the mouth of those South Asian women burned by their husbands. My mouth will be the mouth of those African immigrants sent back to their countries, deprived of the right to try to improve their living conditions, as did millions of Europeans who emigrated to Africa, America, and elsewhere. My mouth will be the mouth of that Palestinian father attempting in vain to shield his son from a rain of bullets. My mouth will be the mouth of the thousands of women murdered each year by their partners. My mouth will be the mouth of my friend Fatima who begged me one day to describe an orgasm to her; of this woman whose sex organs were mutilated in her childhood, for whom sex is synonymous with pain, humiliation, and bitterness.

My mouth will be the mouth of that Spanish girl splashed with acid by her own mother, for daring to denounce the sexual assaults to which she was subjected by her own father.

Was your venom a trick used by destiny to help me become aware of my condition as a woman at war? So be it. I shall assume it from now on without fear. I know that it won't be easy. Who said life was a bed of roses?

There are quite a few visitors at the Reina Sofía museum this Saturday morning. While I am still lost in the contemplation of *Lectura*, somebody gently taps me on the shoulder.

"Excuse me, señora," a woman's high-pitched voice says. "I can't see the painting. Can you move on?"

That high-pitched voice!

I anxiously turn round. The woman raises her lavish eyebrows as our eyes meet. Her full face reddens. She nervously runs her fingers through her jet-black hair. My heart skips several beats. My knees buckle. But I manage to smile and calmly ask, "Move on, Clara?"

Part Seven

Standing
at the Edge of Time
*African Women's Visions
of the Past, Present, and Future*

In this final section, we present the transcription of a roundtable presentation and discussion held at the Center for African Studies at Rutgers University on April 4, 2007. For this roundtable, which was moderated by Dr. Abena P. A. Busia, two of the anthology editors, Pauline Dongala and Omotayo Jolaosho, were joined by contributor Marame Gueye and Rutgers graduate student in anthropology Nimu Njoya in a wide-ranging discussion of their visions for the future of women in Africa, in their home countries as well as in the diaspora. The conversation reached deep into the past as the panelists evoked the struggle of their mothers and grandmothers to propel them to the forefront of education and opportunity, and looked into the future at the new, hybrid culture they are creating for themselves and their children as they begin to establish themselves in the United States. As Marame Gueye concludes, African women today, whether at home in their countries of origin or out in the diaspora, are engaged in a "circle of work and struggle and resistance, and each one of us does whatever we feel we can do to make this thread continue."

The last word in this collection goes to Dr. Abena P. A. Busia, whose poem "Liberation" recounts the struggles between past, present, and future that are being waged in the hearts and minds of so many contemporary African women. As a scholar, teacher, and activist, Dr. Busia is one of a handful of forceful African women scholar-activists who have led the way in strengthening the voices and raising the political profile and clout of African women. "We can laugh beauty into life," Busia says, "and still make you taste / the salty tears of our knowledge." Laughter, beauty, and salty tears bring our exploration of contemporary African women's writing of resistance to a fitting close, awaiting the responses of our sisters and brothers in the ongoing struggle to envision and bring about a world in which all of us—men and women, Africans and other peoples worldwide—can go beyond resistance into a new era of productive, peaceful collaboration for the common good.

"We Are
Our Grandmothers' Dreams"

African Women Envision the Future

**Pauline Dongala,
Marame Gueye,
Omotayo Jolaosho,
Nimu Njoya, and
Abena P. A. Busia**

Dr. Abena P. A. Busia

Good afternoon, everybody, I'm very glad to see you all here.* We have with us today at our roundtable discussion some of the editors and contributors to this wonderful forthcoming volume, *African Women Writing Resistance*, who are going to share with us their visions for a future for Africa and especially for Africa's women. This is very important because, as those of us who work in African studies know, most of the time we're struggling against the tides of the past, and nobody thinks of us as having a future. Certainly nobody thinks of African women as being able to envision a future, so this is important work we will be engaging in today. Our plan is that each of the panelists will say a few words about the topic, and then we will have an open discussion.

*Roundtable transcribed and edited by Jennifer Browdy de Hernandez.

Omotayo Jolaosho

I'm from the Yoruba tribe, and there is a Yoruba proverb about the necessity of looking into the past to envision the future. Translated, the proverb goes, "It is only a child who will keep moving forward when she has fallen; the adult will look back to identify the source of her downfall." This proverb highlights the contribution of the past to present circumstance and its crucial role in the visioning process. It tells us, somewhat counterintuitively, that confronting the past is necessary in order to move forward successfully, in order not to be like that child who, though moving forward, continually falls and thus only achieves a staggered progress.

That word, *progress*, is one I have been thinking about a lot lately. It is one of several words key to the discussion at hand—what would progress mean for women of Africa? I am not here to provide an answer but to offer some reflections on this question. As one of four editors of the anthology *African Women Writing Resistance*, I am in possession of a collection of texts carrying the voices of various contemporary African women. These texts serve as a precious resource for me, because I myself as an African woman recognize the themes that have been recorded in these writings.

Pervasive in some of the writings is a sense of what W. E. B. Du Bois has termed double consciousness. Describing the psychological state of Africans in the American diaspora, he wrote in *The Souls of Black Folk*: "[T]wo souls, two thoughts, two unreconciled strivings; two warring ideals in one dark body, whose dogged strength alone keeps it from being torn asunder." We hear echoes of this description in the words of anthology contributor Diana Mafe, a contemporary mixed-race woman born to a Dutch mother and Nigerian father, who writes about the difficulty of finding her place in the world today:

> I had been reduced to something one-dimensional and inadequate. . . . A white man called me "nigger," a black woman made me kneel. But both read me according to their own rigid ideas about race, gender, and culture before quickly trying to put me in my "appropriate" place. . . .
>
> My place, regardless of citizenships, languages, or accents, may forever be in flux. . . . So I will settle on three things that I know to be firm amid the flux and that represent my own personal resistance, whether to a white man or a black woman, for oppression crosses all boundaries. I write *as a woman*, I write *as a woman of color*, and, simply, *I write*.

For Mafe, writing is the source of dogged strength that keeps her from being torn asunder, the anchor amid the flux. That she has resigned herself to forever being in flux raises the question of whether reconciliation is possible for women like Diana Mafe, whom Audre Lorde calls the hyphenated people of the diaspora.

Like Diana Mafe, I was born and raised in Nigeria, but I have lost a sense of home. I have spent the past eleven years in the United States. Two years ago, when I returned to Nigeria for a visit, a friend told me that I was Nigerian by name and passport but I was not really Nigerian. In my reflections on the experience, you can hear something breaking. I wrote:

> Considering myself Nigerian, I always knew that it would take going back home to reclaim my true self, for pieces of me to be made whole. So to be told that I was Nigerian but not Nigerian put me back in an uncertain territory as to the source of my identity. The result of going home has become much like Eman's from Wole Soyinka's play "The Strong Breed," who said: "This, after all, is what I sought. It was here all the time. And I threw away the part of me that was formed in strange places. I made a home in my birthplace." To claim a home in my native land, I would have to sacrifice those parts of me formed in the "strange place" that is America. I took it for granted that going back to Nigeria would make me whole, but arrived to realize that Nigeria only wants me in pieces. Despite the journey, perhaps because of it, home evades me.

Khanyisa Mjindi, a South African woman, demonstrates that these unreconciled strivings—for home, for place, for identity—are not only diasporic in nature. She describes the divide between her life in the city and the rural area of Eastern Cape in which she grew up, a split that plays out right at the level of her body.

> A week before going home to the deep Transkei, I have to shove food down my little throat like I'll be taken to an abattoir. I do this solely to gain a bit of weight because where I come from, a woman should have a little wheel around the belly, big thighs, and the works. It feels like I am trying too hard to fit in. The part that makes me more sick is the fact that I am trying to fit in with my own people. This is where I come from and today I have to make an effort to be accepted by my own people. I feel out of place in a place I call home. I feel like an outsider in a place where I supposedly belong. A week before I come back to the city, I have to starve myself so I look slim and trim. I must now be a woman for the city.

Khanyisa asks, "Which society do I belong to? Is where I come from more important than where I am going?" Because the histories of our nations, indeed the history of our continent, is written through the details of our individual lives, such questions as Khanyisa's are all the more significant.

The experiences of women like anthology contributor Sybille Ngo Nyeck present another perspective on the question of home and belonging, bringing this question to a dangerous pitch. Sybille lives in the United States, exiled from her native Cameroon. As a lesbian, her life in Cameroon was unsafe, particularly since she was a visible documenter of the trends of homophobia in a country where homosexuality is illegal. "I had met many gays and lesbians in Cameroon and knew the difficulties they faced on a daily basis and decided that someone needed to do something," she said. "So I decided to write about it." When she was arrested in 2004, she applied for and was granted asylum in the United States. The impact of her work is such that her writings represent 80 percent of the resources used by the U.S. Department of Homeland Security and its Citizen and Immigration Services to assess asylum claims based on sexual orientation in Africa.

The danger present in Sybille's experience is echoed in experiences that describe rape as a weapon targeting lesbians and other women who are seen to challenge traditional sex roles. What does the future hold for women like Sybille, forced to flee from home, and for many others for whom danger is a daily experience? What are they striving for? Is it protection, a legally inscribed sense of safety and tolerance, or a more welcoming society? What does the future hold for women like those in a collective in Kinshasa, in the Democratic Republic of Congo, who describe themselves as victims of rape, other sexual violence, and poverty, even though they live in a no-conflict area of a country ravaged by continued warfare?

From the small sampling that I have been able to provide from the anthology, you can see that our experiences are wide-ranging yet our voices resonate with one another. To conclude, I will ask again—what does the future mean for women of Africa and what are the challenges that would cause us to stumble and fall?

Marame Gueye

As I was reflecting on the topic of our roundtable, I began to wonder, what do we mean when we say "the future"? Is it tomorrow, this summer, in three years, in a decade, or twenty years from now? Then I realized that, for me, the future is today and it is all bound up with how I negotiate my dual position as an African woman living in the United States. I started to dwell on my identity and the question of home.

At this moment I call Senegal my home, and I try as much as I can to stay connected to it. However, this so-called connectedness is questionable because every time I go home, I realize that the gap that separates me from my sisters is getting bigger and bigger. Whether I want it or not, I am not the same sister who left eight years ago. My dance moves are questioned and my sense of style is questioned. In our family, dance is very important. My first week at home is very tricky because my sisters always spy on me whenever there is music to see if I still have my moves, and depending on how I perform, they decide to come and start talking to me or they stay away because I'm not doing the moves right.

The reality of my ongoing "outsider-hood" did not hit me until my mom told me that I speak Wolof with an American accent. She was astonished when I started crying in response; she could not understand why I was so upset at that comment. She told one of my sisters that I had become too sensitive, that I could no longer take a joke. Little did she know that this joke brought to light the reality of my displacement and my hybridity. It's all the more painful because the America that she seems to be claiming for me does not perceive me as part of it. I still have to apply for a visa to get into the United States, and at the port of entry I still have to go to the line reserved for visitors. I am an alien. In America I am an African who speaks English with a Wolof accent, and everyone asks me when am I going back home—to Senegal. So it's painful to realize that the place that I called home and thought of as home all my life can let me go so easily.

Should I see America as it sees me? As a place where I work, but to which I do not belong? Or should I make it my own? The second choice seems to me the more desirable because I don't think one can work and live in a place without caring for it. It is just not possible for me. The same question applies to Senegal. Should I close my eyes on the suffering and precariousness of my brothers' and sisters' existence and look on them as strangers? I could never do that. Despite the fact that most people in Senegal think of me as Americanized, they still expect me to claim Senegal as my home. And I do think of myself as Senegalese. Thus the future for me is finding ways to reconcile the two worlds that I live in simultaneously. Is it too much to ask that I want to claim both? Should I favor one over the other? How do I create balance?

Coincidentally, today Senegal is celebrating forty-seven years of independence from France, and our eighty-three-year-old president just won a second term in office. University students have been on strike for more than three months, unemployment has never been higher, and girls still have less chance of attending school than boys. Hospitals are full of dying patients for lack of medications and proper care.

When I think about the future, I think about changes I want to see happen in my two worlds.

In the future, I want to see a proud Africa whose sons and daughters would not feel the need to board boats to leave and escape to Spain in order to survive.

In the future, I want every young boy or girl in every African village to be given the opportunity to attend school.

In the future, I want every African child to go to bed with a full stomach and a roof overhead.

In the future, I want the HIV/AIDS virus, which claims so many African sons and daughters, to be vanquished.

In the future, civil wars and genocides will be history, a history that will never be repeated.

In the future, African women will stop bleaching their skin in order to be someone they will never be.

Also, in the future, there will be an end to "urban renewal" in Harlem, and its residents will live in neighborhoods free of violence, drugs, crime, and prostitution.

In the future, poor black, white, and Latino inner-city children will have good schools and will be given the same opportunities the kids in suburbia have.

In the future, child soldiers will not die for an unjust war.

In the future, Iraqi people will recover their dignity and live in a country free of extremism and bigotry.

In the future, the color of her skin and the accent of her words will not determine how much respect she is given.

In the future, my mother will understand why I speak Wolof with an accent and why I am not ashamed of it anymore.

In the future, I want my two worlds to cohabit within me in harmony.

In the future, my children will be proud to be citizens of the world, a world free of racism, nationalism, poverty, war, fundamentalism, greed, and corruption.

So for me, the future is all the things I want and strive to have today.

Pauline Dongala

I am going to focus on my own experience in my remarks: I am going to explain why I was forced to come to the United States, and how my experiences have shaped my vision for a better future for Africa and for African women, especially. I want to share some stories about violence against women in the civil war that I lived through in my country, Congo-Brazzaville. And then I will share with you some ideas of how I see the future.

When the war started in Brazzaville, the capital of my country, it was horrible. Rival militias bombarded the capital and the neighborhoods, turning them to rubble, and began shooting civilians at random in the city. According to official estimates, the fighting left ten thousand people dead, but some sources believe the number to be much higher, since those who sought refuge in the equatorial rainforests, as I and my family did, were not counted.

Both of the rival militias were raping women and girls, including old women and little girls. The militias did awful things. They plunged bottles and other objects into women's bodies and abused women in many other ways.

Rape and torture of women was used as a weapon of domination over the rival group.

A friend's daughter, who was hiding in our compound, was kidnapped by a group of five gunmen. They kept her for three days. They raped her, cut her hair, gave her a soldier's outfit and brought her back almost dead and confused. She told us they had forced her to smoke marijuana.

Another friend, who witnessed the killing of her father, said: "They caught us by surprise. When the gunmen arrived at our home, I was with my father. They asked me to have sex with him. When my father refused, they killed him and they all raped me. I still vividly recall what happened that day, I can never forget it."

While I was running with my family into the forest, none of the women I saw had a gun. All the women were just victims trying to survive. Some had lost their children, their husbands, their belongings, or had been raped. Later some friends told me that because of the rapes, they ended up having a child they did not want.

In Nkayi and Dolisie, two cities that witnessed fierce combat, women have still not recovered from the trauma of the civil war and still do not want to talk about what they went through. In the words of my sister-in-law, "Women suffered acute spasms of ethnic hatred and violence, and we won't forgive that."

Women paid a heavy price in the civil war in the Congo. They lived and are still living with insecurity. The rate of HIV has doubled, causing a high rate of death among women. In Congo-Brazzaville, the United Nations and Doctors Without Borders have conducted some programs to support the few women who were willing to speak out about their rape. Many women, especially in the countryside, were gang-raped and have received no help since the conflict started. It is hard for them to talk about it—they fear being rejected by their families and peers. This same pattern has occurred in many war-torn African countries: Rwanda, Sudan, the Democratic Republic of Congo, Nigeria, Ethiopia, Burundi, Chad, Somalia, and more.

In answering the question of how I am envisioning the future for African women, I would like to focus on the issue of rape and the future of raped women. I would like to see greater protection, empowerment, and awareness of Congolese women and African women in general. The first step is to reinforce women's security and offer them more protection. In the Congo, after the fighting stopped, the government ran some programs with the United Nations to collect arms and guns in the capital, but in the rest of the country, militia members and civilians still have their guns, with which they commit robberies and killings.

I would like to see Congolese women, and African women generally, enjoy respect and full rights as human beings. I would like to see an end to the cruel practices perpetrated against them, like rape, systematic humiliation, and torture. I would like to see African women who have suffered male violence living free of trauma and psychological trouble. They should not see themselves as victims or feel guilty and shamed. I would like to see self-confidence returning to Congolese women and to all African women whose lives have been disrupted by war.

I envision a world of empowerment for African women, with libraries and meeting centers offering literacy programs, training programs, and counseling programs that help women to flourish. I would like to see a world where Congolese women, and all African women, have access to public lectures and materials on women's rights; a world where women have organizations that will help them to network with other experienced women in order to reach out and engage with each other.

When I look into the future, I envision a future of liberated women in the Congo, and all over the African continent.

Nimu Njoya

A few weeks ago I had a chance to attend the screening of a new film by the award-winning documentary maker Thomas Allen Harris. His film is titled *The Twelve Disciples of Nelson Mandela*, and it's based on the story of the first wave of South African exiles who left the country in 1960 to keep the anti-apartheid movement alive from East Africa, Europe, America, and Cuba. Harris's own father was a member of the twelve.

It's a moving film, but one scene in particular has seized me and refused to let go. In an interview featured in the documentary, one of the original twelve disciples tells the story of how, as a young man, he took up employment with a white farmer over the school holidays to earn some money. He worked day after day, digging and watering and weeding and planting. He worked in all kinds of weather, with abuses raining upon his back the whole time. Finally, after many weeks of hard labor, he came to the Boer employer and asked for his pay. The Boer called the police on him, and they beat him to a pulp and sent him home with nothing to show for his hard work but his wounds. At this point in the narration, the interviewee, now an older gentleman, strengthened and toughened by a life of struggle and exile, begins to break down. That particular experience of brutality, he remembers, brought him to the point where he was unable to envision a future for himself in apartheid South Africa. *He was unable to envision his own future.* Only through the struggle could it begin to come into view once again.

So as I was thinking about the theme for today's roundtable, this scene from the documentary came back to haunt me even more powerfully. Like the people in the film, I felt my imagination giving way before reality. The experiences of racism, imperialism, sexism, and violence mark all aspects of our presence in the world as African women: mind, body, soul, substance, and imagination. Oppression ruptures our experience of time by invalidating and erasing memory, turning the present into chaos, and blocking our ability to envision the future. The tearing apart of time interrupts the processes by which we construct coherent and continuous-seeming selves in the world: it interferes with our capacity to see ourselves as coming from somewhere, standing somewhere, and heading somewhere. As people of African descent, wherever we are in the world, we constantly remind each other that you don't know where you are going unless you know where you came from. For African women to be able to envision the future, therefore, we have a lot of work to do on the past and the present, to figure out their meaning and try to put together the broken pieces in a way that gives our lives some continuity and coherence.

This task includes all the efforts that women's movements in Africa are making to end interpersonal violence, intrastate conflicts, and economic injustice. Women in Africa have called the past to account in their present struggles, rebelling against legacies of colonialism such as the devaluation of agricultural production and the exploitation of a growing industrial labor force. The women's movement is also fighting against the injustices that are perpetrated against women in the name of tradition, such as childhood marriages and female genital mutilation. Writing, storytelling, and oral histories have been very important in the great reckoning that is taking place between the past, the present, and the future of African women. It is in the telling of our own experiences, our mothers' struggles, and our foremothers' visions that it becomes possible to piece together the lives that have been shredded across time and across generations.

African women's lives have also been torn apart and scattered across space. Enslavement, forced migrations, the pressures of scarcity and economic deprivation, environmental devastation, and armed conflict have destroyed the coherence and continuity of life for millions of women. Many, of course, have lost their lives or those of their loved ones. Many more must try to start anew in strange lands where they are treated as second-class citizens or find themselves in increasingly permanent refugee camps. Over half of the world's internally displaced persons are Africans, approximately thirteen million people. For those with greater cultural and economic capital, such as a formal education, the difficulty of piecing together a life in exile is mitigated in many ways. Yet the psychic costs of spatial disintegration, even in the absence of a grave risk of physical harm, make it difficult for African women to reconstruct their lives in exile. It is difficult, but certainly not impossible. More and more women are engaging in a self-conscious and public effort to come together in strange places and mend the broken pieces. This anthology project represents such an effort, and I'm honored to be connected with it and to participate in this conversation.

And yet in these efforts to build coherent and continuous-seeming selves, there will always be gaps that we cannot fill, and we must be ready to respect those silences that are not meant to be broken. In Elechi Amadi's novel *The Concubine*, there is a scene where the heroine, Ihuoma, is sitting in her house weeping. She is a widow and suffers grievously from the brutal affronts of a man who thinks he can do whatever he wants to her, including seizing the produce from her land, simply because she is a woman alone in the world. But Ihuoma is not alone. Her best friend comes into the compound, and when she sees Ihuoma weeping, she puts her arms around her and they weep together quietly: no words are spoken. Only later does she ask Ihuoma, "What is the matter?"

As Gayatri Spivak reminds us in her *Critique of Postcolonial Reason*, we cannot construct a seamless and uninterrupted narrative where there has been a repeated tearing of time. Trying to force all the pieces together, allowing no gaps or cracks, can be a violence in itself. She makes a point that is worth elaborating upon here, because as we try to give African women's lives greater visibility, we sometimes inadvertently cover them up even more. The normative commitment of feminist and Africanist scholars to privilege the "grassroots" as a site for activism or resistance has led us into certain conundrums. Feminist scholar Nancy Naples notes in her *Women's Activism and Globalization* that "the call to reaffirm the grassroots . . . runs through much of the feminist literature on women's movements and political organizing. However," she cautions, "this privileging of the so-called grassroots can also lead to a romanticization of this site of struggle as well as a tendency to 'other' women said to be at the grassroots."

The focus and sense of political purpose that our work gains from privileging the lives of ordinary women has been gained at the expense of losing sight of many other women whose lives do not fit our ideas of "ordinary." Ordinary, or grassroots, in the African context has been taken to mean poor women, mostly in rural areas, who have little formal education and few economic opportunities. Often, we understand their daily lives to be circumscribed by cultural norms and practices that threaten their health and well-being. This is indeed an important constituency for feminism. But we must not lose sight of the complexity of shifting positions in these locations and the multiplicity of lived experiences of African women today: those of us present in this room today; those who came across the Atlantic centuries before us in bondage; the women on the shop floors of factories all over Africa's industrial landscape, in mining villages, on fishing boats and commercial farms, in schools, churches, and urban slums, on dance floors, in prison cells and parliament, driving buses and taxis, at the stock exchange, in refugee camps, and Ellen Johnson-Sirleaf in the Liberian executive mansion. To envision, for me, is always a conscious effort to keep all these locations in sight, and to open myself to the possibility that there are many more that we can bring into view and embrace in sisterhood.

Abena Busia

Thank you all so very much. I think we will go straight to responses and discussion.

Q: I am very interested in what you said, Nimu, about the privileging of the grassroots and how this could be a problem for intellectuals trying to be politically engaged, be it in the women's movement or other political engagements. I'm wondering what gets lost in trying to move beyond the grassroots, in trying to speak for women who were able to enter the diaspora, women who were able to come to the United States or Europe to get an education, a Ph.D., and so on. Does the attention need to be on the most marginalized? How do we practice solidarity as intellectuals? There was a lot of envisioning about the future and what we want to see on this panel, but how do we make this a practice, as opposed to just a utopian statement?

Nimu Njoya: I'll respond to your first question, about the grassroots. What I wanted to emphasize was not so much that we shouldn't be thinking about the women who are facing some of the most difficult challenges today, but rather that the idea of the grassroots sometimes misrepresents the grassroots itself because it focuses on the lack, on the needs, without talking about the resources that are there in the first place. So we end up with an image of a grassroots African woman as sort of standing on an open landscape, barefoot, nothing in the head, nowhere to go, coming from nowhere, heading nowhere, and in need of help, with no resources of her own. Because I've been very interested in funding for women's projects and that's been my main area of research, I've seen donors start their programs with the idea that because these women are facing so many problems, they're all needs and no resources. They don't start out with the idea that these are people who are already living and working in an environment and pulling together whatever little resources they can. They often end up with completely misconceived programs because of a misconception of what the grassroots really means. So the problem is not simply that we are focusing on the grassroots, but that we have an idea of it that is in not in line with what the lived realities really are.

Marame Gueye: I wanted to add that sometimes those of us who have been to school at home or abroad, or who have the opportunity to live abroad, feel that we have arrived, in the sense of having sufficient economic resources, since we always talk about life in terms of material resources. But when we talk about how we position ourselves in the world, sometimes I feel like I am the one who has *not* arrived. Sometimes I feel that that woman that you might have seen in a vacant landscape, barefoot, has more than I do, because at least she has a sense of herself, which sometimes I am lacking. I want us to think about that.

Abena Busia: Sometimes our vision of the term grassroots includes neither "grass" nor "rootedness," and that's a very key point. The issue you raise, Marame, is a very political one, based partly on an idea of authenticity, an idea of the real—when in fact all of these complex issues are based more in mythology than in the ways in which we actually live our lives. It is never an either/or, and that's the struggle for a lot of us. You don't come *either* from Great Barrington, Massachusetts, *or* from Bamako, you come from *both*.

Omotayo Jolaosho: In terms of the question of how we practice solidarity, the example that Nimu just gave of funding schemes for women's projects is certainly one site we can look at because the intention in these projects is to act in solidarity. I was also thinking about silence and listening in terms of practicing solidarity. The importance of being silent is something that we don't always think enough about, particularly as scholars. And also when we're thinking about healing, it seems to me that weeping, and doing nothing but weeping, is sometimes really a way of acting in solidarity.

Pauline Dongala: I would like to add a word about networking. Opening up to other women is crucial to the practice of solidarity. When you reach out, when you open up, when you receive and when you give, you are acting in solidarity.

Nimu Njoya: What Pauline is saying is very important. One of the greatest challenges in trying to build an international women's movement is that too often women who feel they have a lot to *give* are not always willing to *receive*. Solidarity doesn't just mean being willing to aid someone else's struggle, but also to let someone else's struggle transform your own life. That's what real solidarity is about.

Abena Busia: For me, in terms of envisioning a future, one of the most exciting things that's happened to me personally in the last five years was being asked to be one of the founding board members of the African Women's Development Fund. On the board were African women, all of them born in Africa, some of them working somewhere else other than home, some of them still where they were born, having gone away and come back. We sat and thought about all these issues—who gives, who receives, what the conditions are, etc.—and we decided that one of the most important things African women need is to be able to mobilize our own resources, with none of the foreign strings attached. So we created a foundation that raises money to give to African women's organizations.

On the day we announced it for the first time, I was asked to emcee a reception at the Beijing +5 conference. It was just our friends, and a lot of the people present were women from women's organizations who had supported each other to get to that conference. It wasn't a fundraiser, we just said this is what we are, this is what we're going to do. It wasn't a fundraiser, I repeat—but our sisters were so excited that we raised $14,000 in a ninety-minute cocktail party, just from women coming up to us and pledging.

Since then, in the five years we've been in existence, we have raised enough money to give away nearly $4 million to about 250 African women's organizations in forty-five countries. It's an organization run by black women, and we only fund black women's organizations from the grassroots. We fund projects as small as a group of women in northern Ghana who needed a tractor, to continent-wide organizations like FIDA [International Federation of Women Lawyers] and WiLDAF [Women in Law and Development in Africa]. And we have done it. We've done it because we talked to each other and we realized that the grassroots are not barren spaces, not at all.

Q: What I like very much about your anthology is what Nimu presented so beautifully by saying that there is more than one type of site of resistance. Resistance has to be problematized. It comes in a diversity of spaces and forms and uses different tools. I am impressed that your volume covers some of the areas that are problematic even for African feminists. For example, the whole question of homosexuality is one of the most volatile questions in African studies, and your volume includes that, and I appreciate that very much. And to cover the whole range from verbal art to political action in the traditional sense is very important, and makes me think of a comment that Wole Soyinka made at one of his lectures at Ohio State. He said, "Today people know me as the Nobel Prize winner, but the people who really saved me are the women who fed me in their homes and created subversive structures that diverted the attention of my oppressors." So there are many types of resistance, and women play a role in just about all of them. I am glad to see that you tried not to exclude different types of resistance in your anthology.

Abena Busia: I was struck by something that I want to share with you. You know the wonderful African American dramatist Anna Deavere Smith? She maintained that all of us, whenever we are telling stories, switch from prose to poetry when we get to the dramatic and emotional core of our story. Listening to you speak today, there were so many places where your prose turned to poetry: Marame's litany of the way things will be in the future, Pauline's vision of what she would like to see in the future, and that last sentence of Nimu's that began in mining villages and fishing boats and ended with Ellen Johnson-Sirleaf in the Liberian executive mansion. Give me that sentence and I will turn it into a poem for you! You have three marvelous poems right there. It was extraordinary listening to you speak, because when each one of you got to that moment when the prose turned to poetry, there was that extraordinary lyrical quality, and the poet in me was saying, oh my goodness I want to sit with you and take those words and you will have four poems with which to punctuate the essays in this volume. It was really wonderful!

Marame Gueye: There were moments when I was talking that I could feel my tears coming. I did get very emotional.

Abena Busia: You could hear it, and it was very powerful.

Q: Listening to Pauline Dongala's description of what women go through in armed conflict, I'm wondering why women don't empower themselves with guns in situations when they are so vulnerable to attack. Do they not want to fight violence with violence? Are they afraid of using guns? Is it hard for them to get guns?

Pauline Dongala: To begin with, violence is not the answer to violence. The history of women in Africa, in my recollection, has never been violent. Women tend to be more nurturing. In the Congo specifically, we don't have many women in the army. So for a woman to take a gun and protect herself wasn't really a possibility, at least for Congolese women. They were caught by surprise, they were taken in their daily life. They were just victims. Taking guns and organizing as women to protect themselves—it just wasn't something they could do. Also, most of the victims, talking about women, don't know how to get arms.

Abena Busia: The one group of women we have on record, in terms of having given testimony about fighting, are the Zimbabwean women. And the picture isn't pretty. Here we have women who joined the armed resistance struggle, but even when they did, what did they face? Rape. They had to service the male comrades beside whom they were fighting. And then when the war was over, they were as delegitimized as the women who had not been fighting. There was no place for them in the new revolutionary Zimbabwe. To the point when they brought out the documentary *Black Fire*, the comrades now in power asked, "How can you tell this story and diss us?"

The only women who have taken part in an armed struggle who've had a heroic film made about them are the Algerian women in *The Battle for Algiers*. Those women were on the frontlines, but not in the conventional way. They were in dangerous situations, they were passing bombs and carrying guns, but they were not on the frontlines of combat like the men were. We have to remember that resistance is always gendered: women resist in very different ways than men do and have a different relationship to weapons of war.

Q: I am a first-generation American and a lot of the experiences of African women have been told to me by my mother and through stories of my grandmother who lived during the Biafran war. For many of us first-generation African American women, we don't know if we're supposed to envision Africa or how we're supposed to do it. There is such a gap. So I wanted to know if the panelists can tell us, how are *we* as American-born African women supposed to envision Africa? I don't know if you can answer this question, but it's an urgent question for me.

Omotayo Jolaosho: I think it's a claim and a connection that you have to make for yourself. You need to create a space of belonging in which you can make that connection back to Africa. These are issues that we African-born women who live in the diaspora have to struggle with too, in terms of living between two places. I would say that you have access, in terms of your mother and the women in your family, and those are the people you should go to with questions and with the intention of listening. If you can, go to Africa! It's a personal journey and it's a personal reconciliation, and it's a question that we cannot answer except by speaking of our experience and our own search as well.

Marame Gueye: I have a daughter who was born here, and every time I sit and talk to her I start asking myself that very question—how is she going to envision Africa for herself? The way I see it is that later in life it will be her choice. Maybe when she grows up she will say, I don't want to have anything to do with Africa. I am not going to force her to do that, because if she has never been to Africa, I cannot force her. If she doesn't choose to connect with Africa, I cannot force her to do that. All I can do is give her the tools and see what she does with them. We talk to her in Wolof and French and also English because she has all these cultures that come together in one space.

One day I was having a conversation with a friend who brought his children to our house. It was during Christmas and we had a Christmas tree, and to him it was very odd because we are Muslims. As the child came into the house, he said, "Oh, I always wanted a Christmas tree, but my mom says we are Muslims and we don't have Christmas trees." So all of a sudden I found myself having to answer the question of why we have a Christmas tree.

Our perspective is that our daughter was born in America and is probably going to embrace American culture. The way I see it is that Christmas for many people here is cultural rather than religious, so I wanted to introduce her to that part of the culture because when she goes to school she will probably have children coming with their toys, saying this is what I got for Christmas, and she will want to have that. At the same time, we are introducing her to the Muslim faith—she sees us praying, we also celebrate the Muslim holidays, and she is given a Muslim name. When she grows up, she will have to make these choices for herself.

Q: The sense of in-betweenness is something that I have gone through being born here in the United States with African parents. Growing up, if my mom packed me a Ghanaian lunch for school, I didn't want to eat it because I didn't want people to see I was different; I wanted to be part of American culture. But then when we'd have our celebrations, my aunts and uncles would want to speak to me in Fanti and I couldn't understand, and I didn't like that either. There's going to come a time in our lives when we have to go back and make our own connections and shape our own sense of Africa.

Omotayo Jolaosho: I want to stress the interconnectedness of our lives and the importance of knowing our place in history. I am reminded of a song by Sweet Honey in the Rock that says something like, "We are our grand-mothers' dreams." When we're talking about the flow of time and being in this present moment, the fact that you are here in the United States because your parents were able to travel here, speaks directly to the vision of the future that they had in the past. You are in that flow of time and you can contribute to that vision. I don't think that you should necessarily feel uncertain about a vision of Africa; it's something that you just have to claim for yourself.

Nimu Njoya: I want to add something about that phrase "We are our grand-mothers' dreams," because I thought about that idea a lot when I was preparing for this roundtable. Whenever I think about representing African women in any sense, it's a frightening thing, it really makes you shake and tremble, because the way the mainstream discourse will pick up that story is so often not the way you intended it. And then there is also always the question of legitimacy, the fear that I'm going to be sitting up here and people are going to be thinking, "Hmph, that is no real African woman."

But then my foremothers' vision keeps coming back to me. When my grandmother was a young girl, the missionaries had just come into her area and set up a school, and she really wanted to attend. But her family was having none of it because they didn't want anything to do with those missionaries, who were just disrupting life left, right, and center. But she was determined to go to school, so she ran away from home so she could attend the mission school. To get her to come back home, her father started to beat her mother, my great-grandmother, until finally her brother came to her at the school and said, "You have to come home, because our father is going to kill our mother if you don't come back home."

Well, when my grandmother had daughters, you can be sure she sent them to school! But it wasn't so easy for her either because the daughters were needed around the house, not just to help her in her own work but because life is a communal thing and women have never been able to bear all the burdens without leaning on other women in their own generation and also in the next generation. Often something is taken from the next generation to spread these heavy burdens, and so my own mother could not go to school when it was time for her to go to school because her aunties had babies that needed care while they went to cultivate food.

When my mother was eight or nine years old, every morning one of her aunties would put a baby in the traditional leather baby carrier, the kind with a strap around your forehead and another around your waist. My mother would stand there and they would strap the baby to her back, and as soon as they stepped away she'd flick the strap from her head, and of course the baby would fall. Her aunties would keep strapping the baby in and she would keep letting the baby fall, and her aunties were so worried that she was going to hurt the baby that in the end they said, "This is useless, send her to school!" And so my mother went to school. When she came home to do her homework, her mother, who hadn't been able to go to school, would sit there adding logs to the fire so my mother had light to read.

When it was my turn to go to school, the little kids went to school early in the morning, worked hard all day, and would come home in the evening with a lot of homework. So I'd come home with a lot of homework, and since my teachers were over-burdened, I didn't always know what I was doing. I was fortunate that my mother, who had been to school, was able to help me with my homework—and we had electricity to work by too! Sometimes when she had to send me to bed she'd actually do my math homework, and in the morning I'd wake up and copy it into my book and go to school and turn it in!

So now that I'm here, can I apologize for being here? Can I say that I am just swimming in privilege because there are grassroots African women and here I am and everything is handed to me? No, it has not been handed to me! This is my foremothers' vision and sweat and work and struggle, it didn't just happen.

Abena Busia: And resistance and subversion too!

Marame Gueye: My mother never went to school—her father sent his sons to school but not his daughters, because he said daughters get corrupted in school. So when we went to school, my mother took our schooling very seriously. My mom was the disciplinarian, and she was always the one who opened our report cards first. Although she didn't know how to read, she knew how to read the word *first*, and even if you came home with an average of ninety-nine you'd get a beating before my dad got home and could read that you had actually gotten a ninety-nine. I got many beatings for being fifth in my class instead of first!

So again, our location today as African women in academia has not been simply handed to us. My mother lived in a very remote village where she had no help and she bore eleven children, and all those children were sent to school because she said she didn't want us to be like her, illiterate.

She worked so hard to keep us in school! So this opportunity has not been handed to us on a silver platter; it is something that our foremothers worked for, and it is like a long thread of struggle that continues in each one of us today. And this thread is also continuing in my daughter. It is a circle of work and struggle and resistance, and each one of us does whatever we feel we can do to make this thread continue.

Liberation

Abena P. A. Busia

We are all mothers,
and we have that fire within us,
of powerful women
whose spirits are so angry
we can laugh beauty into life
and still make you taste
the salty tears of our knowledge—
For we are not tortured
anymore;
we have seen beyond your lies and disguises,
and we have mastered the language of words,
we have mastered speech
And know
we have also seen ourselves raw
and naked piece by piece until our flesh lies flayed

with blood on our own hands.
What terrible things can you do to us
which we have not done to ourselves?
What can you tell us
which we didn't deceive ourselves with
a long time ago?
You cannot know how long we cried
until we laughed
over the broken pieces of our dreams.
Ignorance
shattered us into such fragments
we had to unearth ourselves piece by piece,
to recover with our own hands such unexpected relics
even we wondered
how we could hold such treasure.
Yes, we have conceived
to forge our mutilated hopes
beyond your imaginings
to declare the pain of our deliverance.
So do not even ask,
do not ask what it is we are laboring with this time;
Dreamers remember their dreams
when they are disturbed—
And you shall not escape
what we will make
of the broken pieces of our lives.

Suggestions
for Further Reading

Fiction, Testimonial, and Memoir

Algeria

Djebar, Assia. *Children of the New World*. Marjolijn de Jager, trans. New York: The Feminist Press, 2005.

———. *Fantasia, an Algerian Cavalcade*. Dorothy S. Blair, trans. Portsmouth, NH: Heinemann, 1993.

———. *A Sister to Scheherezade*. Dorothy S. Blair, trans. Portsmouth, NH: Heinemann, 1987.

———. *So Vast the Prison*. Betsy Wing, trans. New York: Seven Stories Press, 1995.

———. *Women of Algiers in Their Apartment*. Marjolijn de Jager, trans. Charlottesville: University Press of Virginia, 1992.

Benin

Ismaili, Rashidah. *Cantata for Jimmy*. Trenton, NJ: Africa World Press, 2003.
———. *Missing in Action and Presumed Dead: Poems*. Trenton, NJ: Africa World Press, 1992.
———. *Rice Keepers: A Play*. Trenton, NJ: Africa World Press, 2006.

Botswana

Head, Bessie. *Maru*. New York: McCall, 1971.
———. *A Question of Power*. New York: Pantheon, 1974.
———. *Serowe, Village of the Rainwind*. London: Heinemann, 1981.
———. *To Stir the Heart*. New York: The Feminist Press, 2007.
———. *A Woman Alone*. London: Heinemann International, 1990.

Cameroon

Beyala, Calixthe. *The Sun Hath Looked upon Me*. Oxford: Heinemann, 1988.
———. *Your Name Shall Be Tanga*. London: Heinemann, 1996.
Etoké, Nathalie. "Bessombé: Between Home and Exile." In *From Africa: New Francophone Stories*, ed. Adele King. Lincoln: University of Nebraska Press, 2004.
Makuchi (Nfah-Abbenyi, Juliana). *Your Madness, Not Mine: Stories of Cameroon*. Athens: Ohio University Press, 1999.

Cameroon/Ivory Coast

Liking, Werewere. *It Shall Be of Jasper and Coral: Love-Across-a-Hundred-Lives*. Marjolijn de Jaeger, trans. Charlottesville: University Press of Virginia, 2001.
———. *The Power of Um, and A New Earth: African Ritual Theater*. Jeanne N. Dingome et al., eds. and trans. Lanham, MD: International Scholars Publications, 1996.

Egypt

Ahmed, Leila. *A Border Passage*. New York: Penguin Books, 1999.
Rifaat, Alifa. *Distant View of a Minaret*. Denys Johnson-Davies, trans. Portsmouth, NH: Heinemann, 1987.
Saadawi, Nawal El. *A Daughter of Isis: The Autobiography of Nawal El Saadawi*. Sherif Hetata, trans. London: Zed Books, 1999.
———. *The Fall of the Imam*. Sherif Hetata, trans. London: Minerva, 1989.
———. *God Dies by the Nile*. Sherif Hetata, trans. London: Zed Books, 1985.
———. *Memoirs from the Women's Prison*. Marilyn Booth, trans. Berkeley: University of California Press, 1994.
———. *Memoirs of a Woman Doctor: A Novel*. Catherine Cobham, trans. San Francisco: City Lights Books, 1988.

———. *Two Women in One*. Osman Nusairi and Jana Gough, trans. Seattle: Seal Press, 1986.

———. *Woman at Point Zero*. Sherif Hetata, trans. London: Zed Books, 1979.

Soueif, Ahdaf. *In the Eye of the Sun*. New York: Anchor Books, 2000.

———. *I Think of You: Stories*. New York: Anchor Books, 2007.

———. *The Map of Love*. New York: Anchor Books, 2000.

Eritrea

Pool, Hannah. *My Father's Daughter*. New York: Free Press, 2009.

Ethiopia

Haile, Rebecca. *Held at a Distance: My Rediscovery of Ethiopia*. Chicago: Academy Chicago Publishers, 2007.

Ghana

Aidoo, Ama Ata. *Changes*. New York: The Feminist Press, 1993.

———. *The Girl Who Can, and Other Stories*. Oxford; Portsmouth, NH: Heinemann, 2002.

———. *No Sweetness Here*. New York: The Feminist Press, 1995.

———. *Our Sister Killjoy*. London: Longman, 1977.

———. *Two Plays: The Dilemma of a Ghost; Anowa*. Harlow, Essex: Longman, 1987.

Darko, Amma. *Beyond the Horizon*. Portsmouth, NH: Heinemann, 1995.

———. *Faceless*. Legon-Accra, Ghana: Sub-Saharan Publishers, African Books Collective, 2003.

———. *The Housemaid*. Portsmouth, NH: Heinemann, 1998.

———. *Not without Flowers*. Legon-Accra, Ghana: Sub-Saharan Publishers, African Books Collective, 2007.

Ivory Coast

Tadjo, Véronique. *As the Crow Flies*. Wangui wa Goro, trans. Portsmouth, NH: Heinemann, 1986.

———. *The Blind Kingdom*. Janis A. Mayes, trans. Oxford: Ayebia Clarke, 2008.

———. *If I Were a King, If I Were a Queen*. Chicago: Milet Publishing Ltd., 2002.

———. *The Shadow of Imana: Travels in the Heart of Rwanda*. Véronique Wakerley, trans. Portsmouth, NH: Heinemann, 2002.

Kenya

Dow, Unity. *Far and Beyon'*. Botswana: Longman, 2000.

———. *Juggling Truths*. North Melbourne, Australia: Spinifex, 2003.

———. *The Screaming of the Innocent*. North Melbourne, Australia: Spinifex, 2002.

Maathai, Wangari. *Unbowed: A Memoir*. New York: Anchor Books, 2007.

Macgoye, Marjorie Oludhe. *Chira*. Nairobi: East Africa Educational Publishers, 1997.

——. *Coming to Birth*. New York: The Feminist Press, 2000.

——. *The Present Moment*. New York: The Feminist Press, 2000.

Ndambuki, Berida, with Claire C. Robertson. *We Only Come Here to Struggle: Stories from Berida's Life*. Bloomington: Indiana University Press, 2000.

Ogot, Grace. *Land without Thunder: Short Stories*. East Lansing: Michigan State University Press, 1968.

——. *The Promised Land*. Nairobi: East African Educational Publishers, 1991.

——. *The Strange Bride*. Okoth Okombo, trans. Nairobi: Heinemann Kenya, 1989.

Lesotho

Nthunya, Mpho M'atsepo. *Singing Away the Hunger: The Autobiography of an African Woman*. Bloomington: Indiana University Press, 1997.

Liberia

Sirleaf, Ellen Johnson. *This Child Will Be Great: Memoir of a Remarkable Life by Africa's First Woman President*. New York: Harper, 2009.

Morocco

Mernissi, Fatima. *Dreams of Trespass: Tales of a Harem Girlhood*. Reading, MA: Perseus Books, 1998.

Oufkir, Malika. *Freedom: The Story of My Second Life*. New York: Hyperion, 2006.

Oufkir, Malika, and Michèle Fitoussi. *Stolen Lives: Twenty Years in a Desert Jail*. New York: Hyperion, 1999.

Mozambique

Momplé, Lilia. *The Eyes of the Green Cobra*. Portsmouth, NH: Heinemann, 1997.

——. *Neighbors: The Story of Murder*. Richard Bartlett and Isaura de Oliveira, trans. Portsmouth, NH: Heinemann, 2001.

——. *No One Killed Suhuru*. Portsmouth, NH: Heinemann, 1988.

Nigeria

Adichie, Chimamanda Ngozi. *Half of a Yellow Sun*. New York: Alfred A. Knopf, 2006.

——. *Purple Hibiscus*. New York: Anchor Books, 2004.

Alkali, Zaynab. *The Stillborn*. Harlow, Essex: Longman, 1989.

Alkali, Zaynab, and Al Imfeld, eds. *Vultures in the Air: Voices from Northern Nigeria*. East Lansing: Michigan State University Press, 1995.

Atta, Sefi. *Everything Good Will Come*. Northampton, MA: Interlink Books, 2005.

Emecheta, Buchi. *The Bride Price*. New York: G. Braziller, 1976.

———. *Destination Biafra*. New York: Allison & Busby, 1982.

———. *Double Yoke*. New York: G. Braziller, 1983.

———. *Head Above Water*. Portsmouth, NH: Heinemann, 1994.

———. *In the Ditch*. Oxford: Heinemann, 1972.

———. *The Joys of Motherhood*. New York: G. Braziller, 1979.

———. *Kehinde*. Portsmouth, NH: Heinemann, 1994.

———. *The Moonlit Bride*. Oxford: Oxford University Press, 1976.

———. *The New Tribe*. Portsmouth, NH: Heinemann, 2000.

———. *The Rape of Shavi*. New York: G. Braziller, 1985.

———. *Second-Class Citizen*. New York: G. Braziller, 1975.

———. *The Slave Girl: A Novel*. New York: G. Braziller, 1977.

Kalu, Anthonia C. *Broken Lives and Other Stories*. Athens: Ohio University Press, 2003.

Nwapa, Flora. *Efuru*. Portsmouth, NH: Heinemann, 1966.

———. *Idu*. Portsmouth, NH: Heinemann, 1970.

———. *Never Again*. Portsmouth, NH: Heinemann, 1975.

———. *One Is Enough*. Trenton, NJ: Africa World Press, 1992.

———. *This Is Lagos, and Other Stories*. Trenton, NJ: Africa World Press, 1992.

———. *Women Are Different*. Trenton, NJ: Africa World Press, 1992.

Rhodesia/Zimbabwe

Lessing, Doris. *African Laughter: Four Visits to Zimbabwe*. New York: Harper-Collins, 1992.

———. *African Stories*. New York: Simon & Schuster, 1981.

———. *The Grass Is Singing*. New York: Perennial Classics, 2000.

Rwanda

Ilibagiza, Immaculé, with Steve Erwin. *Left to Tell: Discovering God amidst the Rwandan Holocaust*. Carlsbad, CA: Hay House, 2006.

Umutesi, Marie-Béatrice. *Surviving the Slaughter: The Ordeal of a Rwandan Refugee in Zaire*. Julia Emerson, trans. Madison: University of Wisconsin Press, 2004.

Senegal

Bâ, Mariama. *Scarlet Song*. Dorothy S. Blair, trans. Harlow, Essex: Longman, 1986.

———. *So Long a Letter*. Portsmouth, NH: Heinemann, 1989.

Bugul, Ken. *The Abandoned Baobab: The Autobiography of a Senegalese Woman*. Chicago: Lawrence Hill Books, 1991.

Somalia

Dirie, Waris. *Desert Children*. London: Virago, 2008.

Dirie, Waris, with Cathleen Miller. *Desert Flower: The Extraordinary Journey of a Desert Nomad*. New York: William Morrow, 1998.

Dirie, Waris, with Jeanne D'Haem. *Desert Dawn*. London: Virago, 2004.

Hirsi Ali, Ayaan. *Infidel*. New York: Free Press, 2007.

Korn, Fadumo. *Born in the Big Rains: A Memoir of Somalia and Survival*. Tobe Levin, trans. New York: The Feminist Press, 2004.

South Africa

Christiansé, Yvette. *Unconfessed*. New York: Other Press, 2006.

Forna, Aminatta. *Ancestor Stones*. New York: Atlantic Monthly Press, 2006.

———. *The Devil That Danced on the Water: A Daughter's Quest*. New York: Grove Press, 2002.

Gordimer, Nadine. *Burger's Daughter*. New York: Penguin, 1980.

———. *Crimes of Conscience*. Portsmouth, NH: Heinemann, 1991.

———. *Get a Life*. New York: Farrar, Straus & Giroux, 2005.

———. *A Guest of Honor*. New York: Penguin, 1973.

———. *The House Gun*. New York: Farrar, Straus & Giroux, 1998.

———. *July's People*. New York: Viking, 1981.

———. *Jump, and Other Stories*. New York: Penguin, 1992.

———. *My Son's Story*. New York: Penguin, 1991.

———. *None to Accompany Me*. New York: Farrar, Straus & Giroux, 1994.

———. *The Pickup*. New York: Penguin, 2002.

———. *A Sport of Nature*. New York: Penguin, 1988.

Krog, Antjie. *A Change of Tongue*. New York: Random House, 2003.

———. *Country of My Skull: Guilt, Sorrow, and the Limits of Forgiveness in the New South Africa*. New York: Times Books, 1999.

Magona, Sindiwe. *Forced to Grow*. New York: Interlink Books, 1998.

———. *Living, Loving, and Lying Awake at Night*. New York: Interlink Books, 1994.

———. *Mother to Mother*. Boston: Beacon Press, 1999.

———. *Push-Push!* Boston: Beacon Press, 1996.

———. *To My Children's Children*. New York: Interlink Books, 2006.

Maraire, J. Nozipo. *Zenzele: A Letter for My Daughter*. New York: Crown, 1996.

Slovo, Gillian. *Every Secret Thing: My Family, My Country*. Boston: Little, Brown, 1997.

———. *Red Dust*. New York: W.W. Norton, 2002.

Tlali, Miriam. *Amandla*. Johannesburg: Ravan Press, 1980.

———. *Footprints in the Quag: Stories and Dialogues from Soweto*. Cape Town: David Philip, 1989.

———. *Muriel at Metropolitan: A Novel*. Harlow, Essex: Longman, 1987.

Wicomb, Zoe. *The One That Got Away: Short Stories*. New York: New Press, 2009.

———. *Playing in the Light*. New York: New Press, 2006.

———. *You Can't Get Lost in Cape Town: Short Stories*. New York: Pantheon Books, 1987.

Sudan

Aboulela, Leila. *Minaret*. New York: Black Cat, Grove/Atlantic, 2005

———. *The Translator*. New York: Black Cat, Grove/Atlantic, 2006.

Nazer, Mende, with Damien Lewis. *Slave: My True Story*. New York: Public Affairs, 2005.

Togo

Kassindja, Fauziya, with Layli Miller Bashir. *Do They Hear You When You Cry?* New York: Bantam Books, 1999.

Uganda

Keitetsi, China. *Child Soldier: Fighting for My Life*. London: Souvenir Press, 2004.

Kyomuhendo, Goretti. *Waiting*. New York: The Feminist Press, 2007.

Zimbabwe

Dangarembga, Tsitsi. *The Book of Not*. Banbury, England: Ayebia Clarke, 2006.

———. *Nervous Conditions*. New York: Seal Press, 1988.

Fuller, Alexandra. *Don't Let's Go to the Dogs Tonight: An African Childhood*. New York: Random House, 2001.

———. *Scribbling the Cat: Travels with an African Soldier*. New York: Penguin, 2004.

Vera, Yvonne. *Butterfly Burning*. New York: Farrar, Straus & Giroux, 2000.

———. *Nehanda*. Harare, Zimbabwe: Baobab Books, 1993.

———. *The Stone Virgins*. New York: Farrar, Straus & Giroux, 2003.

———. *Why Don't You Carve Other Animals?* Toronto: TSAR Publications, 1992.

———. *Without a Name, and Under the Tongue*. New York: Farrar, Straus & Giroux, 2002.

Anthologies and Collections

Bruner, Charlotte, ed. *The Heinemann Book of African Women's Writing*. Oxford: Heinemann, 1993.

————, ed. *Unwinding Threads: Writing by Women in Africa*. Oxford: Heinemann, 1983.

Daymond, M. J., et al., eds. *Women Writing Africa: The Southern Region*. New York: The Feminist Press, 2003.

Lihamba, Amandina, et al., eds. *Women Writing Africa: The Eastern Region*. New York: The Feminist Press, 2007.

Sadiqi, Fatima, et al., eds. *Women Writing Africa: The Northern Region*. New York: The Feminist Press, 2009.

Sutherland-Addy, Esi, and Aminata Diaw, eds. *Women Writing Africa: West Africa and the Sahel*. New York: The Feminist Press, 2005.

Vera, Yvonne, ed. *Opening Spaces: An Anthology of Contemporary African Women's Writing*. Oxford: Heinemann, 1999.

Nonfiction and Critical Studies by and about African Women

Abusharaf, Rogaia Mustafa, ed. *Female Circumcision: Multicultural Perspectives*. Philadelphia: University of Pennsylvania Press, 2007.

Alidou, Ousseina. *Engaging Modernity: Muslim Women and the Politics of Agency in Postcolonial Niger*. Madison: University of Wisconsin Press, 2005.

Allman, Jean, Susan Geiger, and Nakanyike Musisi, eds. *Women in African Colonial Histories*. Bloomington: Indiana University Press, 2002.

Amadiume, Ifi. *Daughters of the Goddess, Daughters of Imperialism: African Women Struggle for Culture, Power, and Democracy*. London: Zed Books, 2000.

————. *Male Daughters, Female Husbands: Gender and Sex in an African Society*. London: Zed Books, 1987.

————. *Re-inventing Africa: Matriarchy, Religion, and Culture*. London: Zed Books, 1998.

Anyidoho, Kofi, Abena P. A. Busia, and Anne V. Adams, eds. *Beyond Survival: African Literature and the Search for a New Life*. Trenton, NJ: Africa World Press, 1998.

Arnfred, Signe, ed. *Re-thinking Sexualities in Africa*. Uppsala, Norway: Nordic Africa Institute, 2004.

Arnfred, Signe, Bibi Bakare-Yusuf, and Edward Waswa Kisiang'ani, eds. *African Gender Scholarship: Concepts, Methodologies, Paradigms*. Dakar, Senegal: CODESRIA, 2000.

Casenave, Odile. *Rebellious Women: The New Generation of Female African Novelists*. Boulder, CO: Lynne Rienner, 2001.

————. *Afrique sur Seine: A New Generation of African Writers in Paris*. Lanham, MD: Lexington Books, 2006.

Cole, Catherine M., Takyiwaa Manuh, and Stephan F. Miescher, eds. *Africa after Gender?* Bloomington: Indiana University Press, 2007.

Cornwall, Andrea, ed. *Readings in Gender in Africa*. Bloomington: Indiana University Press, 2005.

Goetz, Anne-Marie, and Shireen Hassim, eds. *No Shortcuts to Power: African Women in Politics and Policy Making*. London: Zed Books, 2003.

Gordimer, Nadine. *The Essential Gesture: Writing, Politics and Places*. New York: Knopf, 1988.

Green, December. *Gender Violence in Africa: African Women's Responses*. New York: St. Martin's Press, 1999.

Gruenbaum, Ellen. *The Female Circumcision Controversy: An Anthropological Perspective*. Philadelphia: University of Pennsylvania Press, 2000.

Hernlund, Ylva, and Bettina Shell-Duncan, eds. *Transcultural Bodies: Female Genital Cutting in Global Context*. New Brunswick, NJ: Rutgers University Press, 2007.

Hirsi Ali, Ayaan. *The Caged Virgin: An Emancipation Proclamation for Women and Islam*. New York: Free Press, 2008.

Hodgson, Dorothy, and Sheryl A. McCurdy. *"Wicked" Women and the Reconfiguration of Gender in Africa*. Oxford: Heinemann, 2001.

Imam, Ayesha, Amina Mama, and Fatou Sow, eds. *Engendering African Social Sciences*. Dakar, Senegal: CODESRIA, 2000.

James, Stanlie, and Claire C. Robertson. *Genital Cutting and Transnational Sisterhood: Disputing U.S. Polemics*. Urbana: University of Illinois Press, 2005.

Levin, Tobe, and Augustine H. Asaah, eds. *Empathy and Rage: Female Genital Mutilation in African Literature*. Oxford: Ayebia Clarke, 2009.

Lewis, Desiree. *Living on a Horizon: Bessie Head and the Politics of Imagining*. Trenton, NJ: Africa World Press, 2007.

Maathai, Wangari. *The Challenge for Africa*. New York: Pantheon, 2009.

Mama, Fatima. *Beyond the Masks: Race, Gender, and Subjectivity*. New York: Routledge, 1995.

Mernissi, Fatima. *Beyond the Veil: Male-Female Dynamics in a Modern Muslim Society*. Bloomington: Indiana University Press, 1987.

———. *The Veil and the Male Elite: A Feminist Interpretation of Women's Rights in Islam*. Mary Jo Lakeland, trans. Reading, MA: Addison-Wesley Publishing Company, 1991.

Mikell, Gwendolyn. *African Feminism: The Politics of Survival in Sub-Saharan Africa*. Philadelphia: University of Pennsylvania Press, 1997.

Nfah-Abbenyi, Juliana Makuchi. *Gender in African Women's Writing: Identity, Sexuality, and Difference*. Bloomington: Indiana University Press, 1997.

Nnaemeka, Obioma, ed. *Female Circumcision and the Politics of Knowledge: African Women in Imperialist Discourses*. Westport, CT: Praeger, 2005.

———, ed. *Sisterhood, Feminisms and Power in Africa: From Africa to the Diaspora*. Trenton, NJ: Africa World Press, 1998.

Nzegwu, Nkiru. *Family Matters: Feminist Concepts in African Philosophy of Culture*. Albany: State University of New York Press, 2006.

Oyewumi, Oyeronke. *African Gender Studies: A Reader.* New York: Palgrave Macmillan, 2005.

———. *African Women and Feminism: Reflecting on the Politics of Sisterhood.* Trenton, NJ: Africa World Press, 2004.

———. *The Invention of Women: Making African Sense of Western Gender Discourses.* Minneapolis: University of Minnesota Press, 1997.

Saadawi, Nawal El. *The Nawal El Saadawi Reader.* London: Zed Books, 1997.

Steady, Filomena Chioma, ed. *Black Women, Globalization, and Economic Justice: Studies from Africa and the African Diaspora.* Rochester, VT: Schenkman, 2002.

Thomas, Lynn M. *Politics of the Womb: Women, Reproduction, and the State in Kenya.* Berkeley: University of California Press, 2003.

Tripp, Aili Mari. *Women and Politics in Uganda.* Madison: University of Wisconsin Press, 2000.

Tripp, Aili Mari, Isabel Casimiro, Joy Kwesiga, and Alice Mungwa, eds. *African Women's Movements: Changing Political Landscapes.* New York: Cambridge University Press, 2008.

Wangila, Mary Nyangweso. *Female Circumcision: The Interplay of Religion, Culture, and Gender in Kenya.* Maryknoll, NY: Orbis Books, 2007.

Selected Online Resources on African Women

African Gender Institute, University of Cape Town. An extensive hub for links to sites about African women, gender, and development. http://web.uct.ac.za/org/agi/links%20ngos.htm

The African Women's Development and Communication Network (FEMNET). http://www.femnet.or.ke/

African Women's Development Fund (AWDF). http://www.awdf.org/

African Writing Online. http://www.african-writing.com/hol/

Association for Women's Rights in Development. Resources and links on women's rights in Africa (and other regions). http://www.awid.org

Feminist Africa (print and online journal). http://www.feministafrica.org/

The Green Belt Movement. http://www.greenbeltmovement.org/

Jenda Journal (print and online journal). http://www.jendajournal.com/index.htm

United Nations Development Fund for Women. Extensive resources about women's rights in Africa (and other regions). http://www.unifem.org/resources/

Women in Law and Development in Africa (WiLDAF). http://www.wildaf.org/

Women's Environment and Development Organization (WEDO). http://www.wedo.org/

Women's International League for Peace and Freedom. Database by country of
NGOs working on security issues for women. http://www.peacewomen.org/
contacts/conindex.html

Contributors

SUSAN AKONO was born in 1975 in Cameroon. She completed her undergraduate degree in English and French language and literature at the University of Yaoundé in 1994. In 1995 she joined her mother in Spain and earned an M.A. in English philology and an M. Phil. in postcolonial studies at the Universidad Complutense de Madrid. She currently lives in the United Kingdom and works as the director of the African Peoples Advocacy, an NGO focusing on African communities' development. She is the author of *WMD: The Weapons of My Disappointment* (2004) and *Cuentos africanos* (2007).

SEFI ATTA was born in Lagos, Nigeria. She was educated there, in England, and in the United States. A former chartered accountant and CPA, she is a graduate of the creative writing program at Antioch University, Los Angeles. Her short stories have appeared in journals such as the *Los Angeles Review* and the *Mississippi Review* and have won prizes from *Zoetrope* and Red Hen Press. Her radio plays have been broadcast by the BBC. She is the winner of PEN

International's 2004/2005 David T. K. Wong Prize. In 2006 her debut novel *Everything Good Will Come* was awarded the inaugural Wole Soyinka Prize for Literature in Africa. She lives in Mississippi with her husband, Gboyega Ransome-Kuti, a medical doctor, and their daughter, Temi.

ELLEN MULENGA BANDA-AAKU is Zambian and was born in the United Kingdom in 1965. She was raised in Zambia, then lived in the United Kingdom for twelve years and is now based in Cape Town, South Africa, with her two children, where she recently obtained an M.A. in creative writing. She holds a B.A. in public administration from the University of Zambia and an M.A. in finance and social policy from Middlesex University in the United Kingdom. Her children's book, *Wandi's Little Voice*, was published by Macmillan UK and won the 2004 Macmillan New Writer Award for Africa. In 2007 her story "Sozi's Box" won the Africa region and overall 2007 Commonwealth Short Story Competition, selected from more than two thousand entries.

ZINDZI BEDU, born in Nigeria, currently lives in the United States. She is a poet, performer, and cultural activist, driven to continue a legacy based on her grandmother's work of mobilizing women toward a better life. For her, this work includes creating more spaces for African women to connect with one another and be empowered by one another's voices. Her poem "My Grandmother" appeared in the "Activisms" issue of *Women's Studies Quarterly* (Fall/Winter 2007).

ELISABETH BOUANGA was born in 1930 in the village of Issiami Sibiti in the district of the Lekoumou. Madame Bouanga is a widow as well as mother and grandmother of a large family. She lost three children during the Congolese civil war in the 1990s, during which her house was burned and her extended family scattered. Prevented from attending school as a child due to family responsibilities, Madame Bouanga rededicated herself to her studies after she resettled with several of her children in France. After enrolling in an adult education course, she is proud of her new skills in reading and writing, which she wishes for all African women.

JENNIFER BROWDY dE HERNANDEZ earned her M.A. and Ph.D. in comparative literature from New York University, and since 1994 has taught comparative literature and gender studies at Bard College at Simon's Rock. She has also been a member of the faculty of the interdisciplinary Project Renaissance program at the State University of New York, Albany, since 2002. In 2004 she published the anthology *Women Writing Resistance: Essays on Latin America and the Caribbean* (South End Press), which collected essays and poetry from that region's well-known and emerging women writers. In her scholarship, teaching, and activism, she has followed the trail of women's resistance across cultural and geographic boundaries, gravitating to narratives and stories written by women whose voices are not typically heard in mainstream U.S. discourse. Since 2002 she has directed annual conferences in observance of International Women's Day at Bard College at Simon's Rock, and she served for five years as the vice president for programs of the Berkshire Chapter of UNIFEM/USA, as well as two years on the national Board of UNIFEM/USA. Her ongoing mission with her publications, teaching, organizing, and public speaking is to open up a space in which the voices of women writers can gain a wider audience and be recognized and appreciated for their aesthetic beauty and political power.

ABENA P. A. BUSIA earned her B.A. and M.A. from St. Anne's College, Oxford, and her Ph.D. from St. Anthony's College at Oxford. An associate professor of English at Rutgers University, she is codirector of the groundbreaking Women Writing Africa Project, a multivolume anthology. She is also coeditor of *Women Writing Africa: West Africa and the Sahel* (2005) and author of *Theorizing Black Feminisms* (1993) as well as many articles and book chapters on topics including black women's writing, black feminist criticism, and African literature. Her scholarship keeps her actively connected to her native Ghana, where a recent Fulbright-Hays Group Projects Abroad Grant enabled Busia and two historians to lead the interdisciplinary program "Teaching the History of the Slave Trade Routes of Ghana and Benin." She is now at work on a book called *Song in a Strange Land: Narrative and Rituals of Remembrance in the Novels of Black Women of Africa and the African Diaspora*. A poet and short-story writer as well as a scholar, Busia has published a poetry collection called *Testimonies of Exile*. She serves on the advisory board of the Ghana Education Project, as well as the board of the African Women's Development Fund, the first and only pan-African funding source for women-centered programs and organizations. She teaches courses at Rutgers in African American and African diaspora literature.

PATRICIA CHOGUGUDZA was born in Zimbabwe before independence and grew up during the liberation struggle. Initially she trained as an elementary school teacher, but after a few years of teaching, she entered the University of Zimbabwe where she graduated with a degree in English education in 1991. In 2000 she obtained a graduate certificate in women's studies at South Carolina University; in 2001 she earned a master's degree in English education at South Carolina State University; and in 2004 she completed her Ph.D. in humanities, interdisciplinary gender studies, literature, and education at the University of Texas, Dallas. Currently she teaches rhetorical writing and twentieth-century women's literature at Langston University in Oklahoma and is actively engaged in gender issues. Her forthcoming publication, *A Cry in the Dark: Paida a Memoir to Reggie*, is a novel that employs an experimental mix of memoir and fiction to explore the impact of postcolonial patriarchy on Zimbabwean women in the diaspora.

PAULINE DONGALA of Congo-Brazzaville came to the realization that, as an African woman, there were certain topics that made her boil inside but were hard for her to discuss openly. After she fled the Congo in 2000, she went through a long period of depression and inner turmoil, trying to adjust to her new surroundings in the United States and dealing with the untimely and violent deaths of many family members and friends, as she describes in her essay in this collection, "Prayers and Meditation Heal Despair." Dongala believes that spirituality and faith are essential to the empowerment of women and that women must reach out to support one another. It is the latter goal that so attracted her to participate in the work of compiling this anthology, as well as to continue her education by working toward her B.A. in women's studies at Bard College at Simon's Rock.

CHESHE DOW was born and currently lives in Botswana, the daughter of noted human-rights attorney, judge, and author Unity Dow. She graduated from Kenyon College in 2002 with a B.A. in economics and earned a J.D. from the University of Cincinnati College of Law in 2007.

SOKARI EKINE is originally from Rivers State in southeast Nigeria and now lives in London. She is a feminist and social justice activist with a multidisciplinary background in education, technology, gender issues, and human rights. She is particularly interested in the use of technology as a tool for social justice and human rights and is the founder and principal author of Black Looks, a pan-African feminist blog covering a range of Africa-related issues. Ekine currently works as a freelance researcher and writer.

NATHALIE ETOKÉ was born in Paris but spent her childhood in her parents' native Cameroon. In 1995 she moved back to France, where she earned an M.A. in modern literature. She earned her Ph.D. in French from Northwestern University, was a visiting assistant professor in the Department of French Studies at Brown University for several years, and is currently an assistant professor of French and Africana studies at Connecticut College. Her first novel, *Un amour sans papiers*, was published in 1999 to critical acclaim. A second novel, *Je vois du soleil dans tes yeux*, was published in 2008. Her short story "Bessombè: Between Homeland and Exile" was published in the collection *From Africa: New Francophone Stories* in 2004.

MARAME GUEYE, a native of Senegal, is an assistant professor in the Department of English at East Carolina University, specializing in African and

African diaspora literatures, particularly oral literature and constructions of gender. She earned her B.A. and M.A. at Cheikh Anta Diop University, Senegal, and her Ph.D. at the State University of New York, Binghamton. From 2004 to 2007 she held a three-year Andrew Mellon postdoctoral fellowship at Vassar College. Her recent publications include "Singing the *Laabaan*, Teaching Sex and Sexuality" in *The Verbal Art of Women from the Sahel and Savannah* (2010). She is currently working on a book on how African women negotiate voice and space through verbal art.

KASHA N. JACQUELINE was born in 1980 in Uganda. An outspoken activist for the Ugandan LBGT community, she is the chairperson and a cofounder of the only exclusively lesbian organization in Uganda, Freedom and Roam Uganda (FAR-UG; http://www.faruganda.org/), based in Kampala. Established in 2003, FAR-UG seeks equal rights for lesbians and gays in a country where homosexuality is criminalized.

OMOTAYO JOLAOSHO is a doctoral candidate in the Department of Anthropology at Rutgers University. She traces her relationship to resistance through her Nigerian maternal family line. At the feet of her mother's mother, Victoria Adebanke Bedu, she learned the quintessence of resistance—having a goal and pressing on toward that goal no matter what obstacles are encountered along the way. From her mother, Jolaosho learned the resistant value of not necessarily "speaking truth to power" but rather of claiming power by refusing to bow to circumstance. Her ongoing research is focused on arts resistance and the attainment of human rights in South Africa and her native Nigeria.

MAMLE KABU, a writer of Ghanaian and German descent, was born and raised in Ghana and spent ten years in the United Kingdom, during which she studied at Cambridge University. She returned to Ghana in 1992 where she has since been resident. In addition to writing fiction, she does research consultancy in development issues. Other short stories by her are "Human Mathematics," published in *Mixed: An Anthology of Short Fiction on the Multi-racial Experience* (2006), which will be republished in *Perspectives on Diversity: Selected Readings* in 2010; "Beauty," published in *Sable Litmag* (Fall 2007); and "The End of Skill," published in *Dreams, Miracles and Jazz: New Adventures in African Writing* (2008). "The End of Skill" has been nominated for the 2009 Caine Prize for African Writing.

CHINA KEITETSI was born in 1976 in Uganda. In 1984, at the age of eight, she fell into the hands of the Ugandan National Resistance Army and became a child soldier for the next ten years, a brutal experience she recounts in her memoir, *Child Soldier: Fighting for My Life*, published in 2003. She escaped from the army in 1995 and fled to South Africa, where she sought refugee status. In 1999 she applied to the United Nations High Commissioner for refugees and was offered relocation to Denmark, where she currently lives. Keitetsi has become an international spokeswoman for the plight of child soldiers worldwide, and her book has been translated and published in many languages.

TOURIA KHANNOUS is an assistant professor of Arabic and international studies at Louisiana State University, where she teaches courses on postcolonial literature and theory, Moroccan cinema, literatures of the Maghreb, African literature, and international studies. She has published articles on women's writings from the African diaspora, North African women's literature and film, and cultural studies.

ANN KITHAKA of Kenya is a lawyer and the single mother of three girls. She works as a public prosecutor and in her spare time writes poetry, legal articles, and stories. Kithaka's inspiration for her writing comes from her personal experience; unlike many other African women, she says, she is not ashamed to talk or write about her experiences with female genital mutilation, a failed marriage due to spousal battering, and sexual harassment at work. In the future she plans to earn a master's degree in international criminal law.

JANINE LEWIS of South Africa is currently a lecturer in the Department of Drama at the Tshwane University of Technology in Gauteng, South Africa. She earned an M.A. in theater from the Technikon Pretoria in 2001, specializing in social theater for empowerment. She has worked as a performance artist creating site-specific solo and collaborative pieces with a variety of performers, fine artists, and digital artists. Her specializations include physical theater, including movement studies, and applied theater, especially theater for empowerment. She acts, directs, and co-creates public productions and has worked with Augusto Boal (1997), Anne Bogart and SITI Company, Het Waterhuis and the Toneelacademie Maastricht (2006 to present). She has also been a guest lecturer at Ohio State University and the Hunter Gates Physical Theatre Academy in Edmonton, Canada.

WANGARI MAATHAI was born in Kenya in 1940. She earned an undergraduate degree in biological sciences from Mount St. Scholastica College in Kansas in 1964 and a M.S. degree from the University of Pittsburgh in 1966. She pursued doctoral studies in Germany and the University of Nairobi, obtaining a Ph.D. in anatomy in 1971 from the University of Nairobi, where she also taught veterinary anatomy. She became chair of the Department of Veterinary Anatomy and an associate professor in 1976 and 1977, respectively; in both cases, she was the first woman in the region to attain those positions. Wangari Maathai was active in the National Council of Women of Kenya from 1976 to 1987 and was its chairman from 1981 to 1987. While serving on the National Council of Women, she introduced the idea of planting trees with local people in their own communities, a concept she developed into a broad-based, grassroots organization whose main focus is planting trees with women's groups in order to conserve the environment and improve their quality of life. Through the Green Belt Movement she has assisted women in planting more than twenty million trees on their farms, at schools, and church compounds. In 1986 the movement established the Pan-African Green Belt network with the goal of initiating similar tree-planting initiatives in other African countries. In 2002 Professor Maathai was elected to parliament with an overwhelming 98 percent of the vote. She was subsequently appointed Kenya's assistant minister for Environment, Natural Resources and Wildlife. She and the Green Belt Movement have received numerous awards, most notably the 2004 Nobel Peace Prize.

MIA MACDONALD is a Worldwatch senior fellow whose research focuses on gender and population, biodiversity conservation, and reproductive health and rights.

DIANA ADESOLA MAFE was born in a small Dutch city but grew up in the dense metropolis of Lagos, Nigeria. After completing high school in Nigeria, she moved to Ontario, Canada, where she earned her B.A. in fine art and English at McMaster University, her M.A. in English at the University of Guelph, and her Ph.D. in English at McMaster University. Her research aims to situate mixed-race studies in the relatively unexplored sub-Saharan African context. Her work also tracks the literary roles of women of color in African and American discourses. She has published articles in *Research in African Literatures, American Drama, English Academy Review, Frontiers*, and *Safundi*.

CATHERINE MAKONI, born in 1976 in Zimbabwe, is a lawyer by profession and also holds a master's degree in women's law from the Southern and East African Centre for Women's Law at the University of Zimbabwe. She currently works with the Southern Africa Office of the Catholic Agency for Overseas Development as a regional program officer for social and economic justice. Her work within the women's rights movement in Zimbabwe has inspired her writing, which addresses some of the challenges facing young women today, including HIV/AIDS, violence, poverty, relationships with older men, and barriers to negotiating safer sex. She is interested in exploring the political and economic difficulties in Zimbabwe and their impact, at a very personal level, on the decisions young women make.

MAKUCHI (JULIANA NFAH-ABBENYI) is a professor of English and comparative literature at North Carolina State University. She was born and raised in Cameroon and educated at the University of Yaoundé, Cameroon, and at McGill University in Montreal, Canada. She writes fiction under the pen name Makuchi. She is the author of *The Sacred Door and Other Stories: Cameroon Folktales of the Beba* and *Your Madness, Not Mine: Stories of Cameroon*. Her fiction has also appeared in *Callaloo: A Journal of African-American and African Arts and Letters*, *The Toronto Review of Contemporary Writing Abroad*, *Thamyris*, *Worldview*, and *Obsidian: Literature of the African Diaspora*, among other publications. Her scholarly publications include *Gender in African Women's Writing: Identity, Sexuality, and Difference*, as well as many book chapters, articles, and essays in journals. Her work has been reprinted in such anthologies as *The Anchor Book of Modern African Stories*, *The Rienner Anthology of African Literature*, *Canadian Woman Studies: An Introductory Reader*, *African Gender Studies: A Reader*, and *African Literature: An Anthology of Criticism and Theory*.

KHADIJA MAROUAZI was born in Marrakesh in 1961. A member of the Moroccan Organization for Human Rights and general secretary of the Center for the Study of Democracy and Human Rights, she is also a professor of modern literature in the College of Humanities and Social Sciences at Ibn Tufail University in Kenitra. *Biography of Ash* is her first novel. She lives in Rabat, Morocco. Translator Alexander Elinson teaches Arabic language and literature at Hunter College/CUNY and directs the Hunter College Summer Arabic Program.

KAYA A MBAYA is a Babongo woman of about forty years of age, who lives in the forest surrounding the village of Missama in the district of Sibiti, state of Lekoumou, Republic of Congo. She is married and the mother of many children and grandchildren.

SIBONGILE MTUNGWA was born in 1973 in South Africa. She currently works with the South African Women's Leadership and Training Programme, where her main focus is educating women in rural communities about issues related to gender, HIV/AIDS, culture and heritage, and the environment. Mtungwa maintains an ongoing commitment to working collaboratively to help women in South Africa break the chains of oppression and realize their potential at community, national, and global levels.

J. TSITSI MUTITI was born in Mt. Darwin in Zimbabwe. She has worked in logistics for Doctors Without Borders and now teaches business management. Mutiti has published a number of short stories. Her stories are inspired by her experiences and the way in which those who appear powerless can sometimes rise above their weaknesses and win.

Danielle Nierenberg is a senior researcher at the Worldwatch Institute and co-project director of *State of World 2011: Nourishing the Planet.*

Nimu Njoya, born in Kenya, earned her B.A. in political science from Macalester College in 2002 and went on to develop an enduring interest in women's rights through her work with the Women's Foundation of Minnesota. In 2004 she received an M.A. in social sciences from the University of Amsterdam. She is currently a doctoral candidate in political science at Rutgers University, focusing on approaches to the law, justice, and ethics in writing by women of the African diaspora.

Sybille Ngo Nyeck left her native Cameroon in 2001 after a family crisis made her life there unbearable. After accusing a male family member of raping a younger female relative in 2000, Nyeck was outed as a lesbian during a police investigation into the allegations. In Cameroon, homosexuality is a crime, punishable by prison for up to five years. Nyeck spent only one night in jail, but once she gained freedom, her sexual orientation was plastered in government-run and private newspapers, and she was subjected to taunts and death threats. She fled Cameroon in 2001 and sought political asylum in the United States, which was granted in August 2004. She holds an A.A. in liberal arts and international studies from LaGuardia Community College and a B.A. in comparative literature from Swarthmore College. She writes extensively in French and English about sexism, globalization, racism, and homophobia and has written for Amnesty International as well as the U.S. State Department concerning the abuse of gay and lesbian people in Cameroon.

Eve Zvichanzi Nyemba was born in Zimbabwe in 1981. She recently earned an M.S. in international relations at the University of Zimbabwe. She is currently working as an office manager at Word Ablaze Ministries (Zimbabwe), specializing in financial administration and management. She plans to complete a doctorate in international development with a focus on African development. Her short story "To Light a Candle" was the title story in a book entitled *Light a Candle* (2006), and her first poetry collection, *Look Within*, was published in 2008. She performs her poetry at the Book Cafe in Harare, Zimbabwe, and has written various as-yet-unpublished short stories, poems, and novels.

Iheoma Obibi, a Nigerian, traces her interest in women's issues to her childhood when she was forced to witness her mother's repeated physical abuse by her father. Watching her mother struggle to raise her children after divorce impressed upon Obibi the value of education for women, and she earned a B.A. with honors from North East London Polytechnic and an M.A. with distinction in communications/policy studies. She has worked with various international and local agencies in promoting women's issues and rights and currently serves as the executive director of Alliances for Africa (AfA), an African-led international nongovernmental human rights, peace, and sustainable development organization with offices in the United Kingdom and Lagos, Nigeria. A major focus of AfA is the Women in Governance Initiative, aimed at encouraging women in Africa to participate actively in governance, public life, and decision-making processes at all levels in their communities. In 2005 she was elected an Ashoka Fellow, focusing on increasing civic engagement among women in Nigeria. Her short story "Pastor Saul Bottomsup" was published in *The Anthology of Great Writing, Volume I* by the online writers' Web site www.greatwriting.co .uk and is available from www.Lulu.com. She is currently working on her M.A. in creative writing at Manchester Metropolitan University, United Kingdom, through the distance-learning program.

PIERRE PIYA-BOUANGA, born in 1956, is the married father of many children and a professor of French at the Lycée de Sibiti Congo. He is the author of several as-yet-unpublished manuscripts of poetry and essays on the psychology of pedagogy.

NAWAL EL SAADAWI was born in Kafr Tahla village in Egypt in 1931. A novelist and psychiatrist, she writes in Arabic and is the author of more than forty books which have been translated and acclaimed around the world. Her work on the situation of women has had a deep effect on successive generations of young women over the past four decades. She has been awarded several national and international literary prizes, has lectured in many universities, and has organized and participated in international and national conferences. She is the founder and president of the Arab Women's Solidarity Association and has been involved with many other organizations on behalf of women's rights and human rights; as a result, she has frequently been targeted by the Egyptian government. El Saadawi has been imprisoned, lost influential positions, had her writing banned, and received death threats. She remains one of the foremost international defenders of women's (and men's) human rights.

ANNE SERAFIN gained strong family and work values from her parents, the children of Polish immigrants at the turn of the previous century. She taught English at several high schools in the United States and at Newton North High School in Newton, Massachusetts, for more than thirty years. In the early 1990s she received an NEH Teacher-Scholar Award to read and research African literatures, and in 1996 she established an African literature discussion group at the Newton Free Library, which has continued to the present. She has also published articles and reviews in numerous journals, presented papers on African literature and film at academic conferences, and conducted workshops in African literatures for school groups and adult education programs.

KUUKUA DZIGBORDI YOMEKPE immigrated to the United States from her native country, Ghana, in 1996 at age nineteen. She earned a B.A. in English from Old Dominican College and an M.A. in English at the University of Dayton. She is currently pursuing another graduate degree at the Graduate Theological Union in Berkeley. Yomekpe is a member of the National Religious Leaders Roundtable, Call to Action, Critical Resistance, and Incite!, as well as the Beatitudes Society in Berkeley. She is proud to be an African woman and a politically queer woman of color who believes strongly in justice and equality for all peoples, and she lives this calling through her social justice work in the communities to which she belongs. A talented choreographer of liturgical and African dance forms, Yomekpe has worked nationally with several organizations in expressions of spirituality and healing through dance, as well as through other art forms.